TurningPoints

LITTLE ROCK
NINE

JAN 09

CH

ALSO AVAILABLE

TurningPoints
SONS OF LIBERTY
BY MARSHALL POE
ILLUSTRATED BY LELAND PURVIS

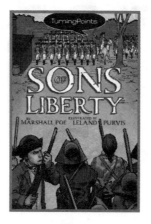

COMING SOON . . .
A HOUSE DIVIDED

LITTLE ROCK
NINE

BY **MARSHALL POE**
ILLUSTRATED BY **ELLEN LINDNER**

ALADDIN PAPERBACKS
NEW YORK   LONDON   TORONTO   SYDNEY

This book is dedicated to Julianna and Isaiah—M.P.

For Stephen—E.L.

In this book, history is fleshed out with fictionalized details, and conversations have been added to make the stories come alive to today's reader, but every reasonable effort has been made to make the stories consistent with the events, ethics, and character of their subjects and the historical time period.

☛ ALADDIN PAPERBACKS • An imprint of Simon & Schuster Children's Publishing Division 1230 Avenue of the Americas, New York, NY 10020 • Copyright © 2008 by Marshall Poe and Ellen Lindner • All rights reserved, including the right of reproduction in whole or in part in any form • ALADDIN PAPERBACKS, Turning Points and logo, and colophon are trademarks of Simon & Schuster, Inc. • The text of this book is set in Turning Points, created by Dalton Webb Manufactured in the United States of America • First Aladdin Paperbacks edition July 2008
10 9 8 7 6 5 4 3 2 1
Library of Congress Control Number 2007937918
ISBN-13: 978-1-4169-5066-0 • ISBN-10: 1-4169-5066-4

ACKNOWLEDGMENTS:

MARSHALL POE

In writing *Little Rock Nine*, I felt a little like a traveler in an unfamiliar country. I needed a lot of guidance. Happily, I got it. First, from my agent, Bob Mecoy, who pointed the way. Next from Ellen Lindner, who drew an excellent map. Then, when I was too thick to understand the said map, from the remarkable Carla Jablonski, who put me (and the book) firmly back on track. And finally from my editor at Simon & Schuster, Liesa Abrams, and from Matt Madden, who both greeted me when I arrived, at long last, safe and sound.

ELLEN LINDNER

Special thanks to Sólveig Rolfsdóttir for production assistance, Emily Ryan Lerner for invaluable visual reference, Bob Mecoy and Matt Madden for their hard work behind the scenes, Leland Purvis for his advice and encouragement, and the Lindner and Betts families for their help and generosity.

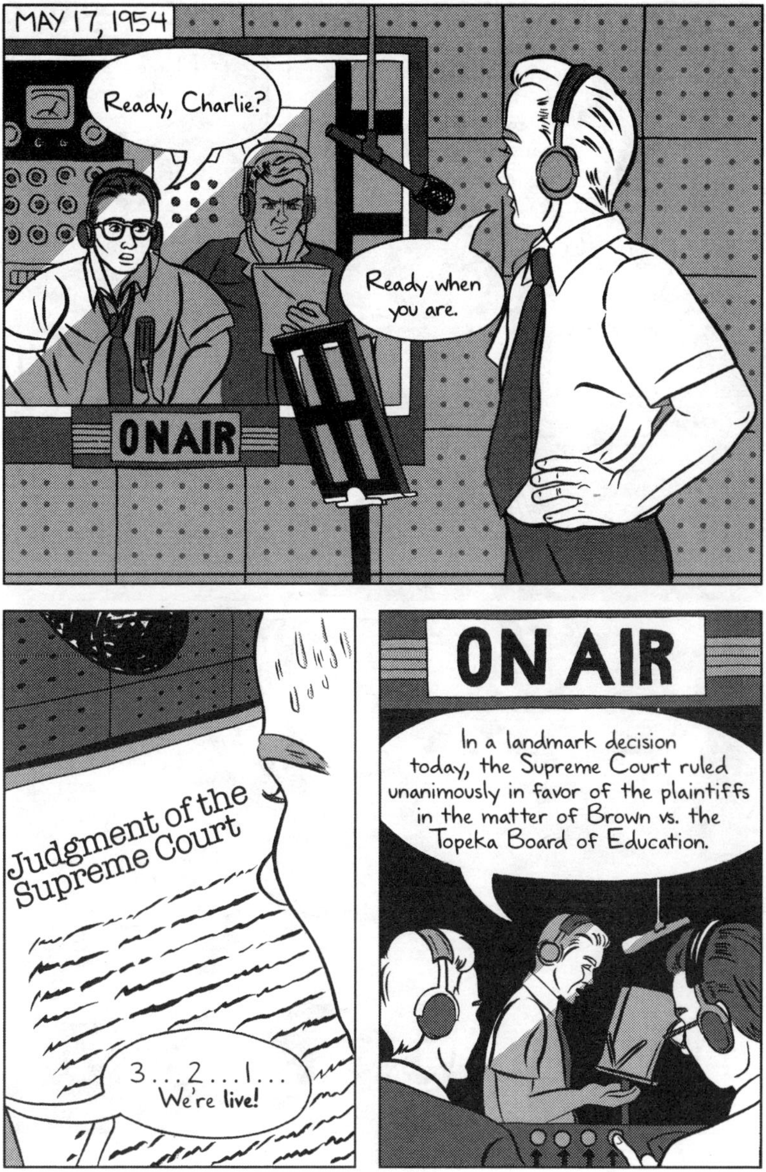
MAY 17, 1954
Ready, Charlie?
Ready when you are.
ON AIR
Judgment of the Supreme Court
3...2...1... We're live!
ON AIR
In a landmark decision today, the Supreme Court ruled unanimously in favor of the plaintiffs in the matter of Brown vs. the Topeka Board of Education.

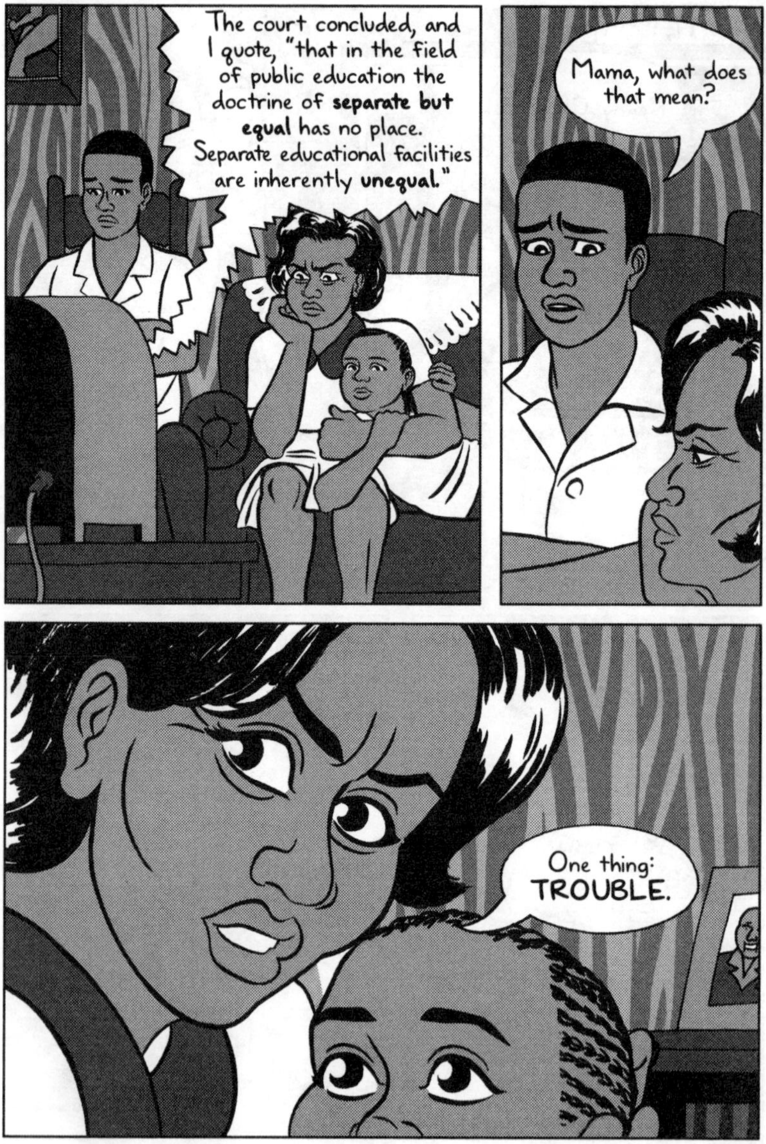
The court concluded, and I quote, "that in the field of public education the doctrine of **separate but equal** has no place. Separate educational facilities are inherently **unequal.**"
Mama, what does that mean?
One thing: TROUBLE.

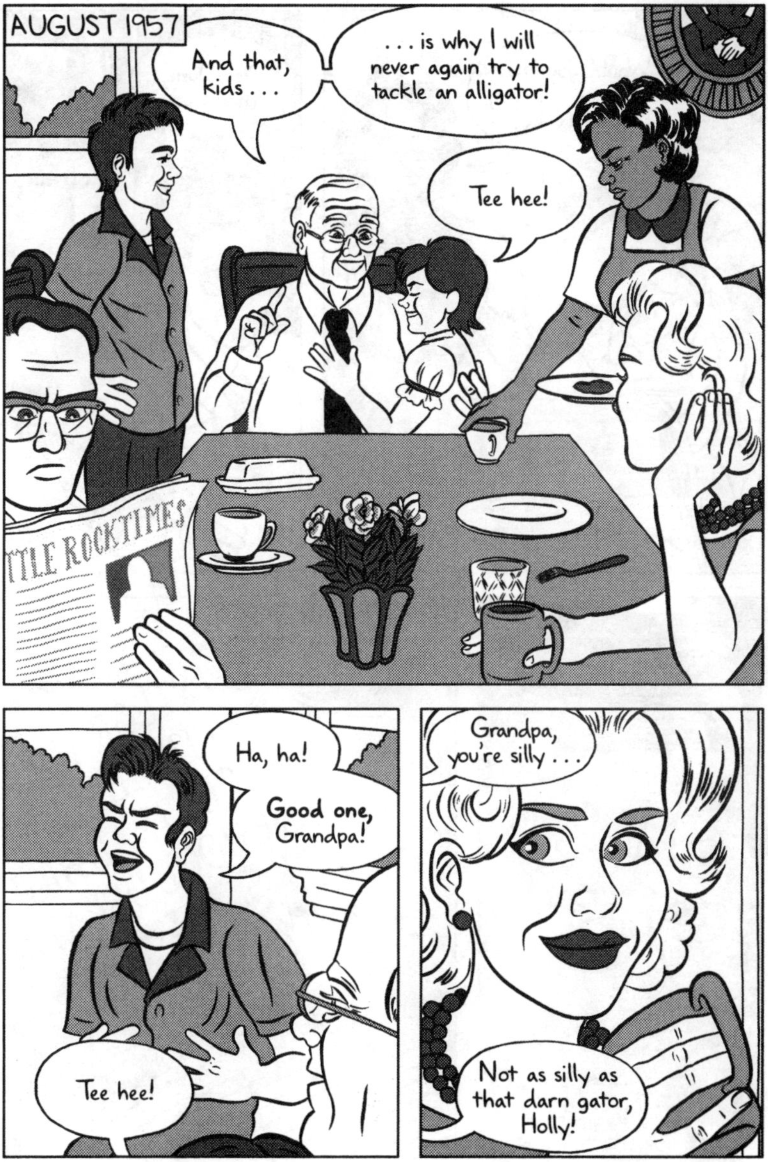
AUGUST 1957
And that, kids . . .
. . . is why I will never again try to tackle an alligator!
Tee hee!
Ha, ha!
Good one, Grandpa!
Tee hee!
Grandpa, you're silly . . .
Not as silly as that darn gator, Holly!

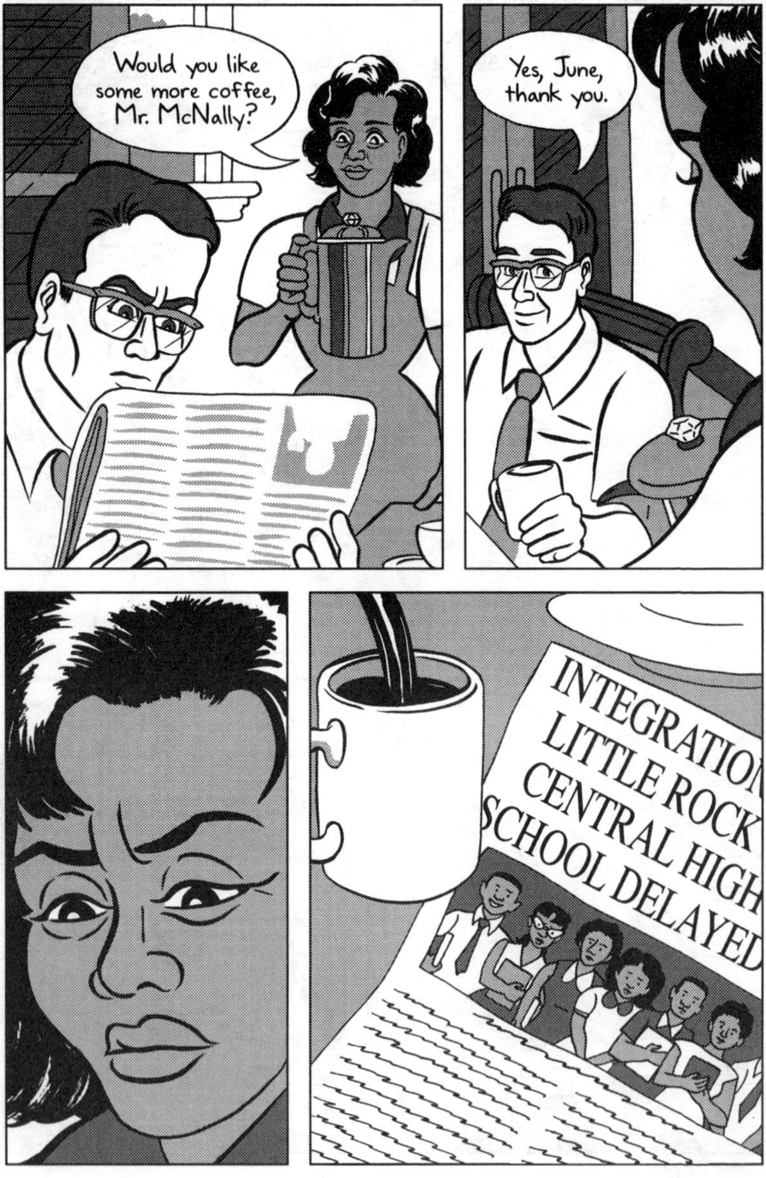
Would you like some more coffee, Mr. McNally?
Yes, June, thank you.
INTEGRATION LITTLE ROCK CENTRAL HIGH SCHOOL DELAYED

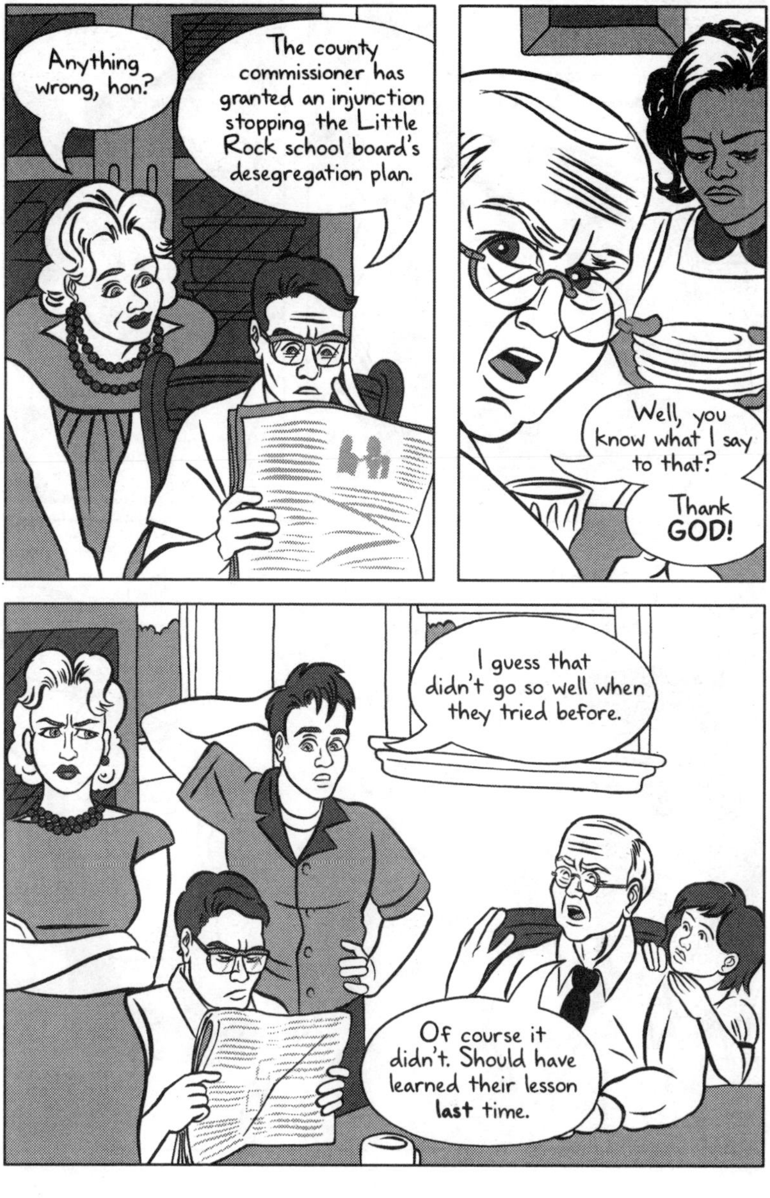
Anything wrong, hon?
The county commissioner has granted an injunction stopping the Little Rock school board's desegregation plan.
Well, you know what I say to that?
Thank **GOD!**
I guess that didn't go so well when they tried before.
Of course it didn't. Should have learned their lesson **last** time.

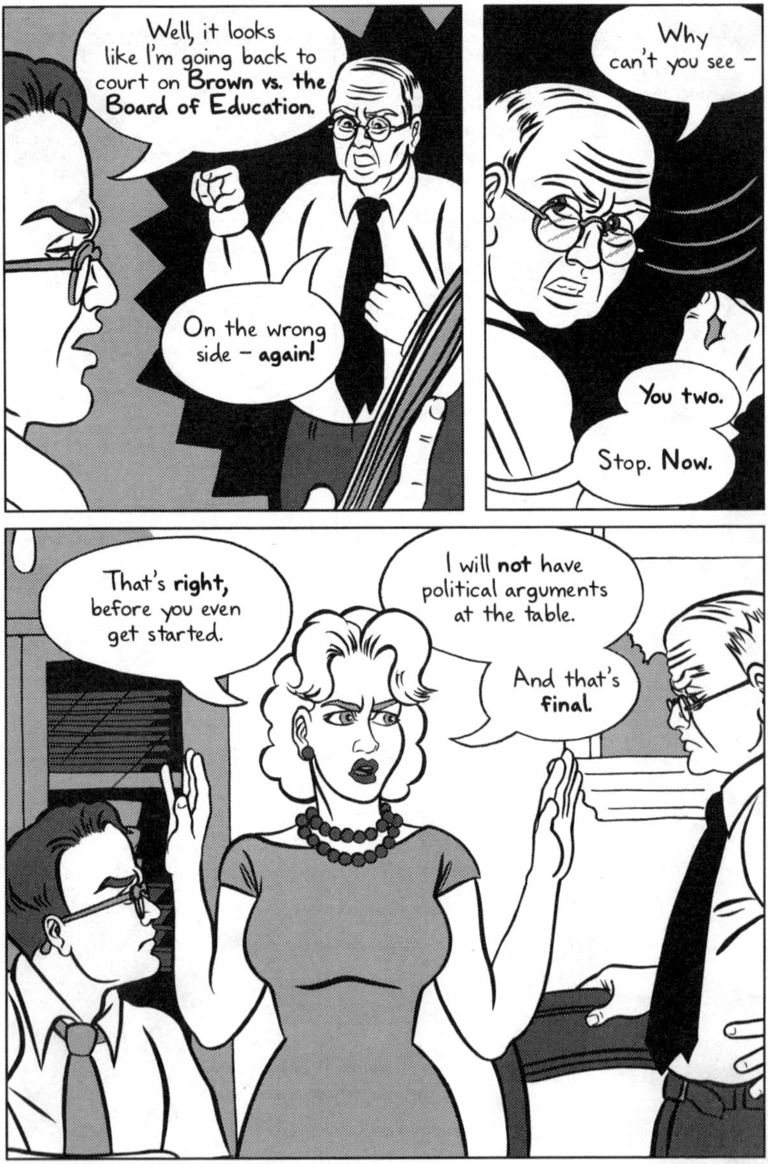
Well, it looks like I'm going back to court on **Brown vs. the Board of Education.**
On the wrong side – **again!**
Why can't you see –
You two.
Stop. **Now.**
That's **right,** before you even get started.
I will **not** have political arguments at the table.
And that's **final.**

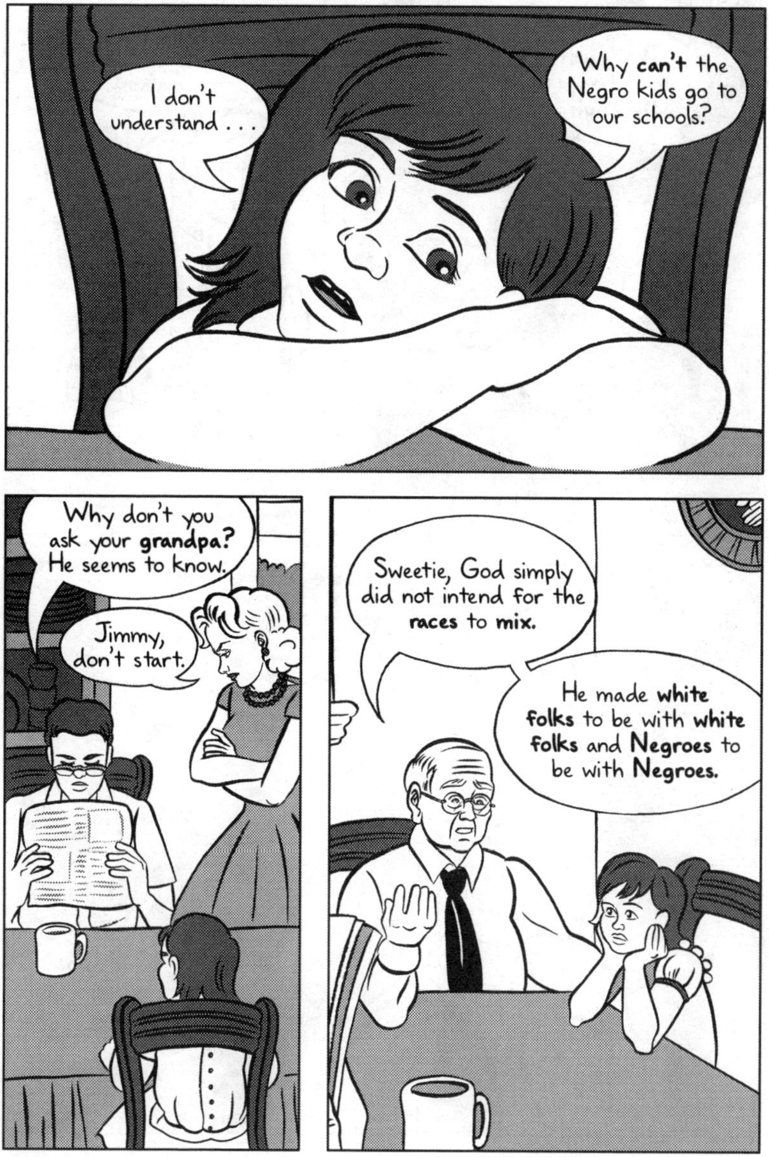
I don't understand . . .
Why **can't** the Negro kids go to our schools?
Why don't you ask your **grandpa?** He seems to know.
Jimmy, don't start.
Sweetie, God simply did not intend for the **races** to **mix.**
He made **white folks** to be with **white folks** and **Negroes** to be with **Negroes.**

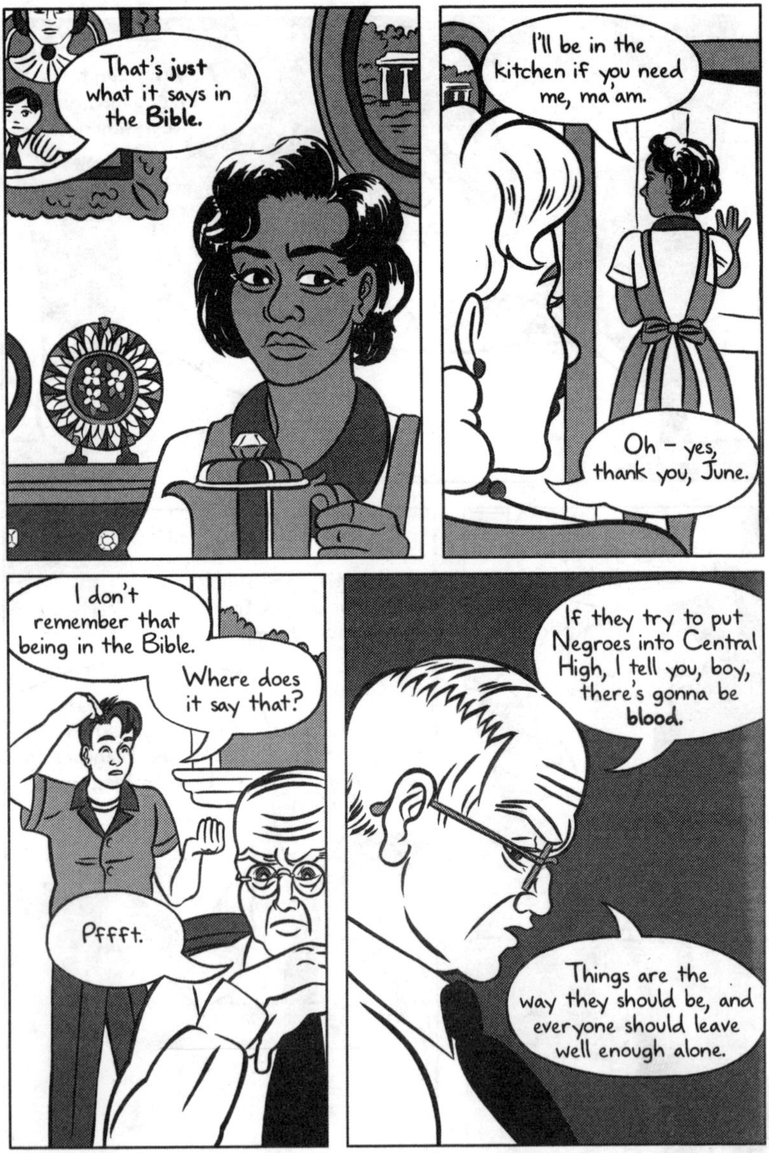
That's **just** what it says in the **Bible.**
I'll be in the kitchen if you need me, ma'am.
Oh – yes, thank you, June.
I don't remember that being in the Bible.
Where does it say that?
Pffft.
If they try to put Negroes into Central High, I tell you, boy, there's gonna be **blood.**
Things are the way they should be, and everyone should leave well enough alone.

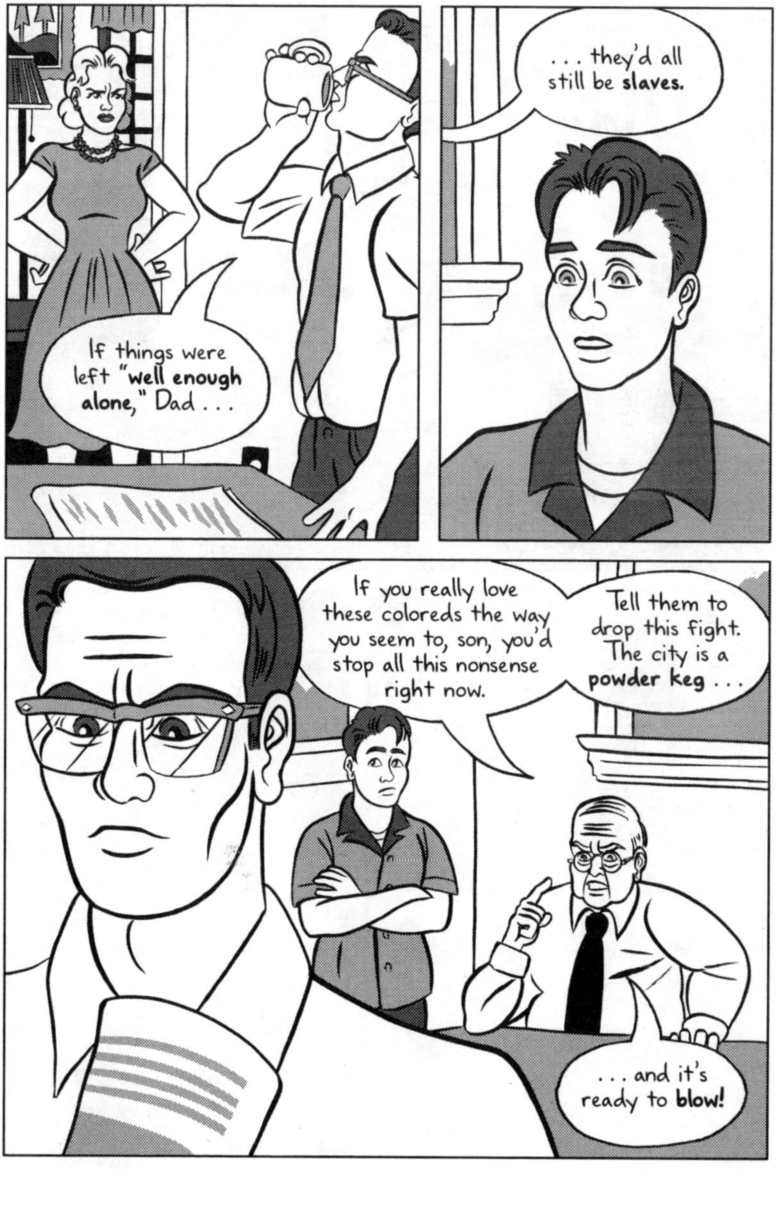
If things were left "well enough alone," Dad . . .
. . . they'd all still be slaves.
If you really love these coloreds the way you seem to, son, you'd stop all this nonsense right now.
Tell them to drop this fight. The city is a powder keg . . .
. . . and it's ready to blow!

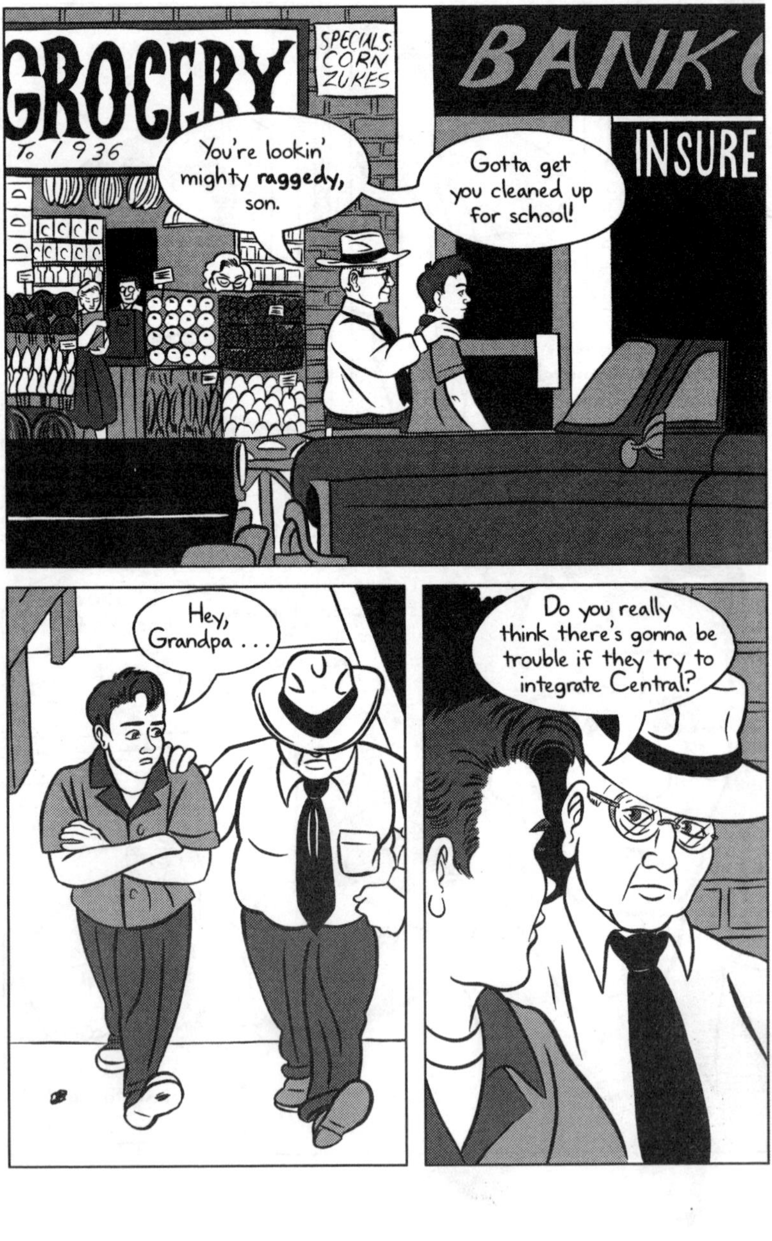
GROCERY
To 1936
SPECIALS: CORN ZUKES
BANK
INSURE
You're lookin' mighty **raggedy,** son.
Gotta get you cleaned up for school!
Hey, Grandpa . . .
Do you really think there's gonna be trouble if they try to integrate Central?

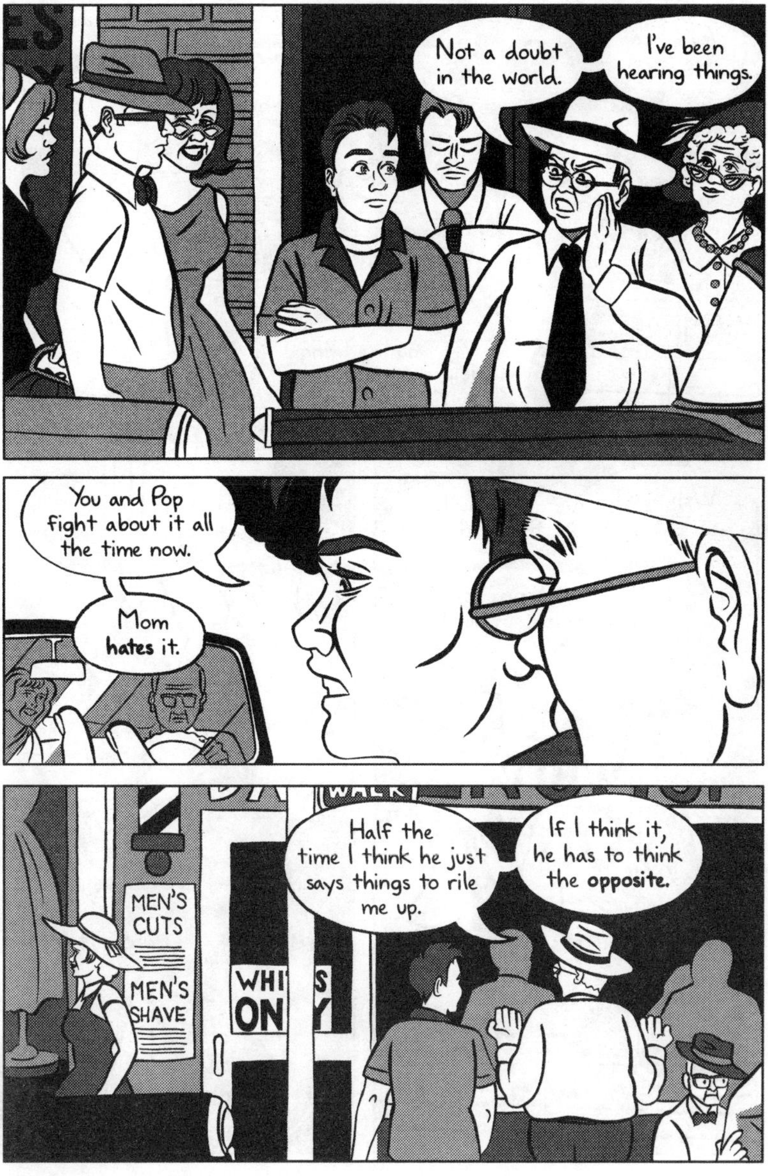
Not a doubt in the world.
I've been hearing things.
You and Pop fight about it all the time now.
Mom **hates** it.
WALK
Half the time I think he just says things to rile me up.
If I think it, he has to think the **opposite.**
MEN'S CUTS
MEN'S SHAVE

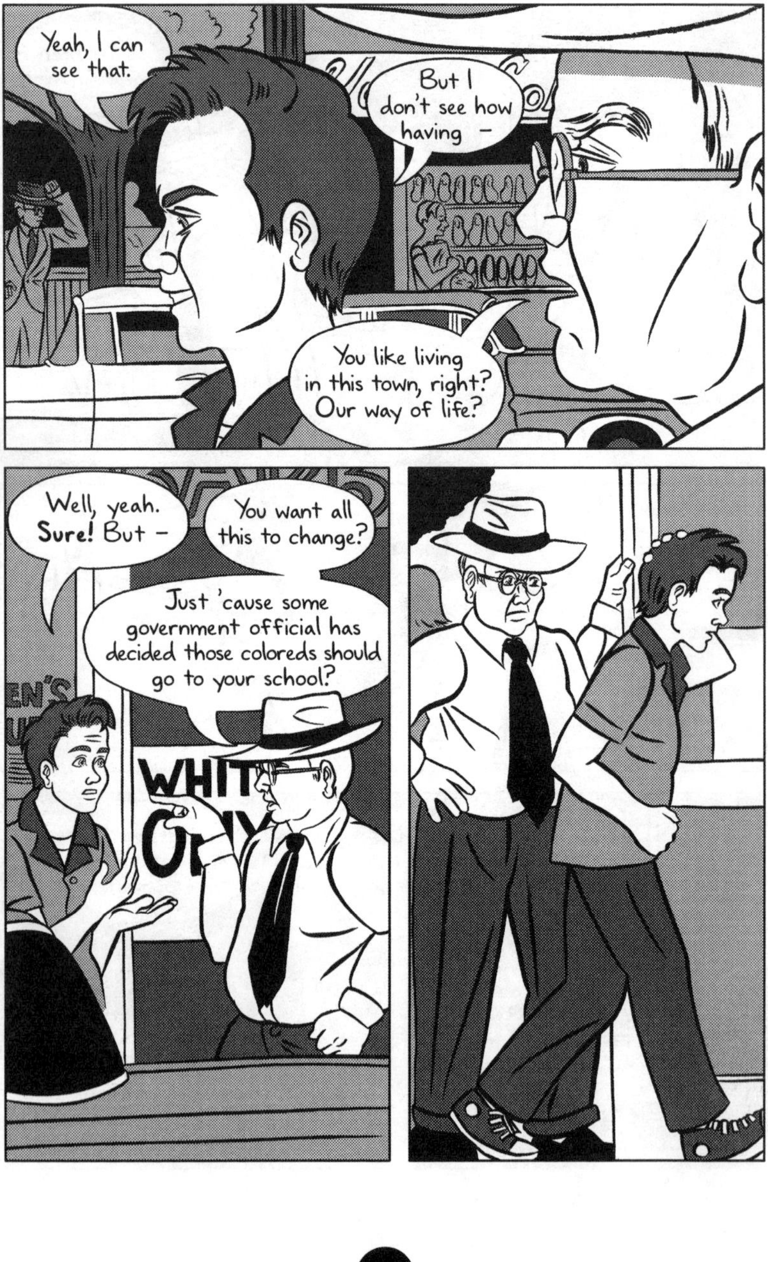
Yeah, I can see that.
But I don't see how having –
You like living in this town, right? Our way of life?
Well, yeah. **Sure!** But –
You want all this to change?
Just 'cause some government official has decided those coloreds should go to your school?
WHIT
ON

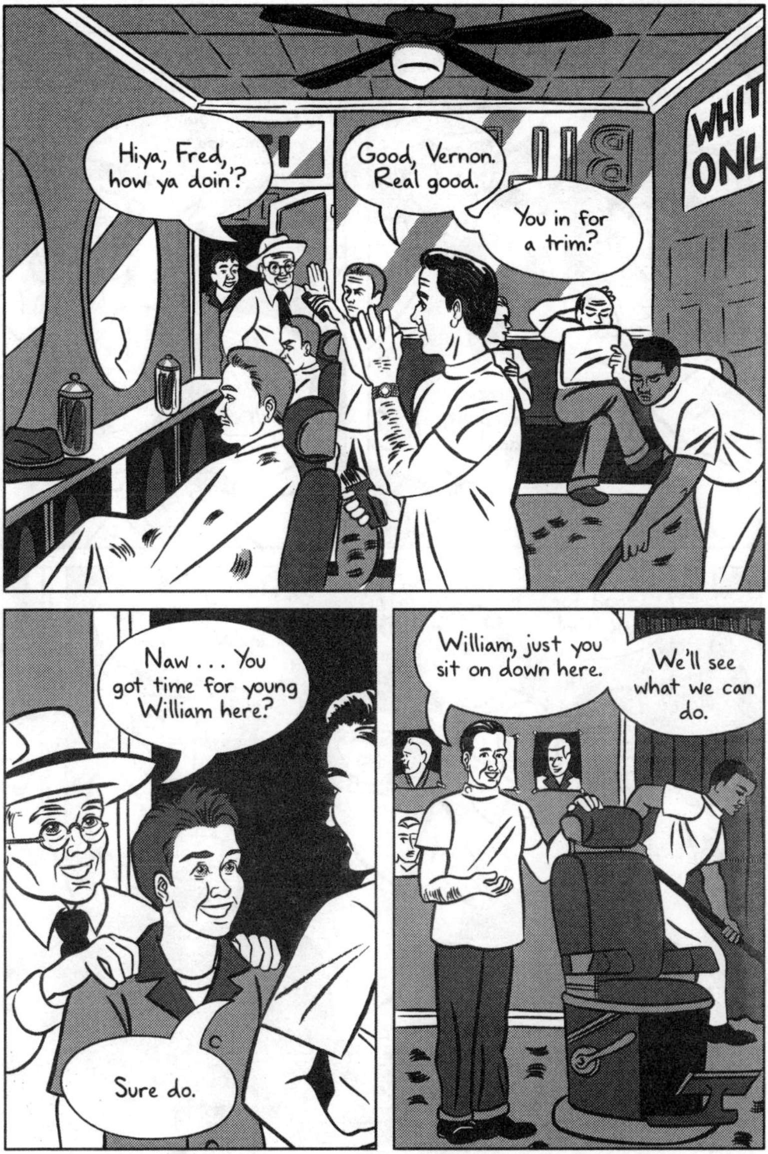
Hiya, Fred, how ya doin'?
Good, Vernon. Real good.
You in for a trim?
WHIT
ONL
Naw . . . You got time for young William here?
Sure do.
William, just you sit on down here.
We'll see what we can do.

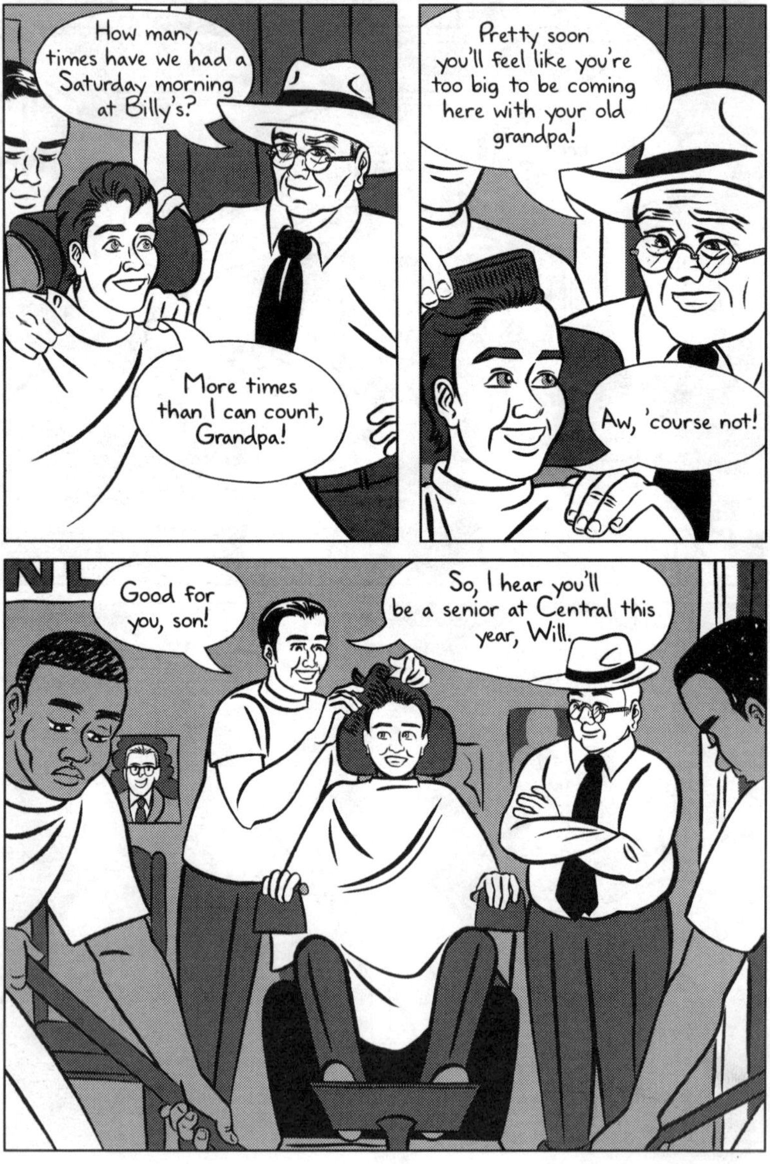
How many times have we had a Saturday morning at Billy's?
More times than I can count, Grandpa!
Pretty soon you'll feel like you're too big to be coming here with your old grandpa!
Aw, 'course not!
Good for you, son!
So, I hear you'll be a senior at Central this year, Will.

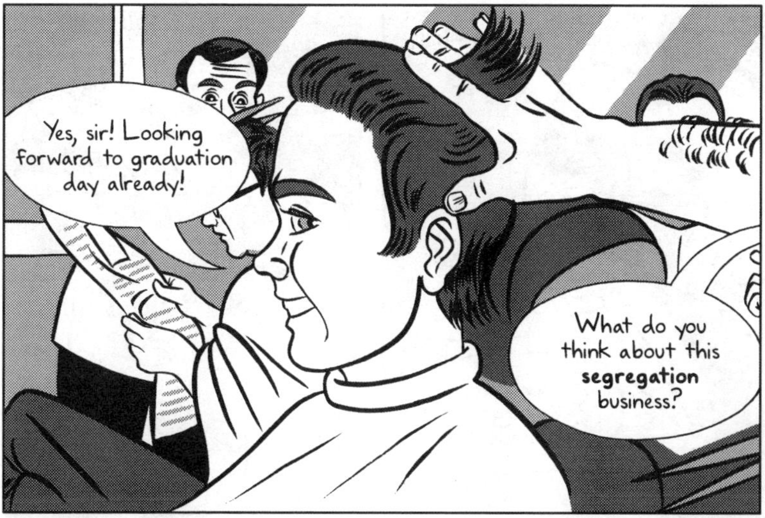
Yes, sir! Looking forward to graduation day already!
What do you think about this **segregation** business?

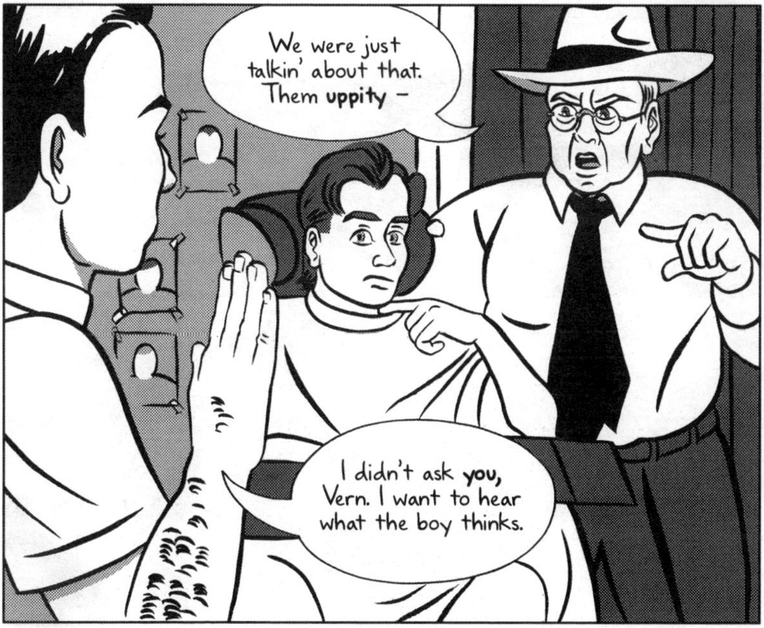
We were just talkin' about that. Them **uppity** –
I didn't ask **you,** Vern. I want to hear what the boy thinks.

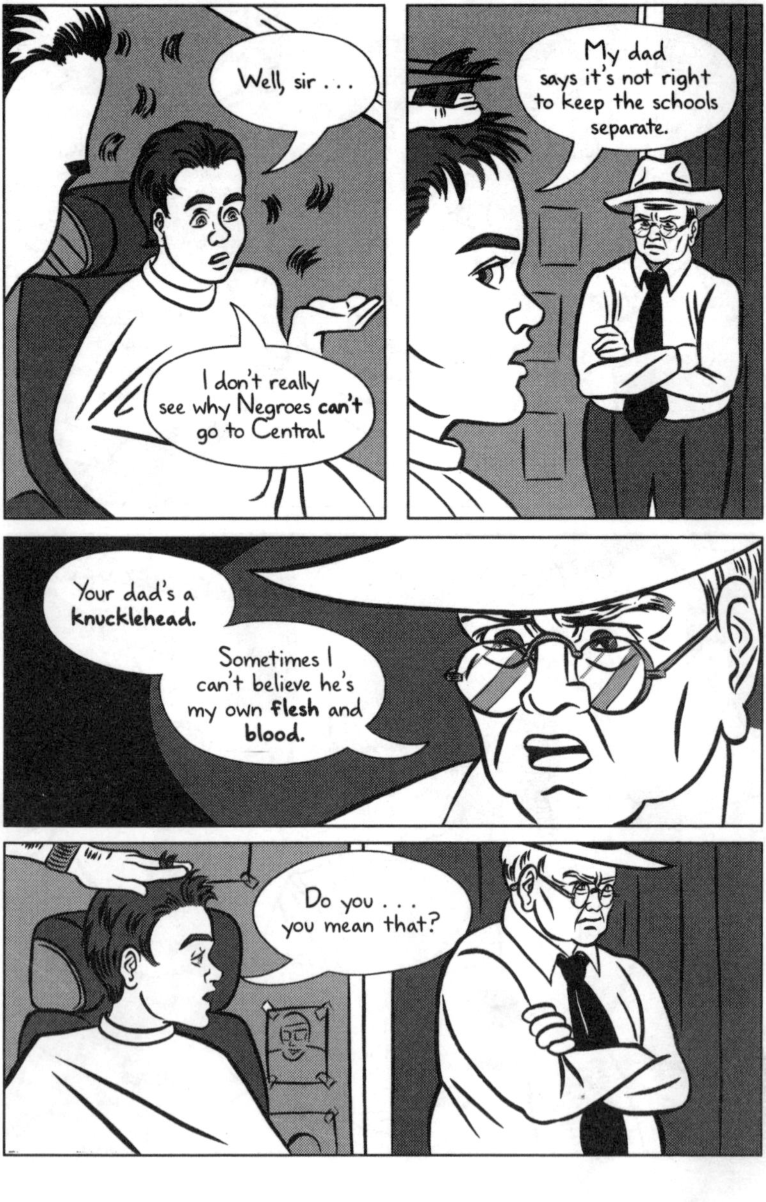
Well, sir . . .
I don't really see why Negroes **can't** go to Central
My dad says it's not right to keep the schools separate.
Your dad's a **knucklehead.**
Sometimes I can't believe he's my own **flesh** and **blood.**
Do you . . . you mean that?

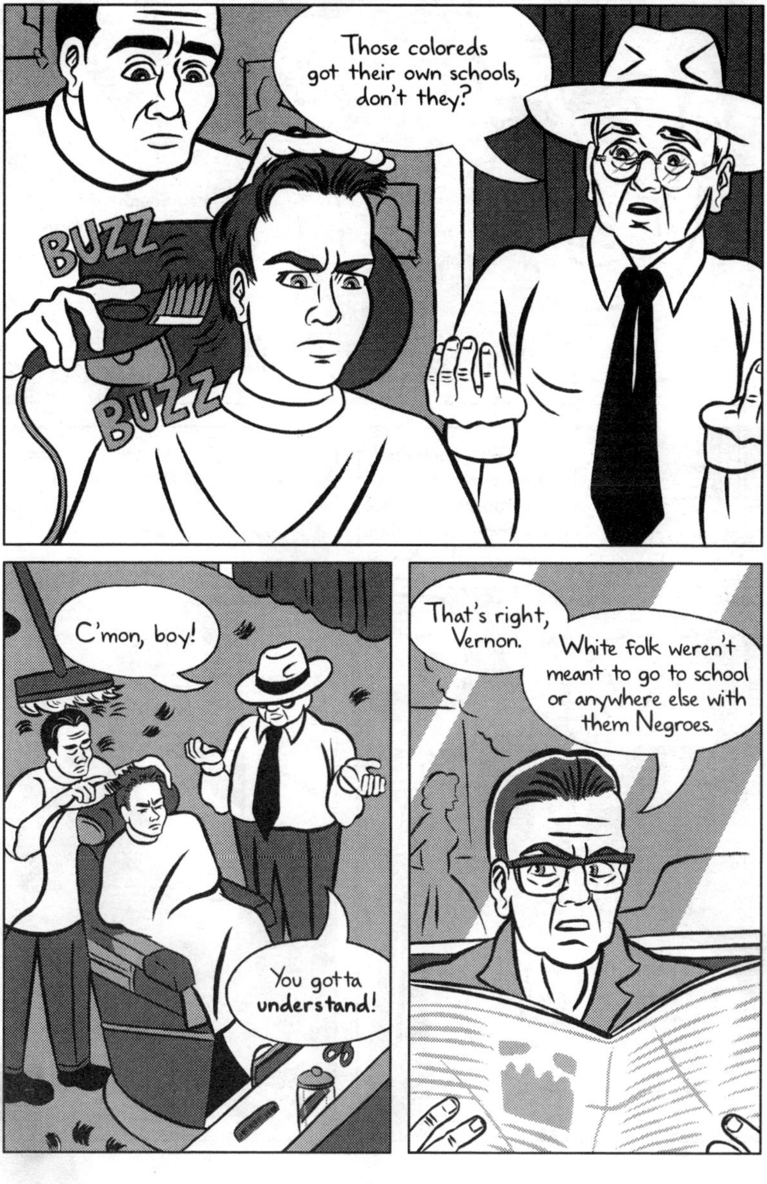

Those coloreds got their own schools, don't they?
BUZZ
BUZZ
C'mon, boy!
You gotta **understand!**
That's right, Vernon.
White folk weren't meant to go to school or anywhere else with them Negroes.

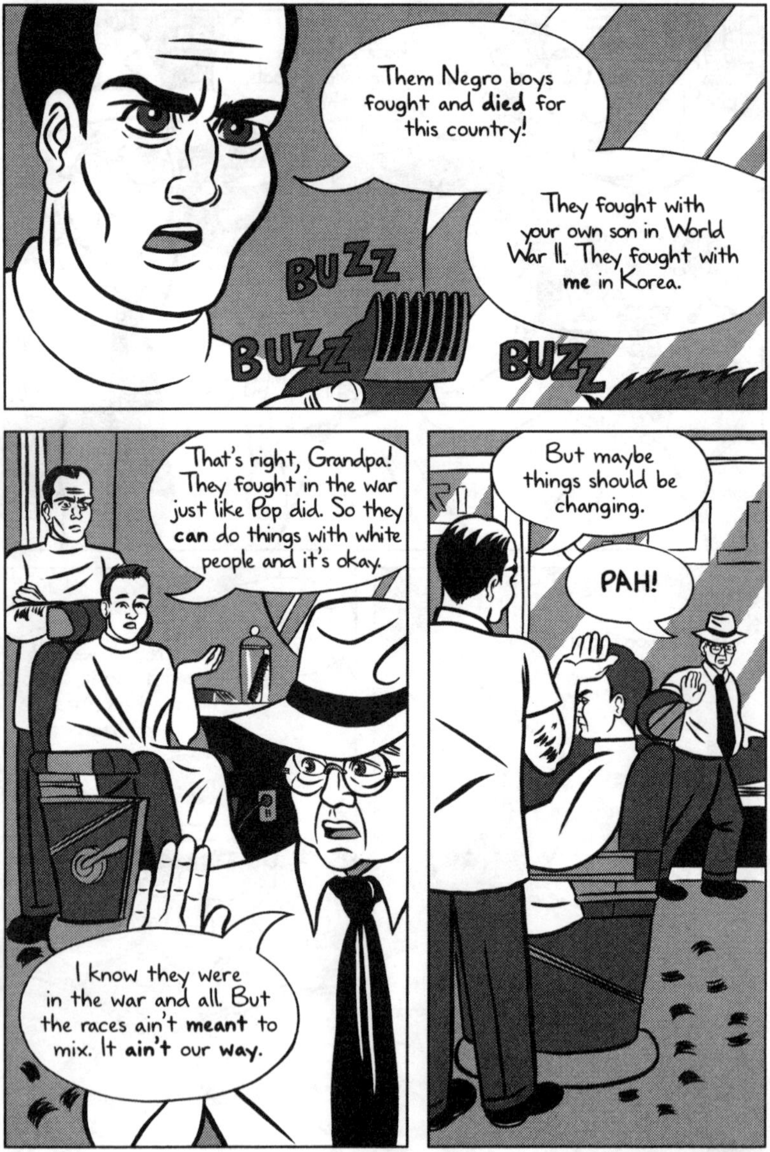
Them Negro boys fought and **died** for this country!
They fought with your own son in World War II. They fought with **me** in Korea.
BUZZ
BUZZ
BUZZ
That's right, Grandpa! They fought in the war just like Pop did. So they **can** do things with white people and it's okay.
I know they were in the war and all. But the races ain't **meant** to mix. It **ain't** our **way**.
But maybe things should be changing.
PAH!

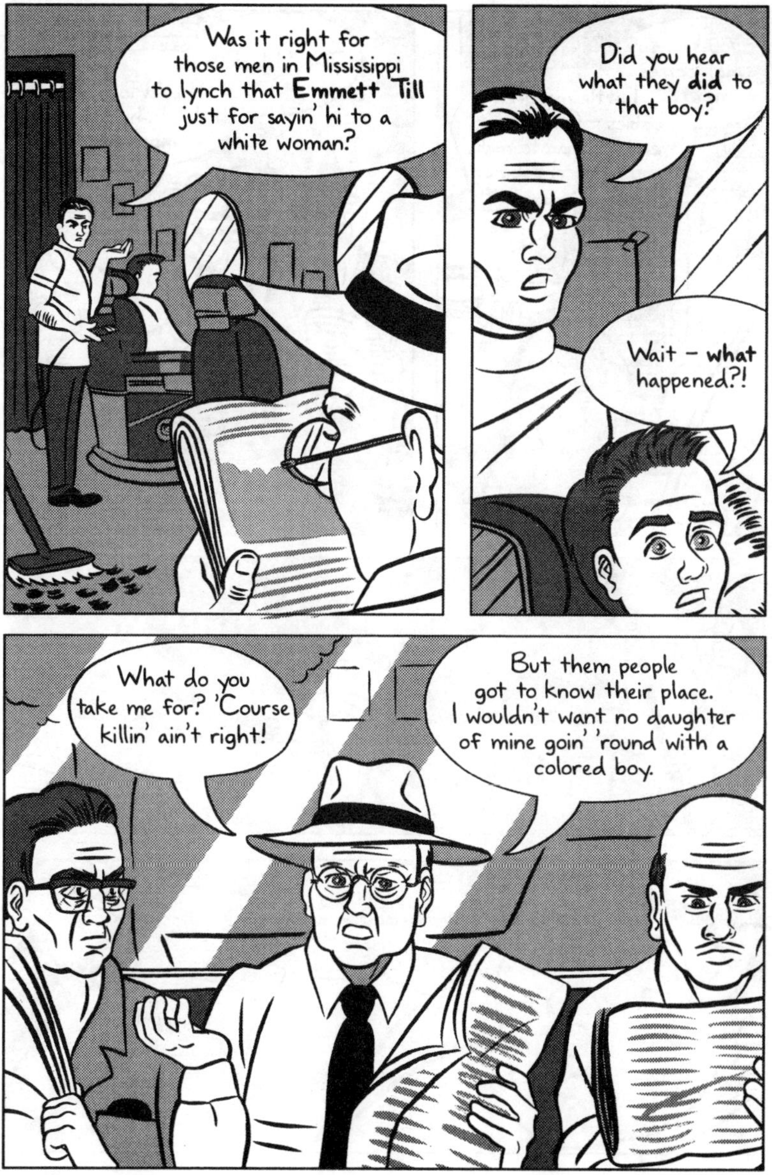
Was it right for those men in Mississippi to lynch that **Emmett Till** just for sayin' hi to a white woman?
Did you hear what they **did** to that boy?
Wait – **what** happened?!
What do you take me for? 'Course killin' ain't right!
But them people got to know their place. I wouldn't want no daughter of mine goin' 'round with a colored boy.

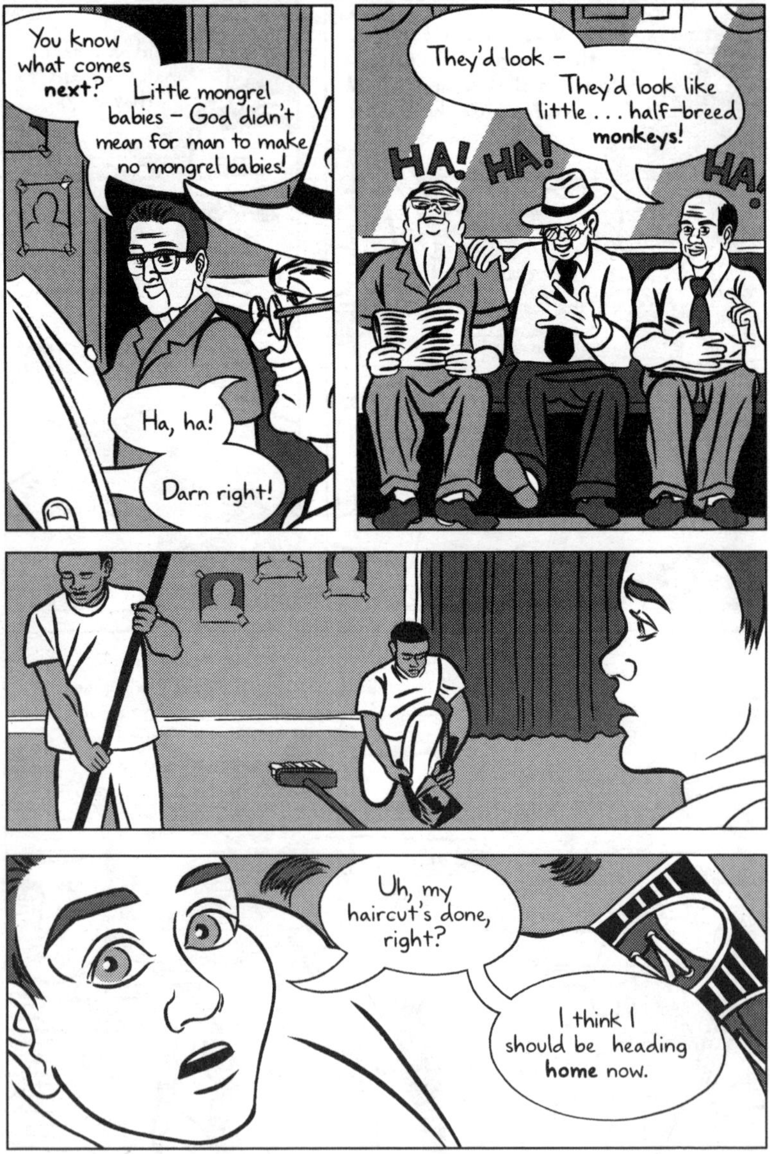
You know what comes **next**?
Little mongrel babies – God didn't mean for man to make no mongrel babies!
Ha, ha!
Darn right!
They'd look –
They'd look like little . . . half-breed **monkeys**!
HA! HA! HA!
Uh, my haircut's done, right?
I think I should be heading **home** now.

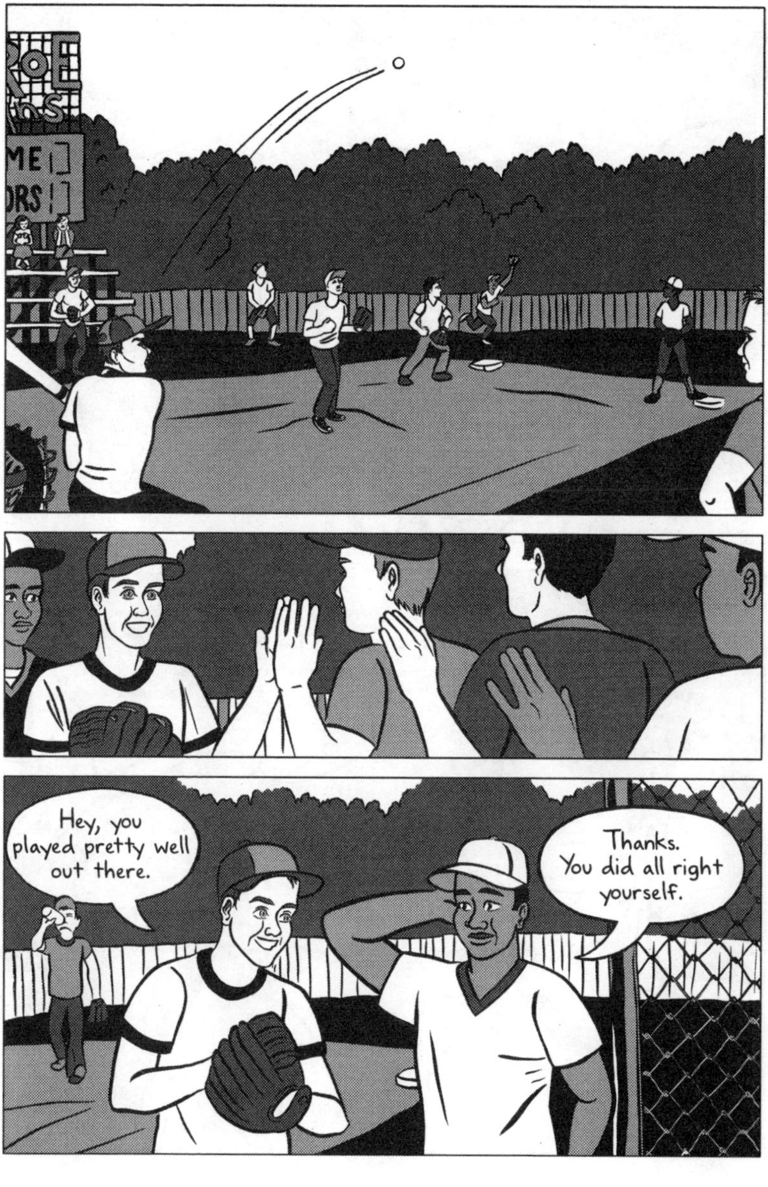
Hey, you played pretty well out there.
Thanks. You did all right yourself.

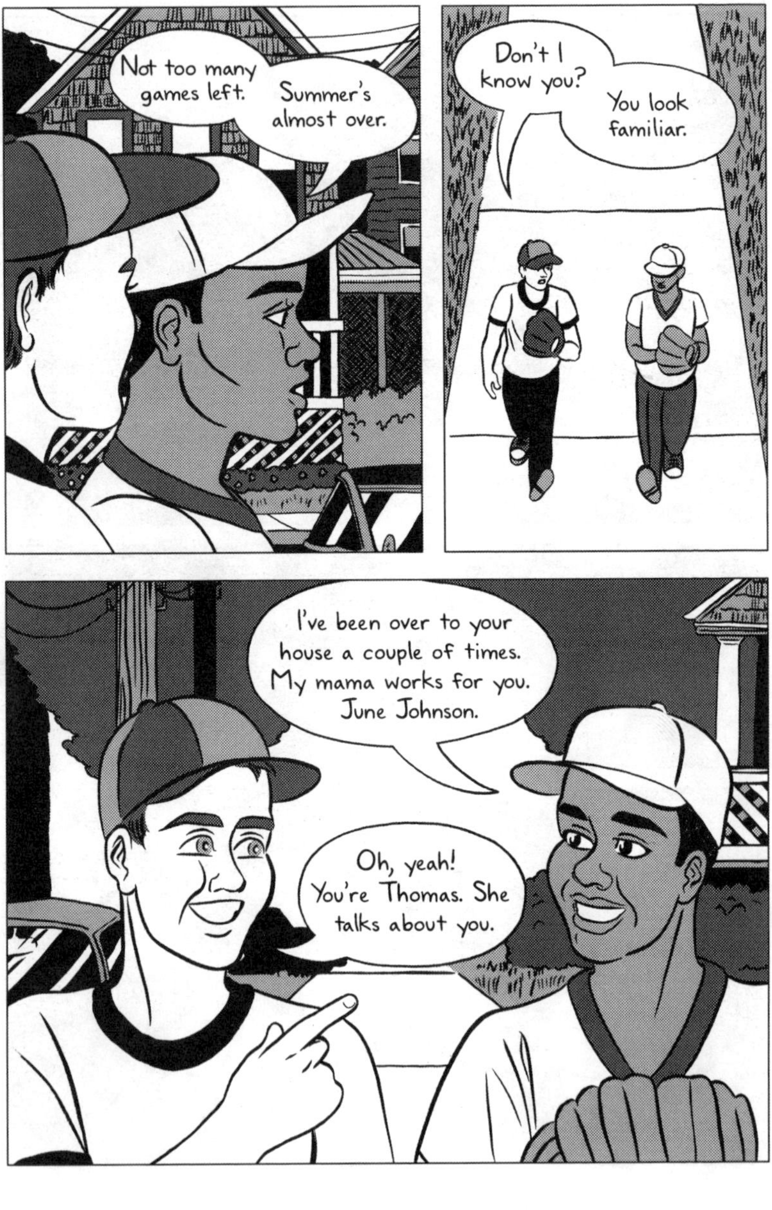
Not too many games left.
Summer's almost over.
Don't I know you?
You look familiar.
I've been over to your house a couple of times. My mama works for you. June Johnson.
Oh, yeah! You're Thomas. She talks about you.

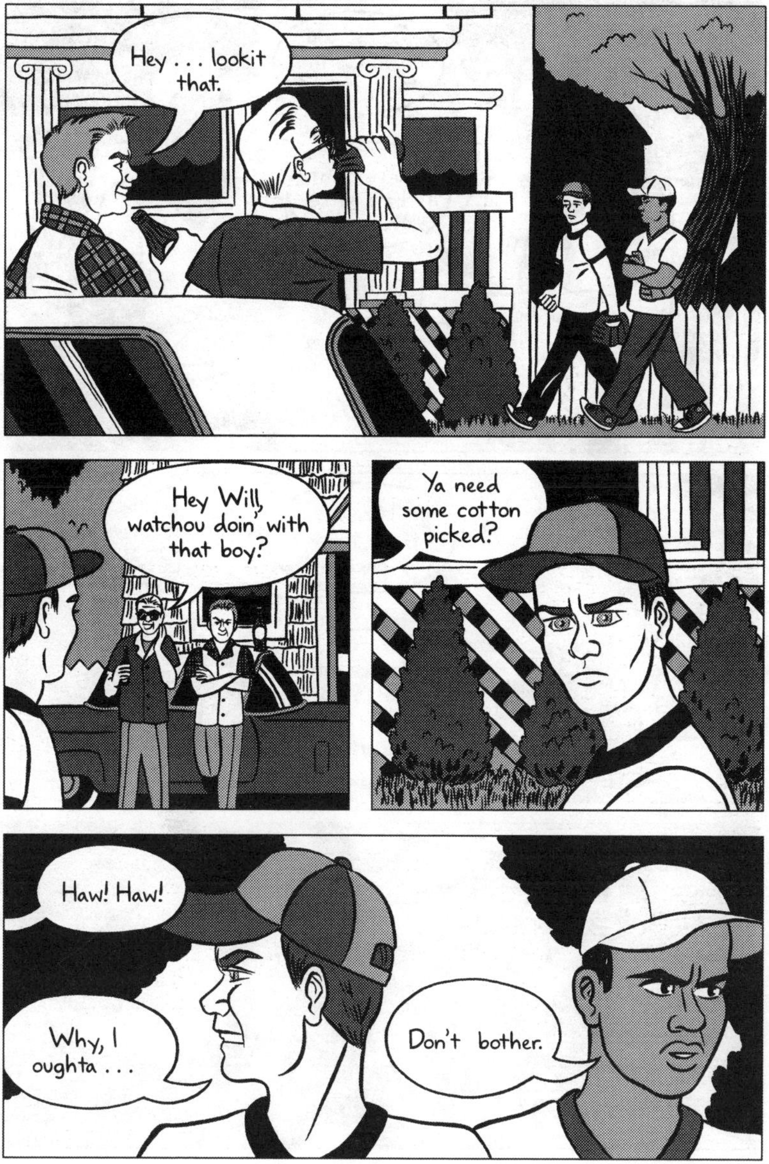
Hey . . . lookit that.
Hey Will, watchou doin' with that boy?
Ya need some cotton picked?
Haw! Haw!
Why, I oughta . . .
Don't bother.

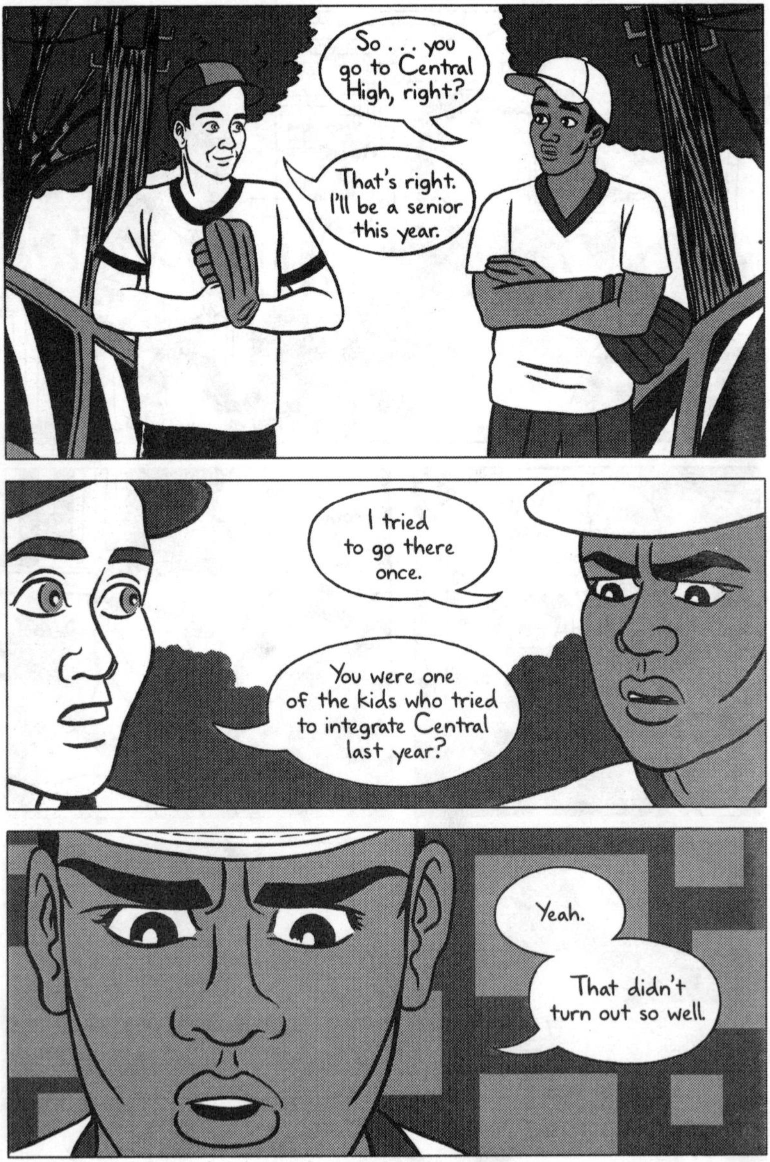
So . . . you go to Central High, right?
That's right. I'll be a senior this year.
I tried to go there once.
You were one of the kids who tried to integrate Central last year?
Yeah.
That didn't turn out so well.

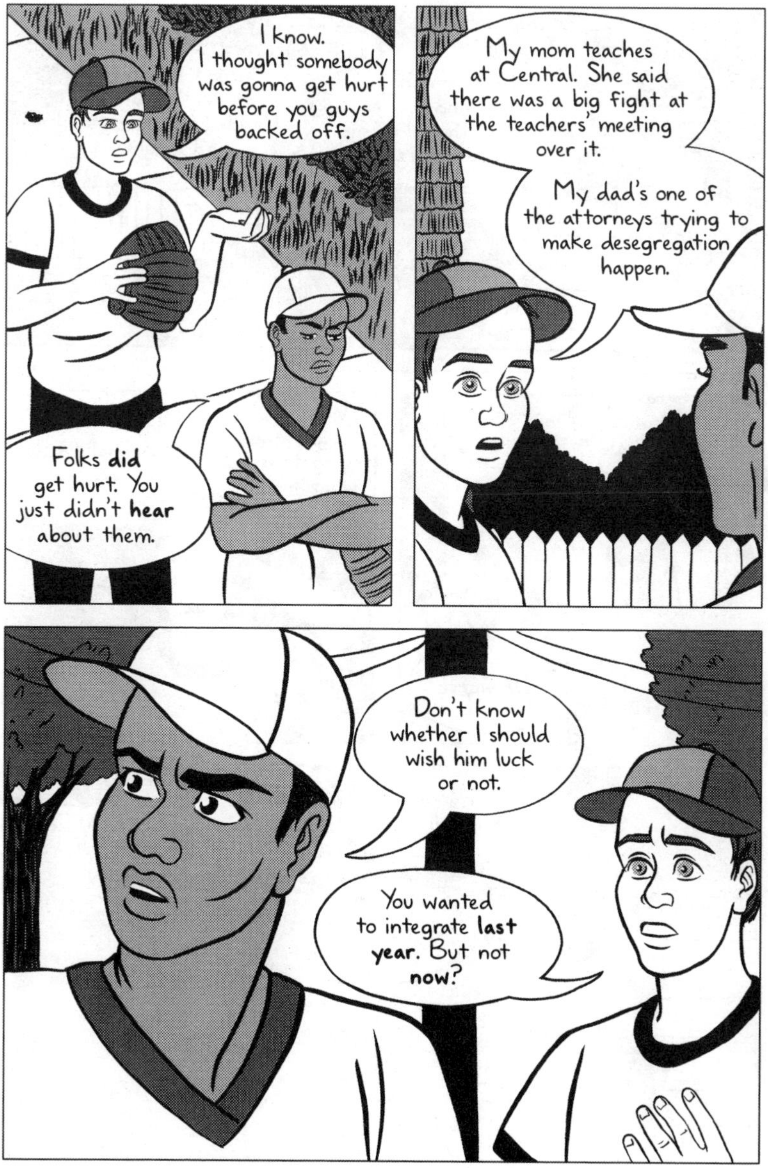
I know. I thought somebody was gonna get hurt before you guys backed off.
Folks **did** get hurt. You just didn't **hear** about them.
My mom teaches at Central. She said there was a big fight at the teachers' meeting over it.
My dad's one of the attorneys trying to make desegregation happen.
Don't know whether I should wish him luck or not.
You wanted to integrate **last year**. But not **now**?

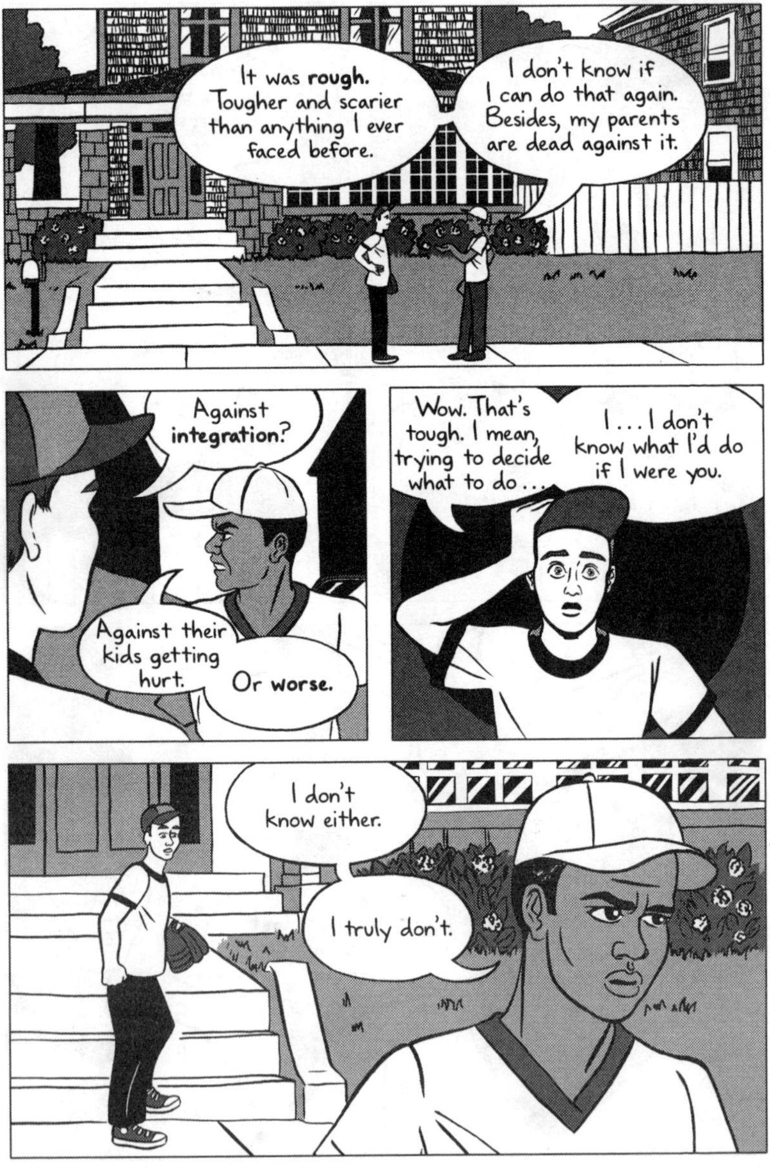
It was **rough.** Tougher and scarier than anything I ever faced before.
I don't know if I can do that again. Besides, my parents are dead against it.
Against **integration?**
Against their kids getting hurt.
Or **worse.**
Wow. That's tough. I mean, trying to decide what to do . . .
I . . . I don't know what I'd do if I were you.
I don't know either.
I truly don't.

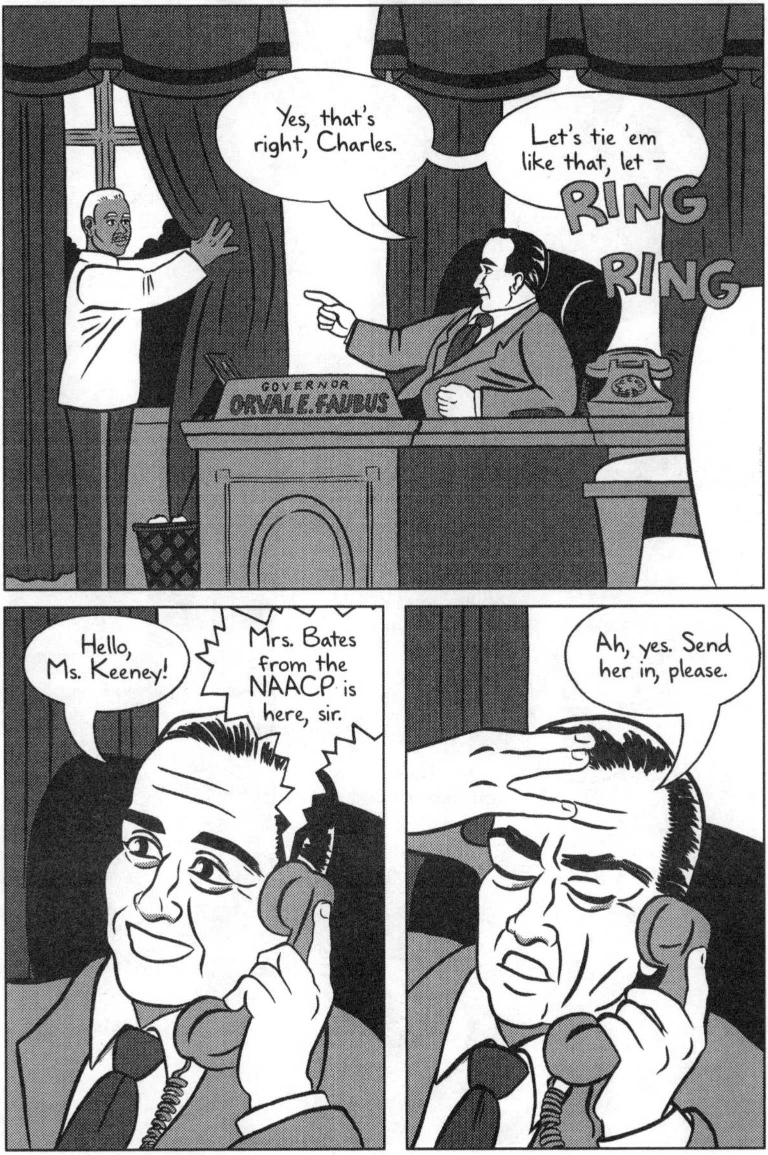
Yes, that's right, Charles.
Let's tie 'em like that, let –
RING
RING
GOVERNOR ORVAL E. FAUBUS
Hello, Ms. Keeney!
Mrs. Bates from the NAACP is here, sir.
Ah, yes. Send her in, please.

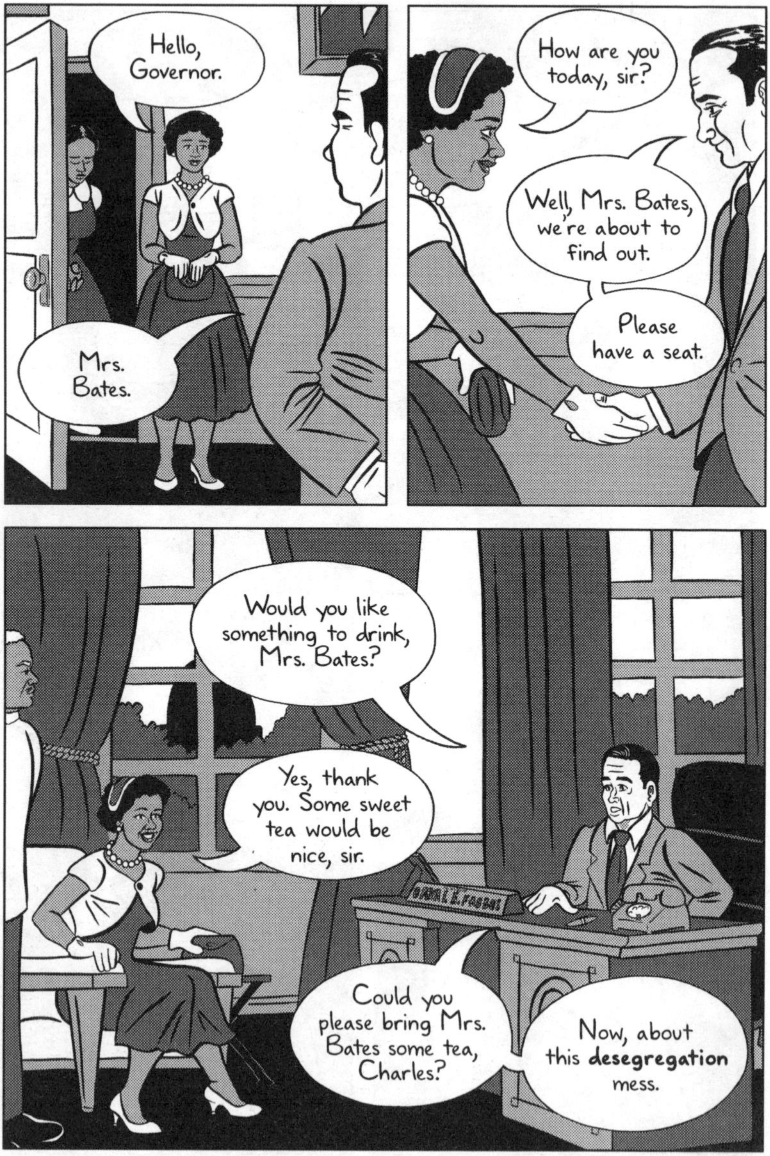
Hello, Governor.
Mrs. Bates.
How are you today, sir?
Well, Mrs. Bates, we're about to find out.
Please have a seat.
Would you like something to drink, Mrs. Bates?
Yes, thank you. Some sweet tea would be nice, sir.
Could you please bring Mrs. Bates some tea, Charles?
Now, about this **desegregation** mess.

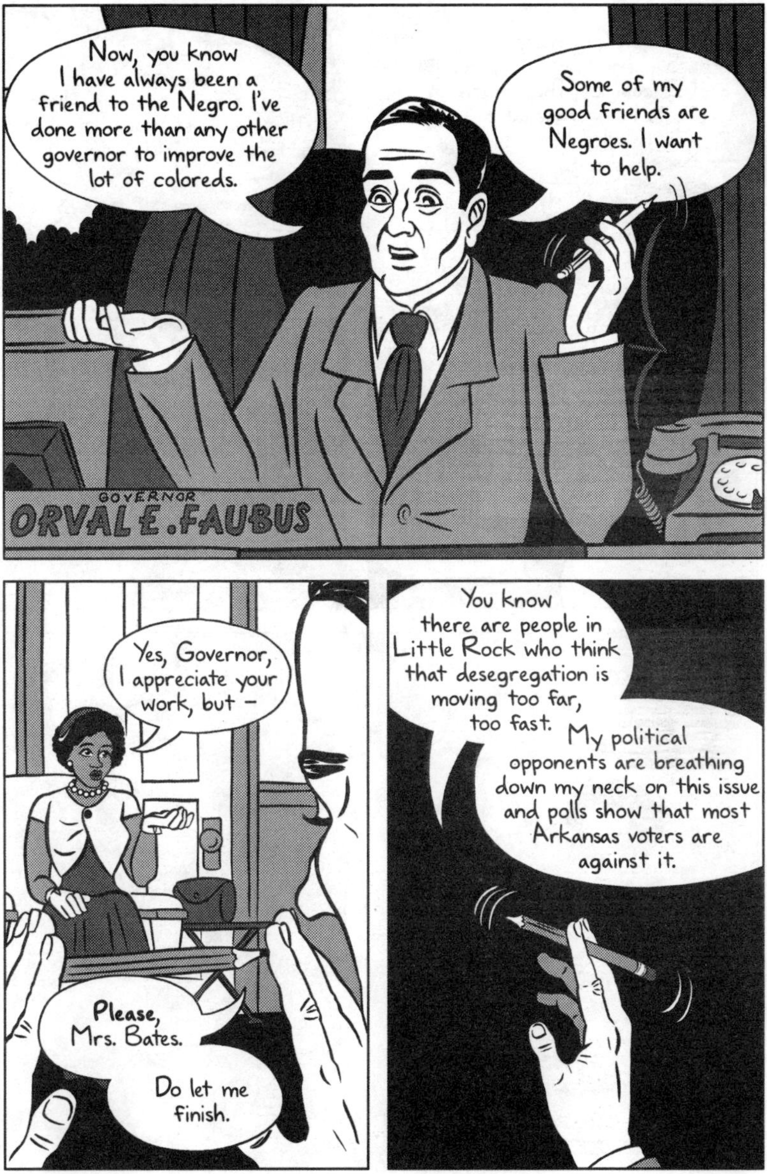
Now, you know I have always been a friend to the Negro. I've done more than any other governor to improve the lot of coloreds.
Some of my good friends are Negroes. I want to help.
GOVERNOR
ORVAL E. FAUBUS
Yes, Governor, I appreciate your work, but –
Please, Mrs. Bates.
Do let me finish.
You know there are people in Little Rock who think that desegregation is moving too far, too fast.
My political opponents are breathing down my neck on this issue and polls show that most Arkansas voters are against it.

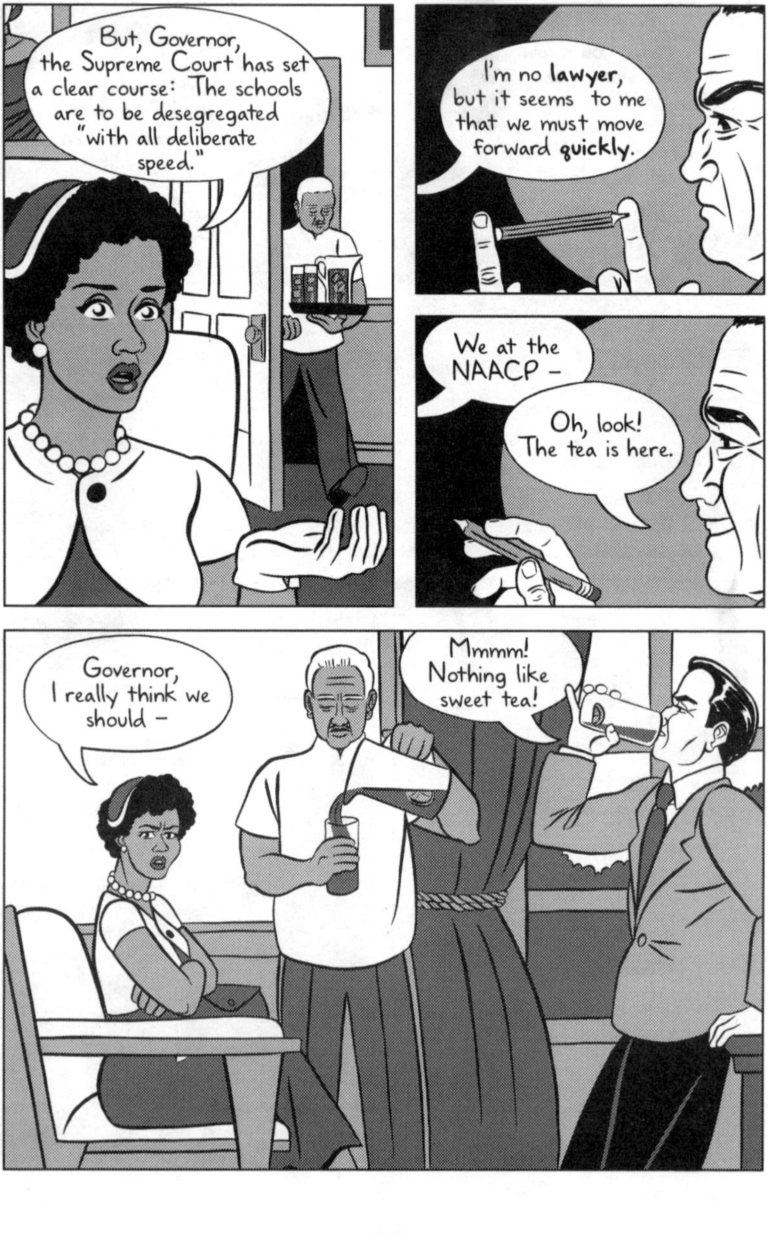
But, Governor, the Supreme Court has set a clear course: The schools are to be desegregated "with all deliberate speed."
I'm no **lawyer**, but it seems to me that we must move forward **quickly**.
We at the NAACP –
Oh, look! The tea is here.
Governor, I really think we should –
Mmmm! Nothing like sweet tea!

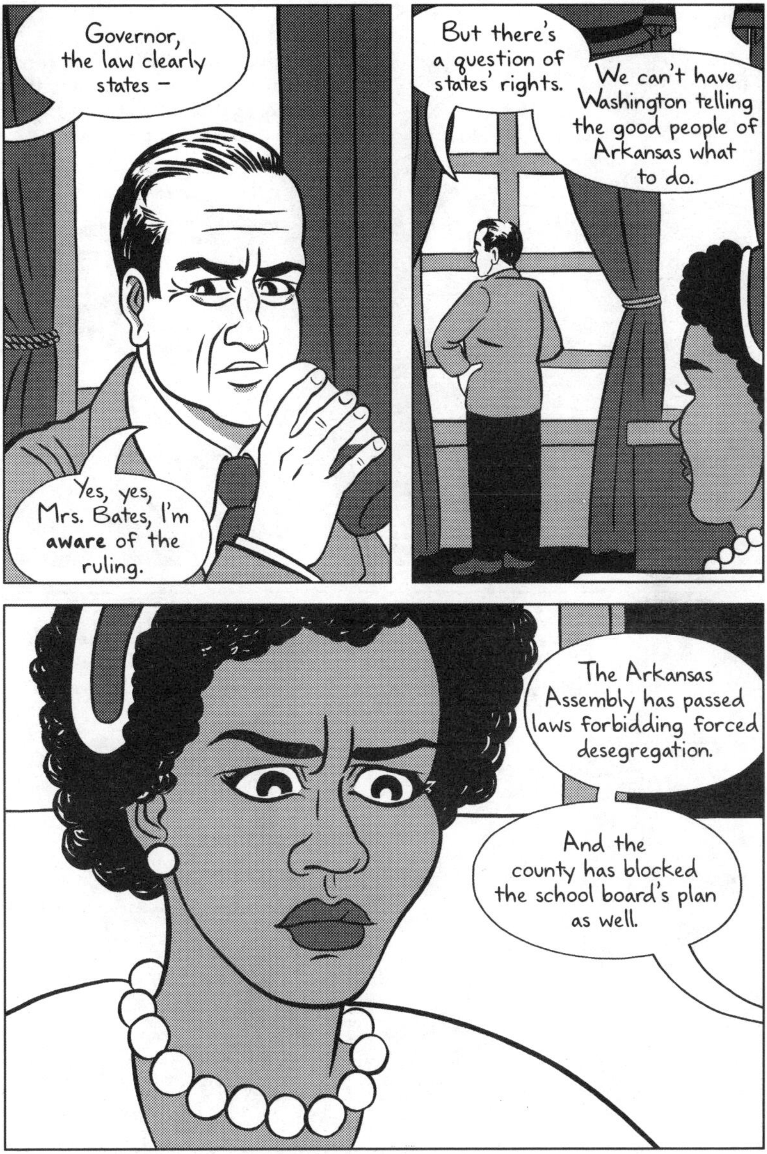
Governor, the law clearly states –
Yes, yes, Mrs. Bates, I'm **aware** of the ruling.
But there's a question of states' rights.
We can't have Washington telling the good people of Arkansas what to do.
The Arkansas Assembly has passed laws forbidding forced desegregation.
And the county has blocked the school board's plan as well.

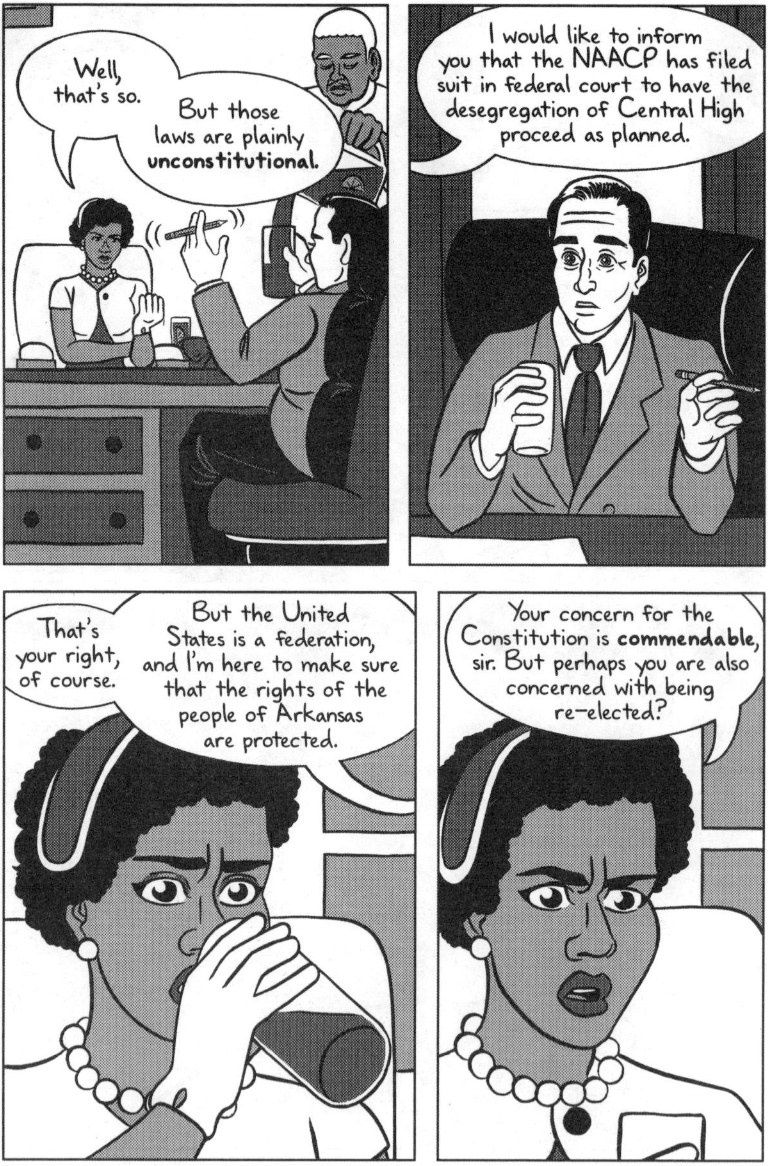
Well, that's so.
But those laws are plainly **unconstitutional.**
I would like to inform you that the NAACP has filed suit in federal court to have the desegregation of Central High proceed as planned.
That's your right, of course.
But the United States is a federation, and I'm here to make sure that the rights of the people of Arkansas are protected.
Your concern for the Constitution is **commendable,** sir. But perhaps you are also concerned with being re-elected?

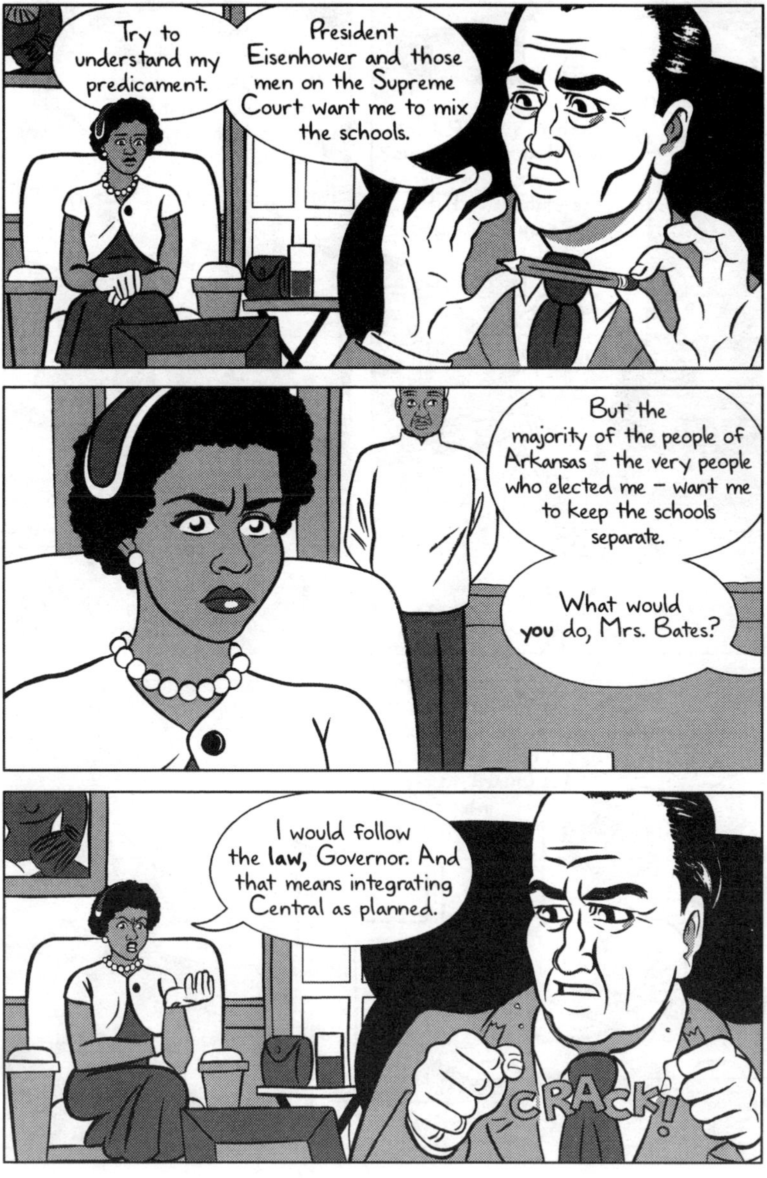
Try to understand my predicament.
President Eisenhower and those men on the Supreme Court want me to mix the schools.
But the majority of the people of Arkansas – the very people who elected me – want me to keep the schools separate.
What would **you** do, Mrs. Bates?
I would follow the **law,** Governor. And that means integrating Central as planned.
CRACK!

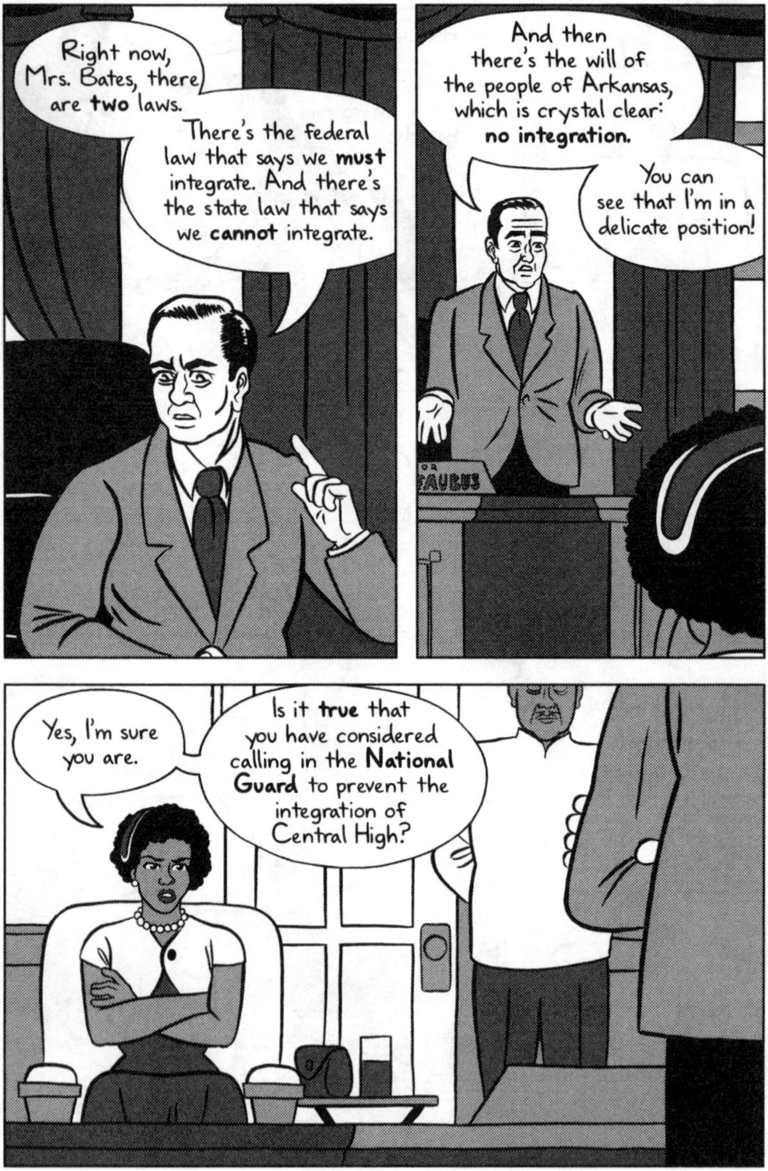
Right now, Mrs. Bates, there are **two** laws.
There's the federal law that says we **must** integrate. And there's the state law that says we **cannot** integrate.
And then there's the will of the people of Arkansas, which is crystal clear: **no integration.**
You can see that I'm in a delicate position!
FAUBUS
Yes, I'm sure you are.
Is it **true** that you have considered calling in the **National Guard** to prevent the integration of Central High?

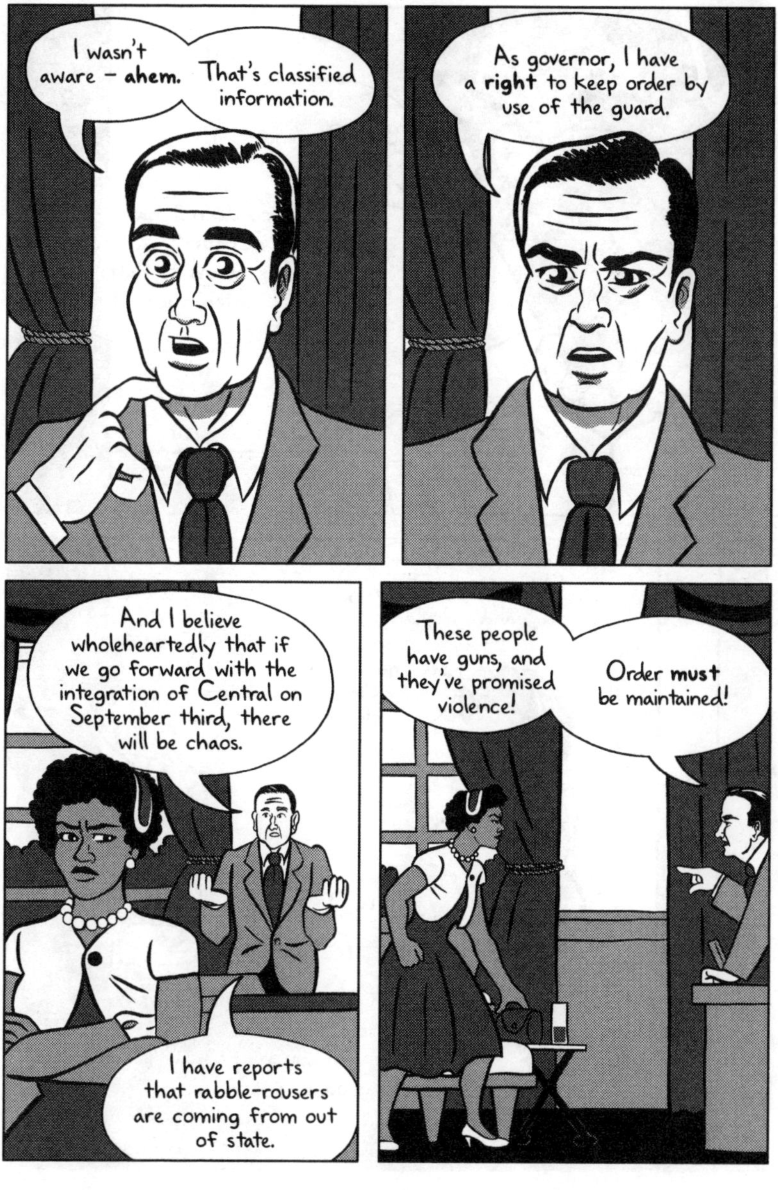
I wasn't aware – **ahem.**
That's classified information.
As governor, I have a **right** to keep order by use of the guard.
And I believe wholeheartedly that if we go forward with the integration of Central on September third, there will be chaos.
I have reports that rabble-rousers are coming from out of state.
These people have guns, and they've promised violence!
Order **must** be maintained!

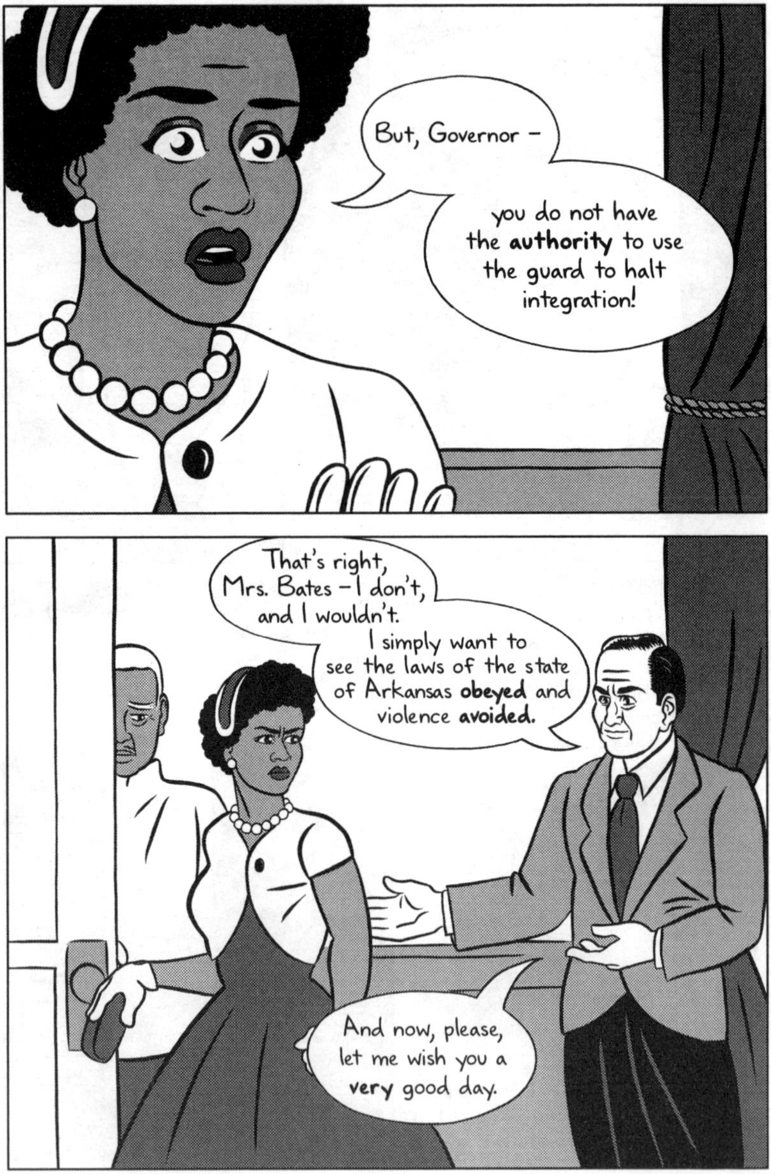

But, Governor –
you do not have the **authority** to use the guard to halt integration!
That's right, Mrs. Bates – I don't, and I wouldn't.
I simply want to see the laws of the state of Arkansas **obeyed** and violence **avoided.**
And now, please, let me wish you a **very** good day.

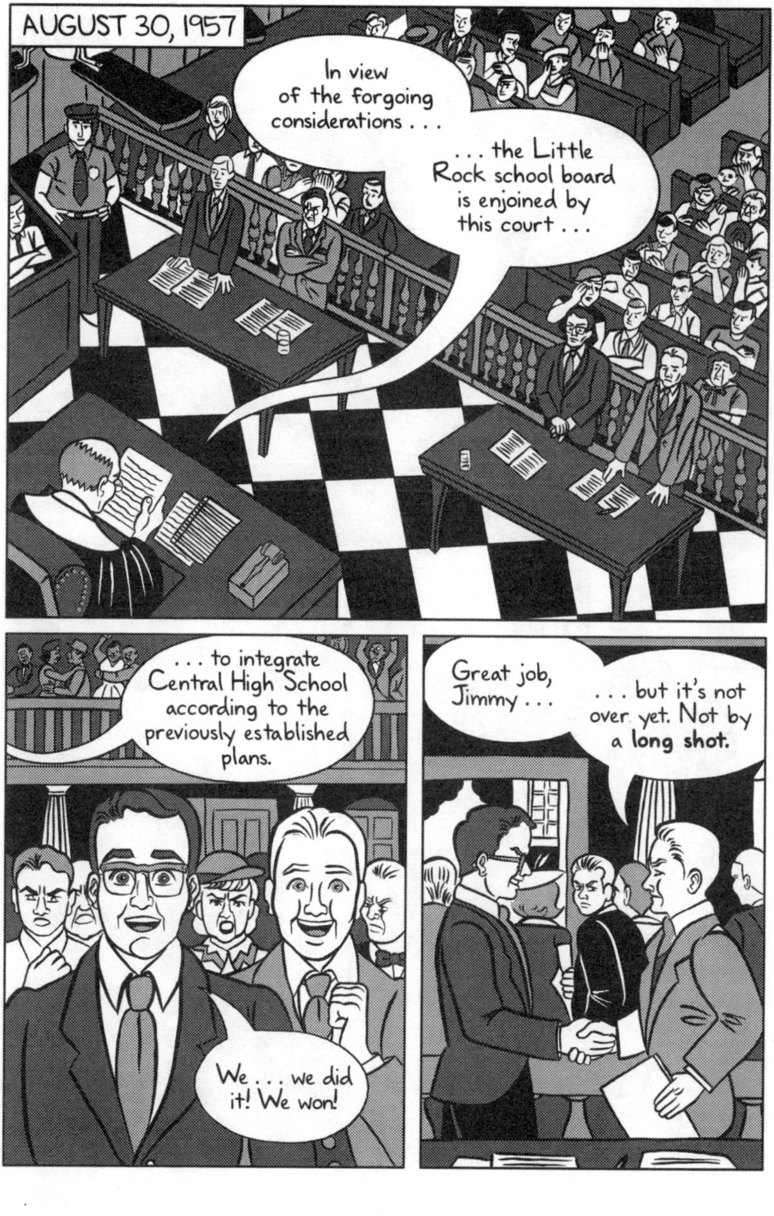
AUGUST 30, 1957
In view of the forgoing considerations . . .
. . . the Little Rock school board is enjoined by this court . . .
. . . to integrate Central High School according to the previously established plans.
We . . . we did it! We won!
Great job, Jimmy . . .
. . . but it's not over yet. Not by a **long shot.**

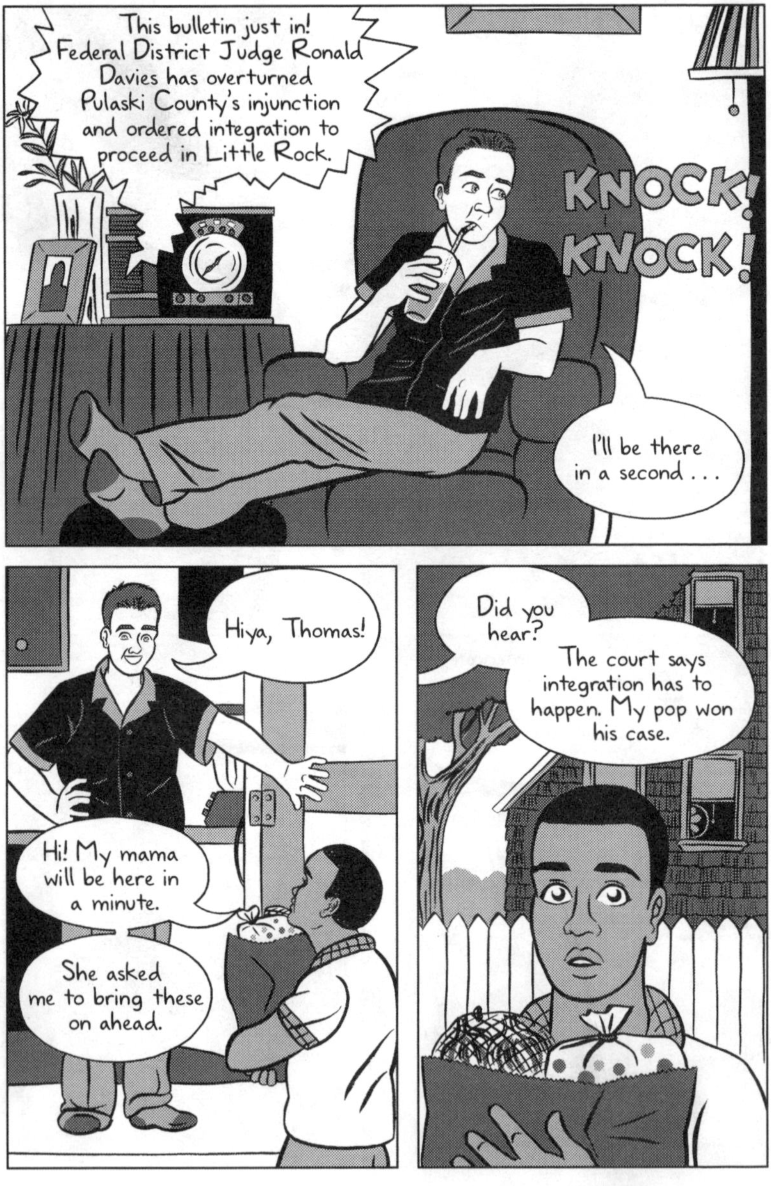
This bulletin just in! Federal District Judge Ronald Davies has overturned Pulaski County's injunction and ordered integration to proceed in Little Rock.
KNOCK! KNOCK!
I'll be there in a second . . .
Hiya, Thomas!
Hi! My mama will be here in a minute.
She asked me to bring these on ahead.
Did you hear?
The court says integration has to happen. My pop won his case.

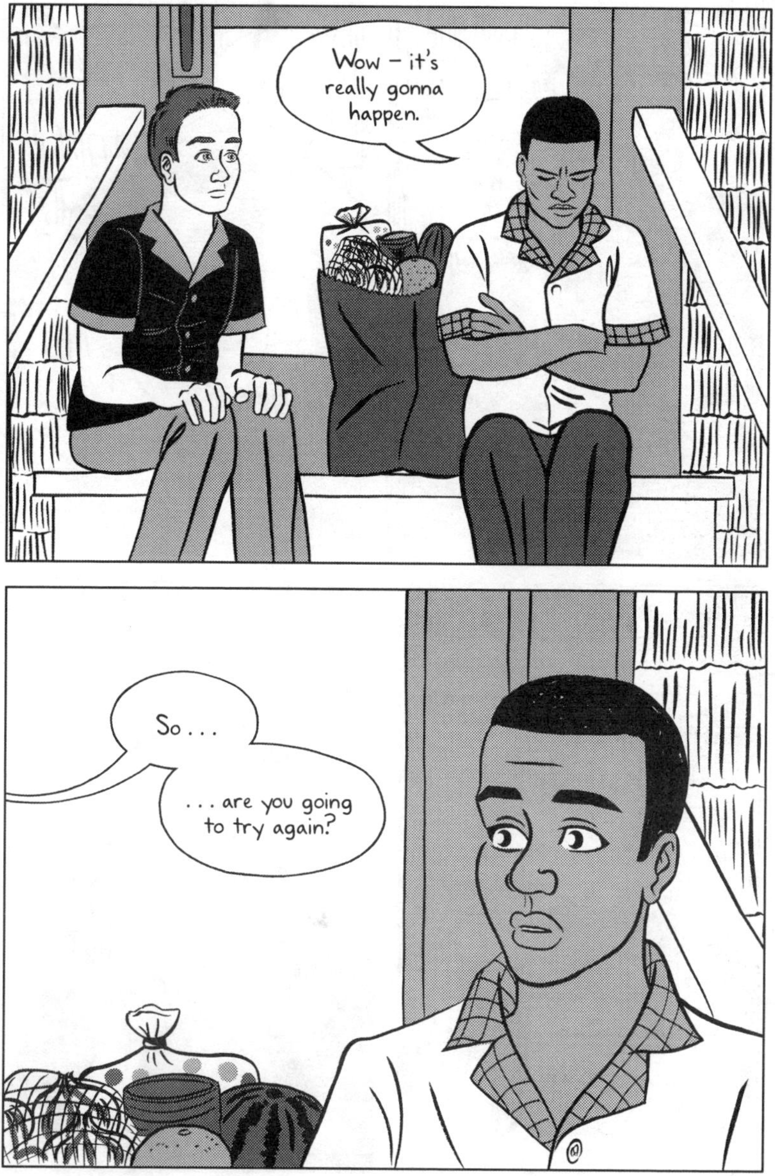
Wow – it's really gonna happen.
So . . .
. . . are you going to try again?

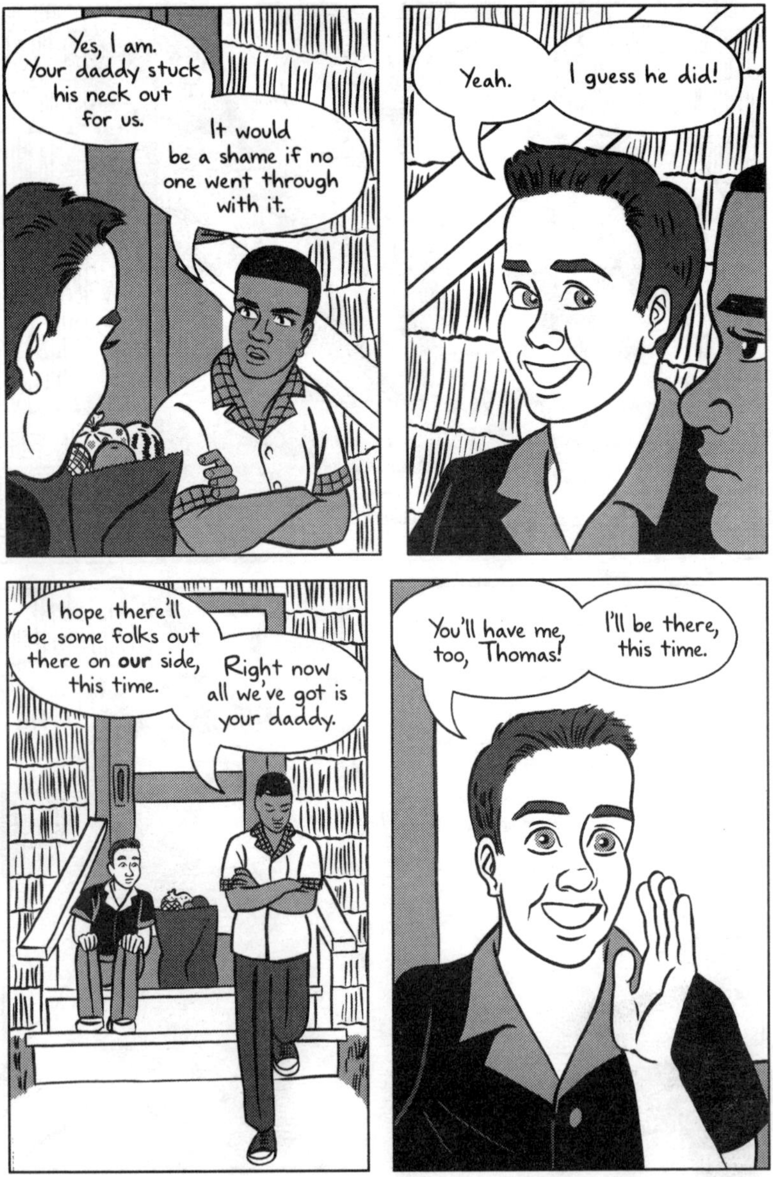
Yes, I am. Your daddy stuck his neck out for us.
It would be a shame if no one went through with it.
Yeah.
I guess he did!
I hope there'll be some folks out there on **our** side, this time.
Right now all we've got is your daddy.
You'll have me, too, Thomas!
I'll be there, this time.

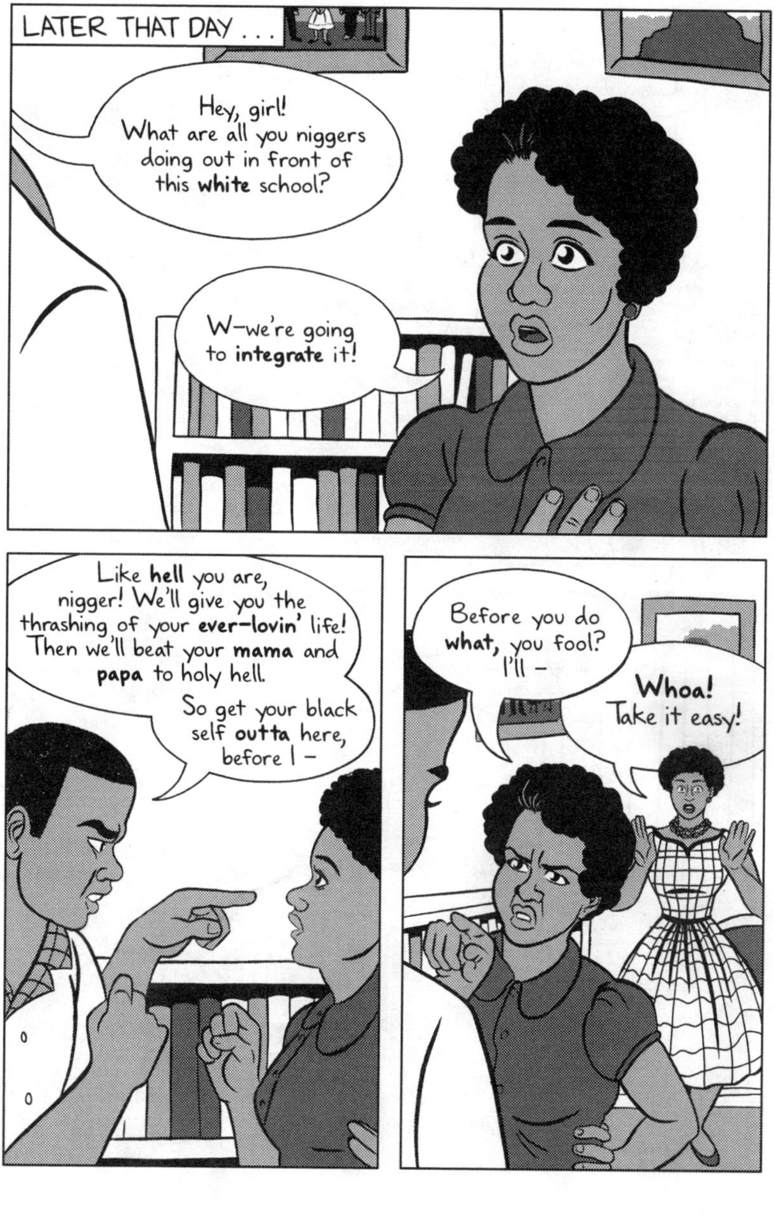
LATER THAT DAY . . .
Hey, girl! What are all you niggers doing out in front of this white school?
W-we're going to integrate it!
Like hell you are, nigger! We'll give you the thrashing of your ever-lovin' life! Then we'll beat your mama and papa to holy hell.
So get your black self outta here, before I –
Before you do what, you fool? I'll –
Whoa! Take it easy!

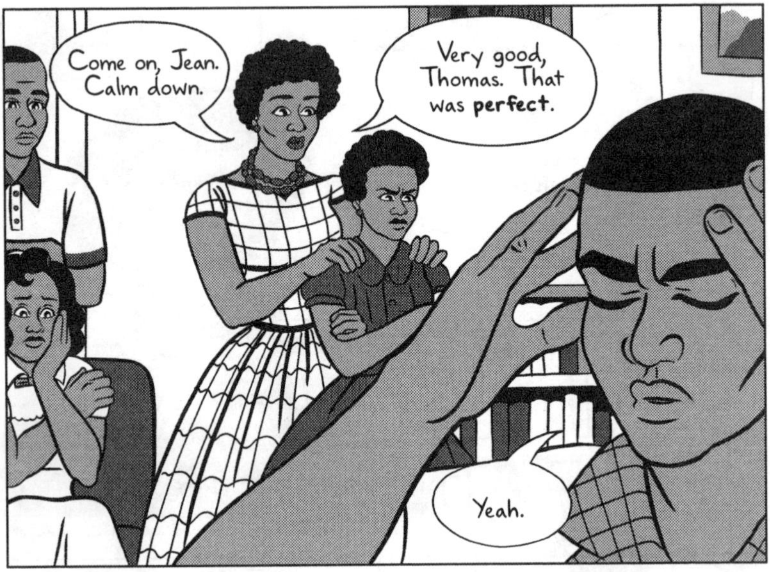
Come on, Jean. Calm down.
Very good, Thomas. That was **perfect**.
Yeah.

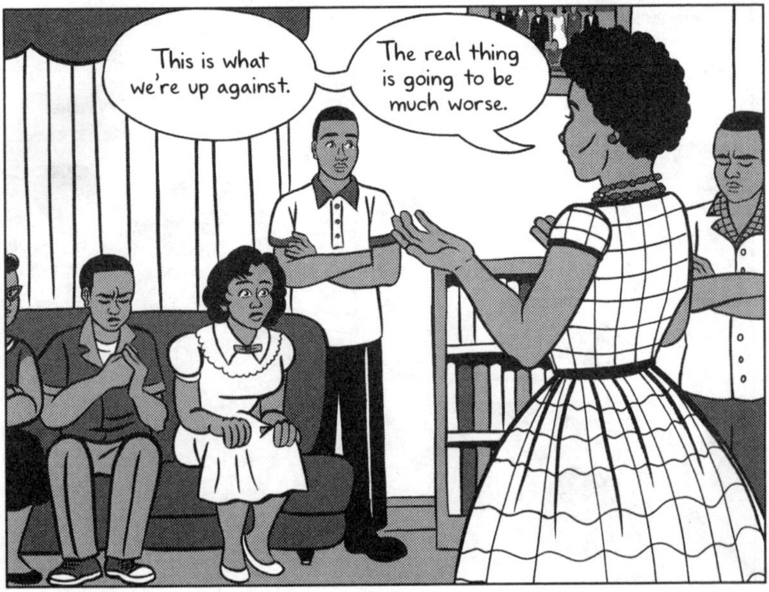
This is what we're up against.
The real thing is going to be much worse.

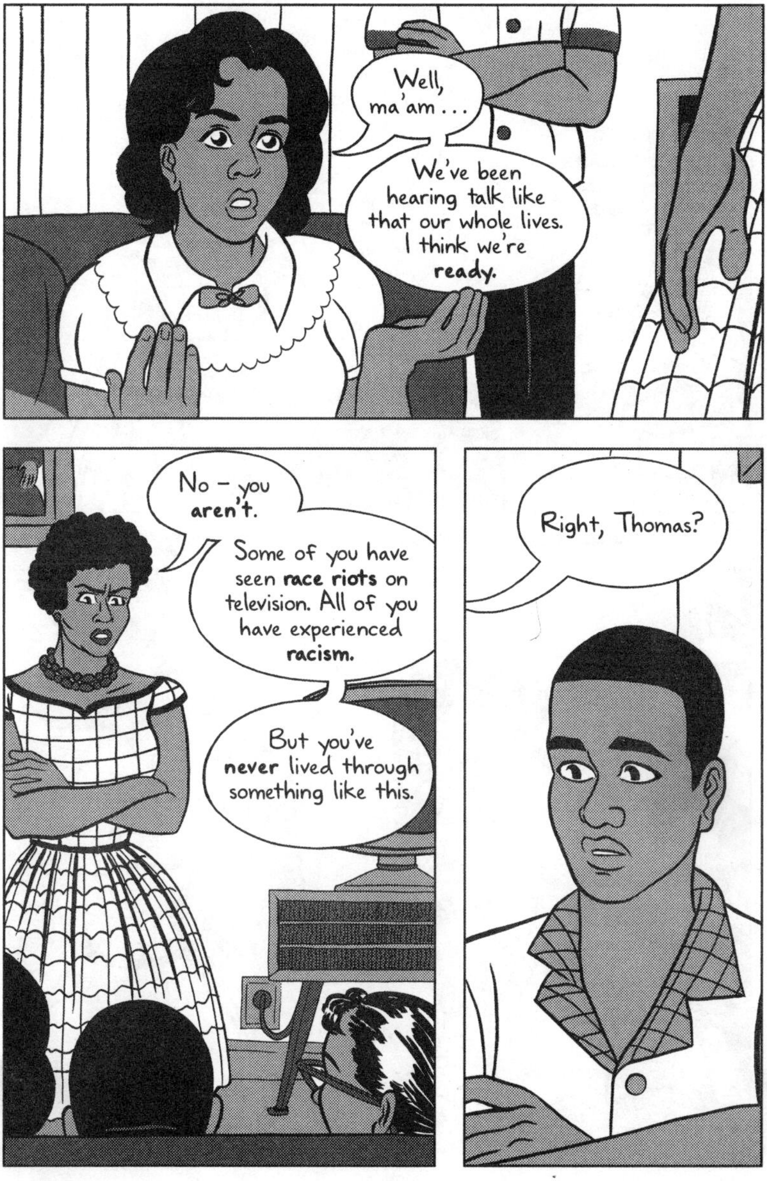

Well, ma'am . . .
We've been hearing talk like that our whole lives. I think we're **ready.**
No – you **aren't.**
Some of you have seen **race riots** on television. All of you have experienced **racism.**
But you've **never** lived through something like this.
Right, Thomas?

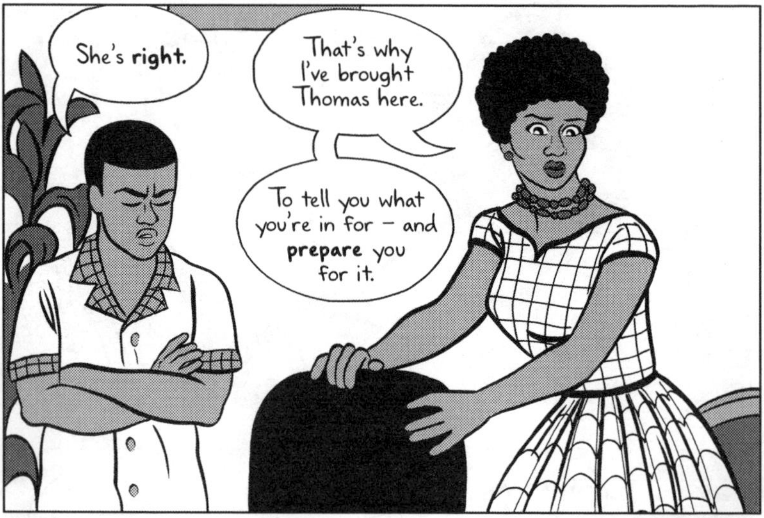
She's **right.**
That's why I've brought Thomas here.
To tell you what you're in for – and **prepare** you for it.

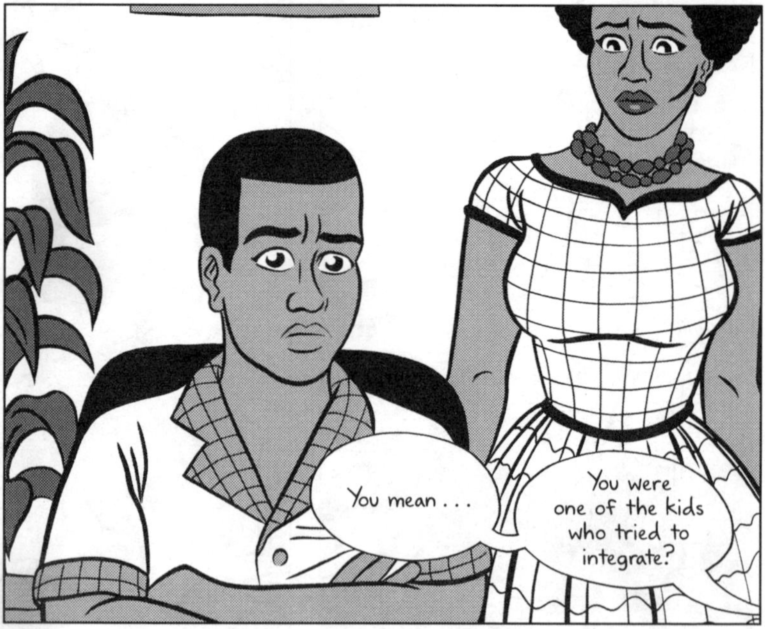
You mean . . .
You were one of the kids who tried to integrate?

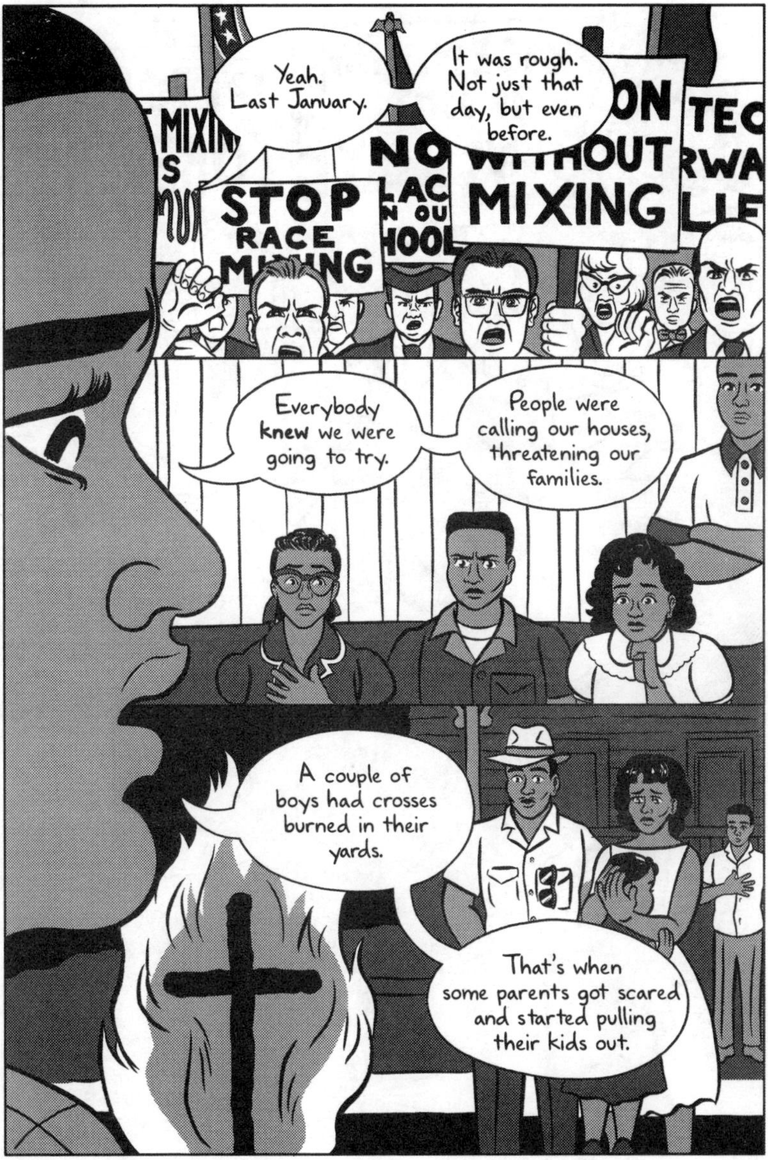
MIXIN
STOP RACE MIXING
NO
WITHOUT MIXING
Yeah. Last January.
It was rough. Not just that day, but even before.
Everybody knew we were going to try.
People were calling our houses, threatening our families.
A couple of boys had crosses burned in their yards.
That's when some parents got scared and started pulling their kids out.

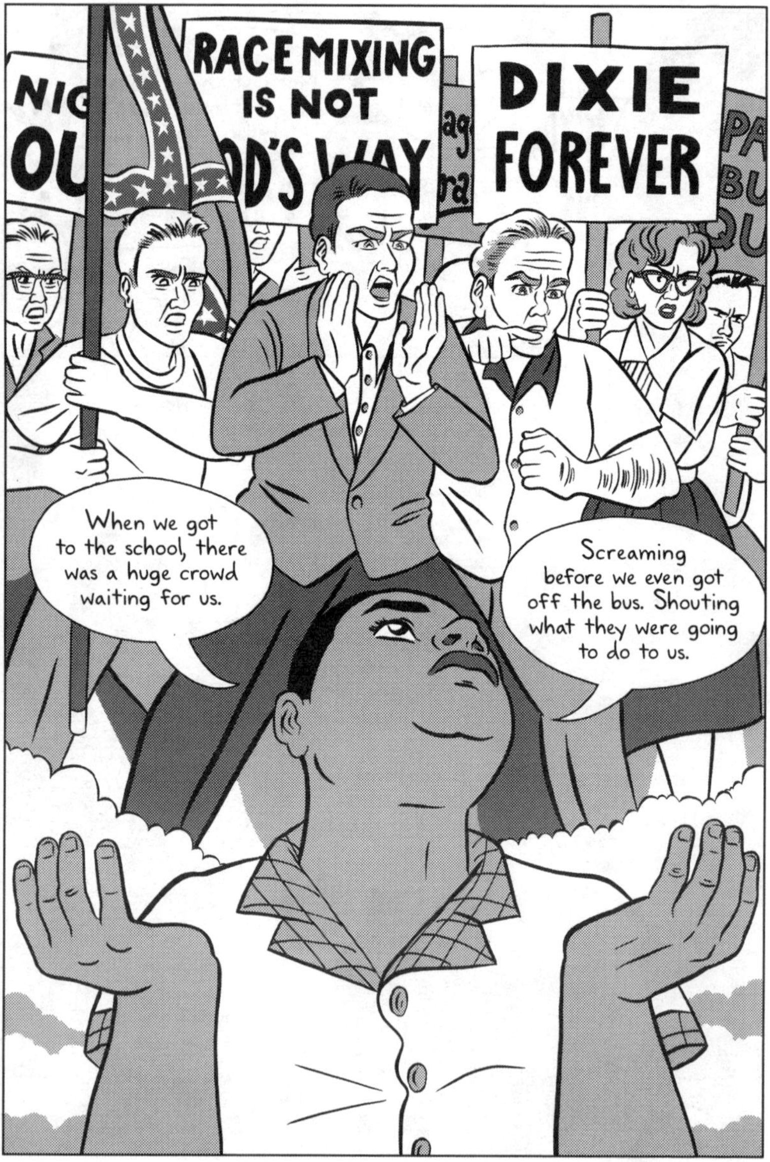
RACE MIXING IS NOT
DIXIE FOREVER
When we got to the school, there was a huge crowd waiting for us.
Screaming before we even got off the bus. Shouting what they were going to do to us.

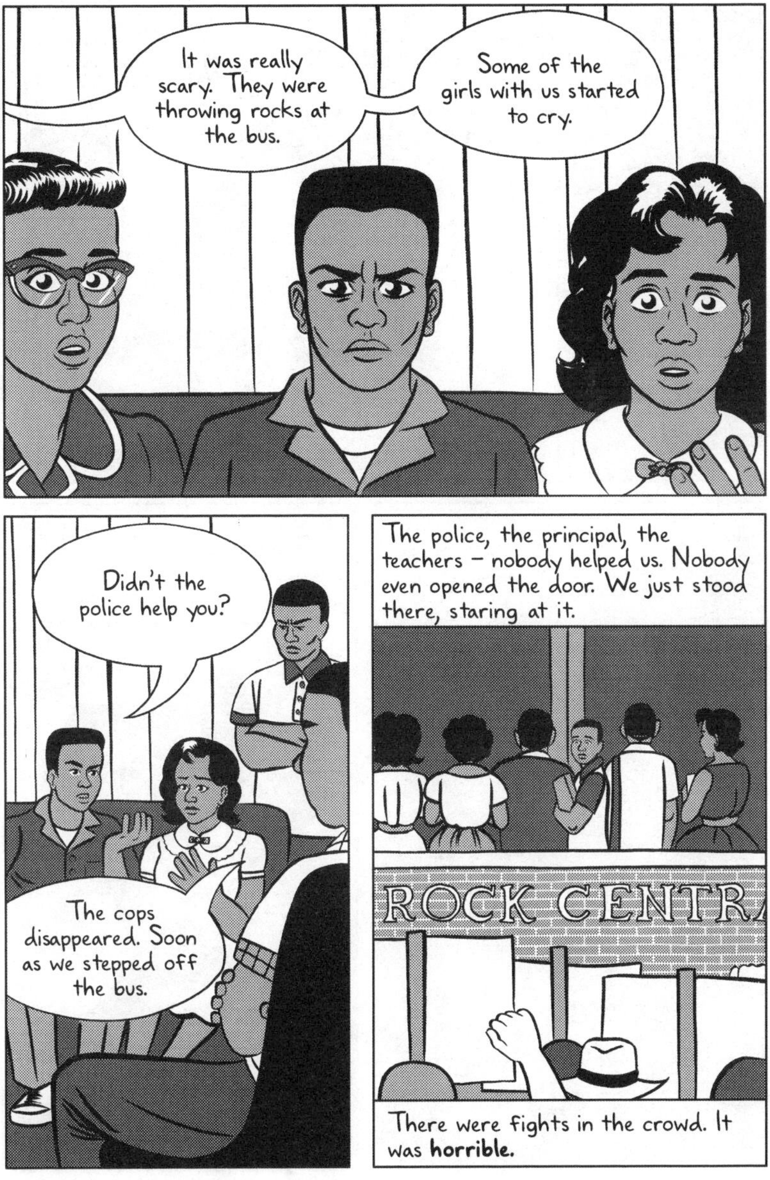
It was really scary. They were throwing rocks at the bus.
Some of the girls with us started to cry.
Didn't the police help you?
The cops disappeared. Soon as we stepped off the bus.
The police, the principal, the teachers – nobody helped us. Nobody even opened the door. We just stood there, staring at it.
ROCK CENTRA
There were fights in the crowd. It was **horrible.**

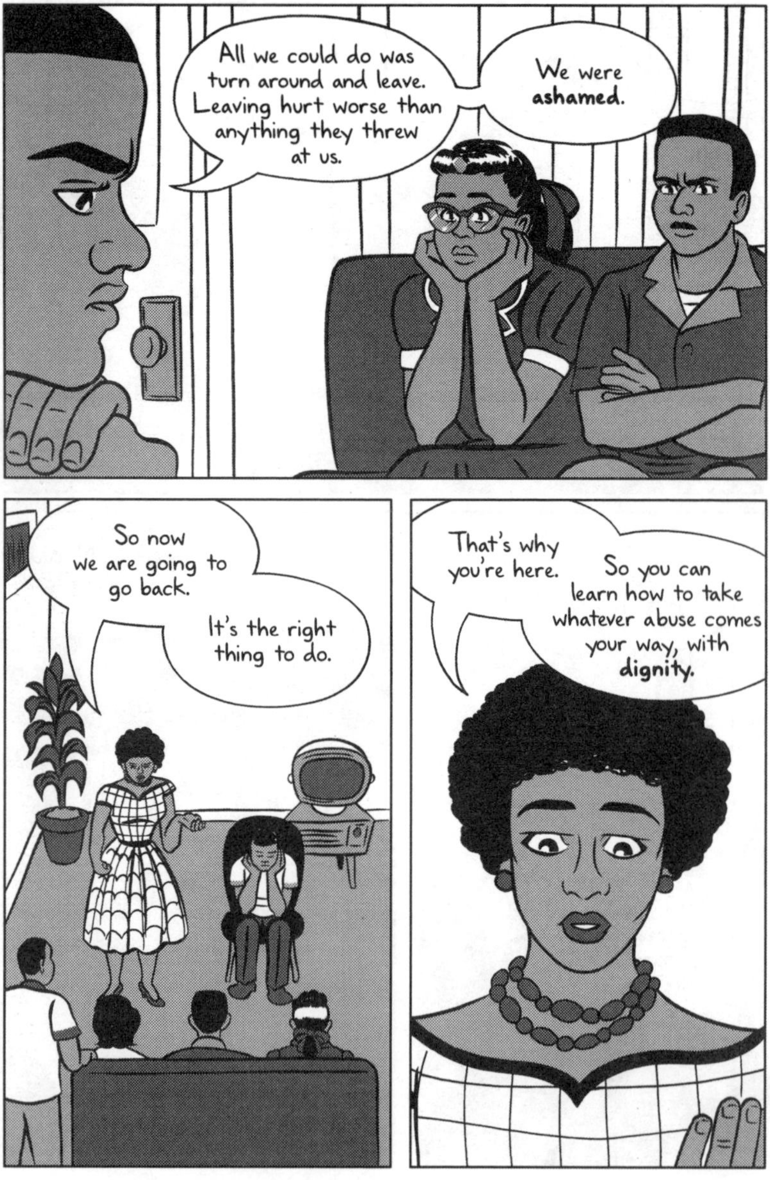
All we could do was turn around and leave. Leaving hurt worse than anything they threw at us.
We were **ashamed.**
So now we are going to go back.
It's the right thing to do.
That's why you're here.
So you can learn how to take whatever abuse comes your way, with **dignity.**

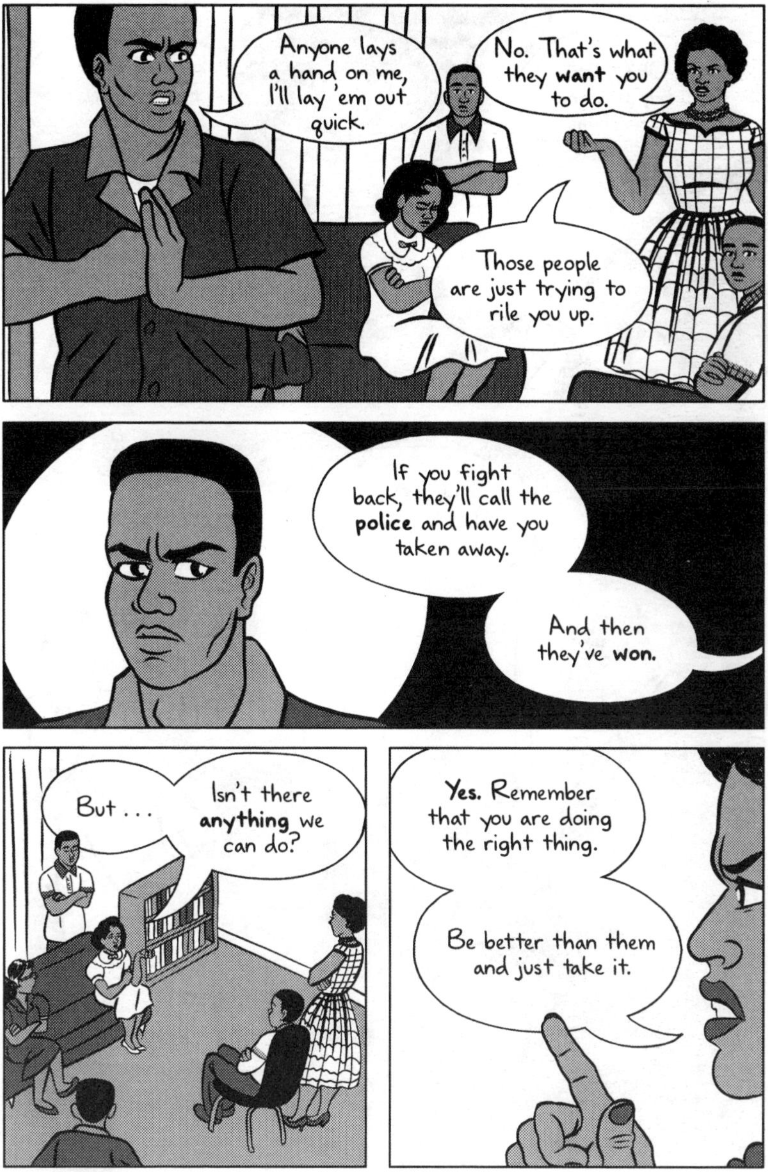
Anyone lays a hand on me, I'll lay 'em out quick.
No. That's what they **want** you to do.
Those people are just trying to rile you up.
If you fight back, they'll call the **police** and have you taken away.
And then they've **won.**
But . . .
Isn't there **anything** we can do?
Yes. Remember that you are doing the right thing.
Be better than them and just take it.

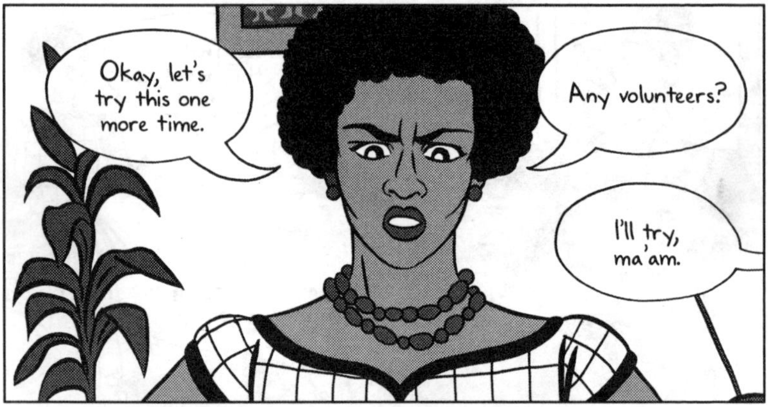
Okay, let's try this one more time.
Any volunteers?
I'll try, ma'am.

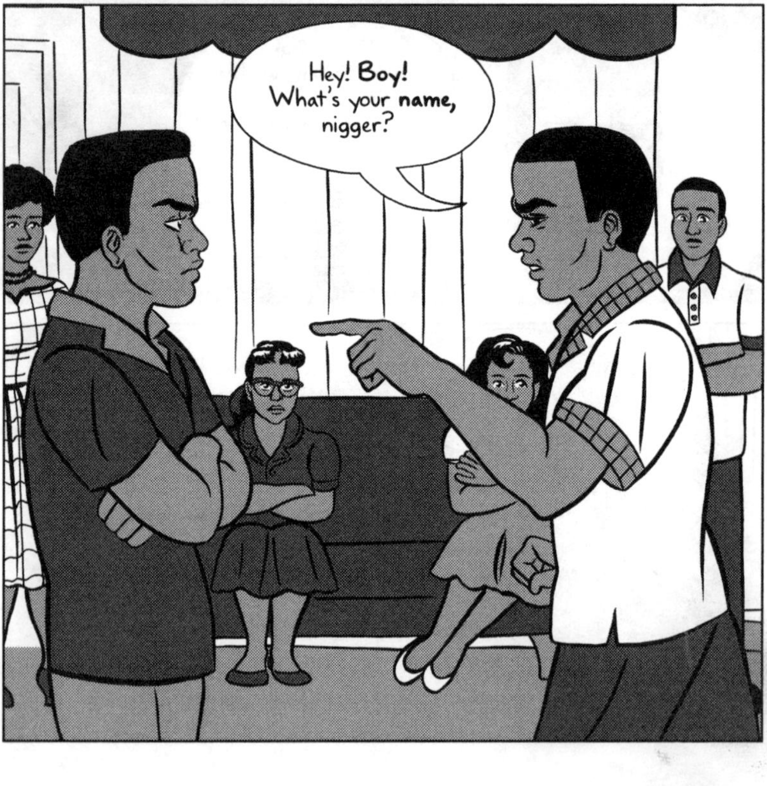
Hey! **Boy!** What's your **name,** nigger?

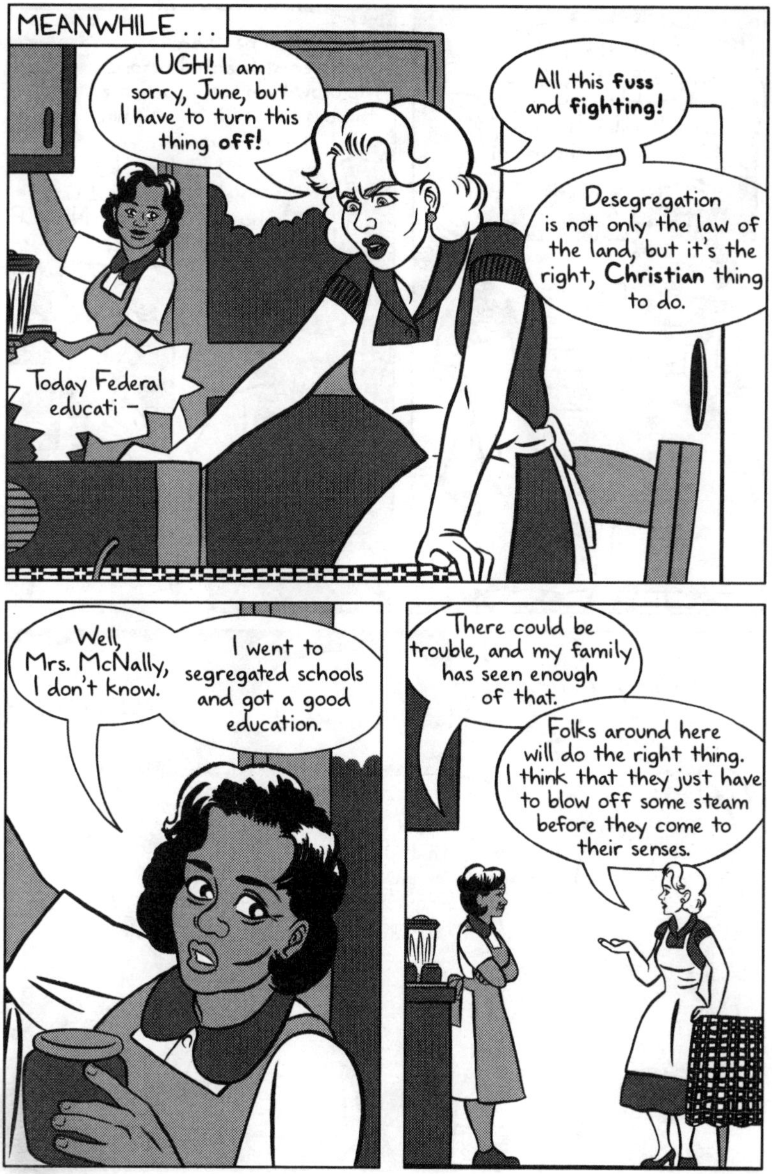
MEANWHILE . . .
UGH! I am sorry, June, but I have to turn this thing off!
Today Federal educati –
All this fuss and fighting!
Desegregation is not only the law of the land, but it's the right, Christian thing to do.
Well, Mrs. McNally, I don't know.
I went to segregated schools and got a good education.
There could be trouble, and my family has seen enough of that.
Folks around here will do the right thing. I think that they just have to blow off some steam before they come to their senses.

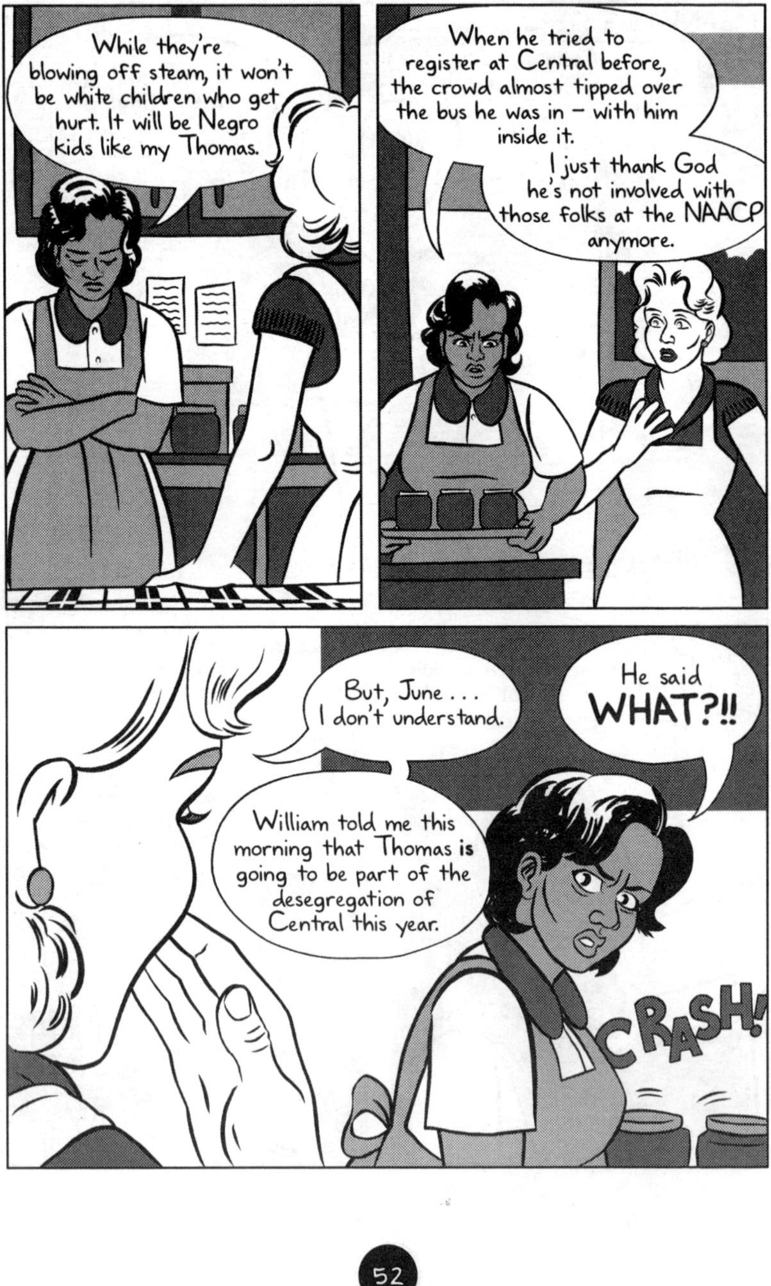
While they're blowing off steam, it won't be white children who get hurt. It will be Negro kids like my Thomas.
When he tried to register at Central before, the crowd almost tipped over the bus he was in – with him inside it.
I just thank God he's not involved with those folks at the NAACP anymore.
But, June . . . I don't understand.
William told me this morning that Thomas **is** going to be part of the desegregation of Central this year.
He said **WHAT?!!**
CRASH!

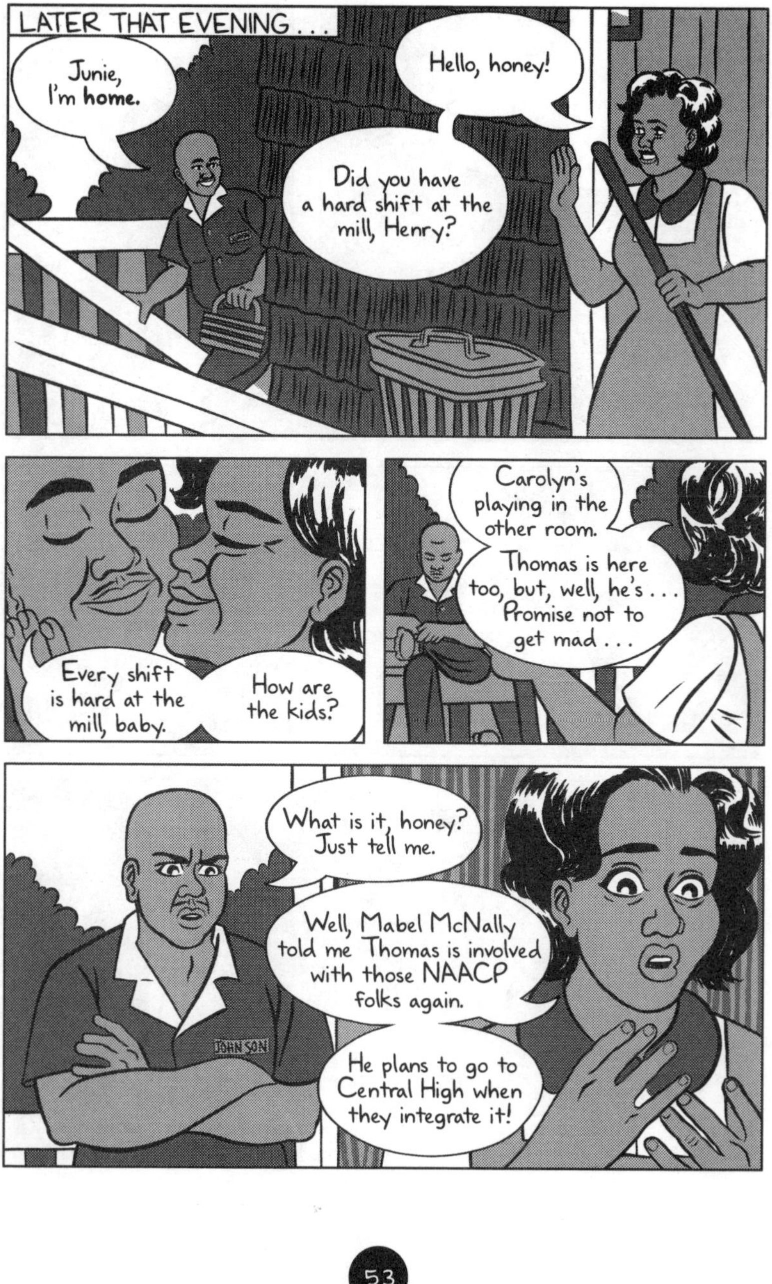
LATER THAT EVENING . . .
Junie, I'm **home.**
Hello, honey!
Did you have a hard shift at the mill, Henry?
Every shift is hard at the mill, baby.
How are the kids?
Carolyn's playing in the other room.
Thomas is here too, but, well, he's . . . Promise not to get mad . . .
What is it, honey? Just tell me.
Well, Mabel McNally told me Thomas is involved with those NAACP folks again.
He plans to go to Central High when they integrate it!
JOHNSON

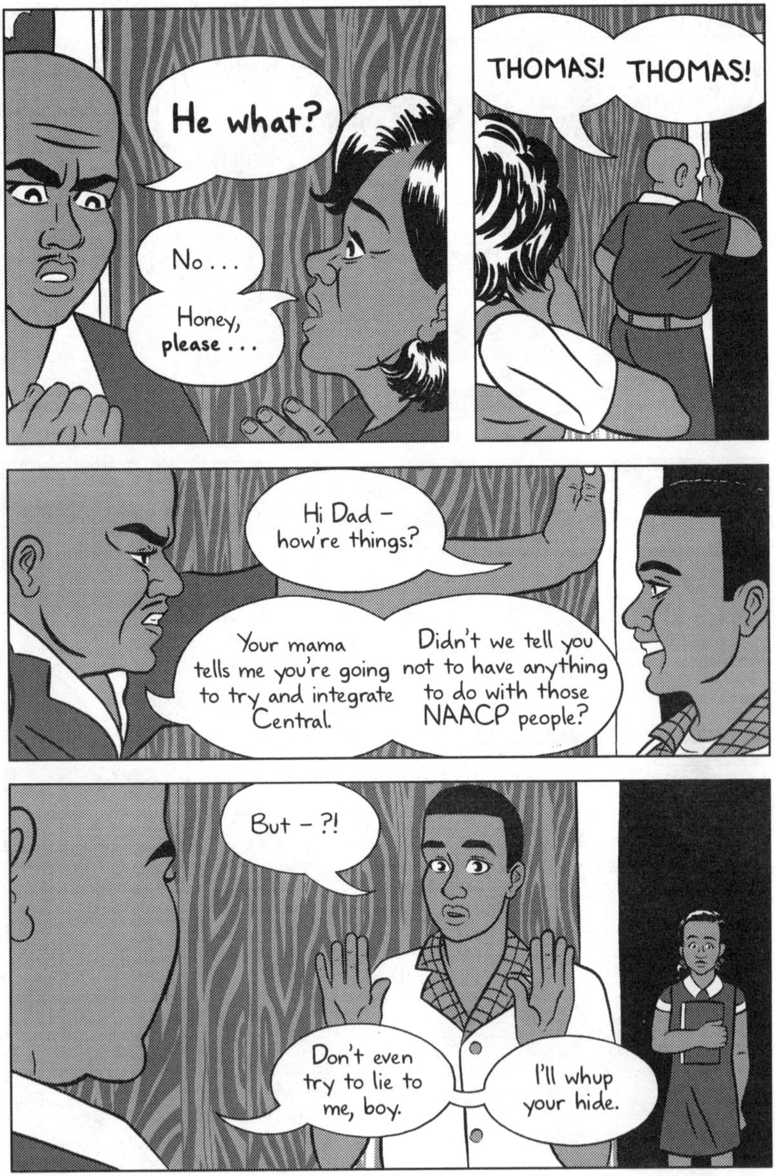
He what?
No . . .
Honey, please . . .
THOMAS! THOMAS!
Hi Dad – how're things?
Your mama tells me you're going to try and integrate Central.
Didn't we tell you not to have anything to do with those NAACP people?
But – ?!
Don't even try to lie to me, boy.
I'll whup your hide.

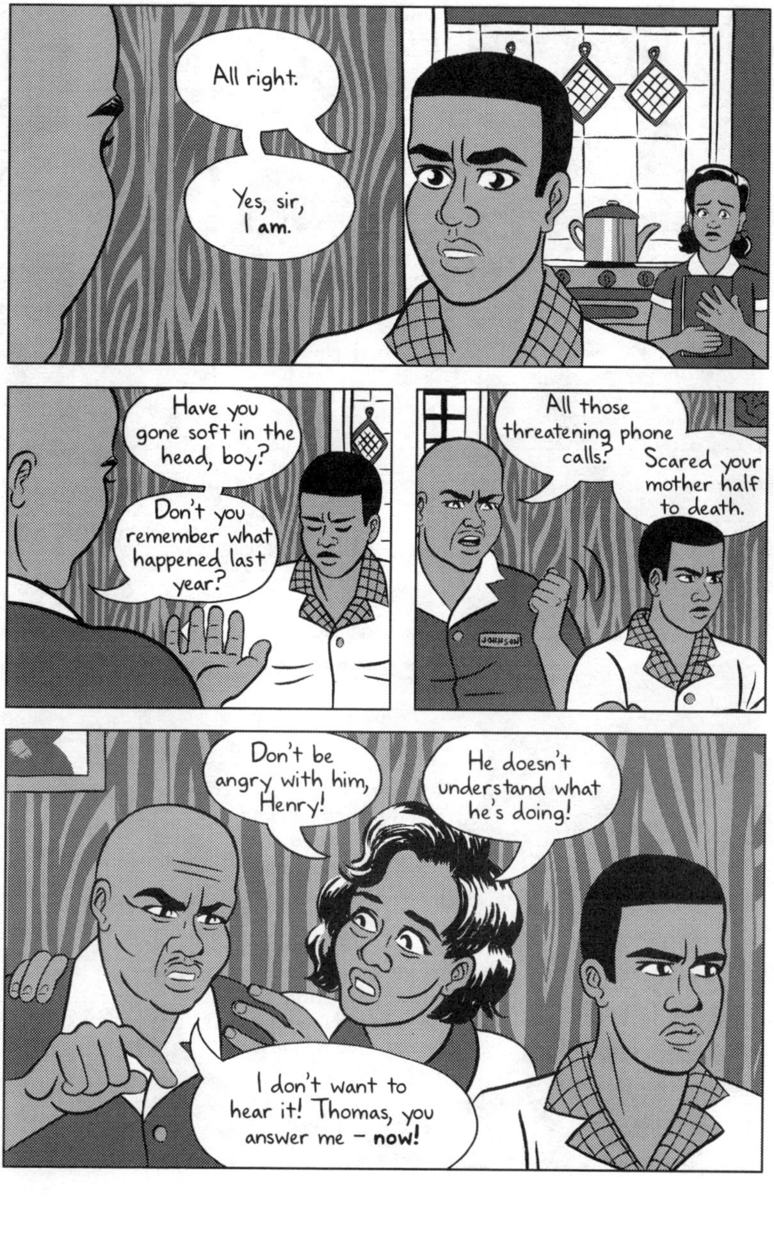
All right.
Yes, sir, I am.
Have you gone soft in the head, boy?
Don't you remember what happened last year?
All those threatening phone calls?
Scared your mother half to death.
JOHNSON
Don't be angry with him, Henry!
He doesn't understand what he's doing!
I don't want to hear it! Thomas, you answer me – now!

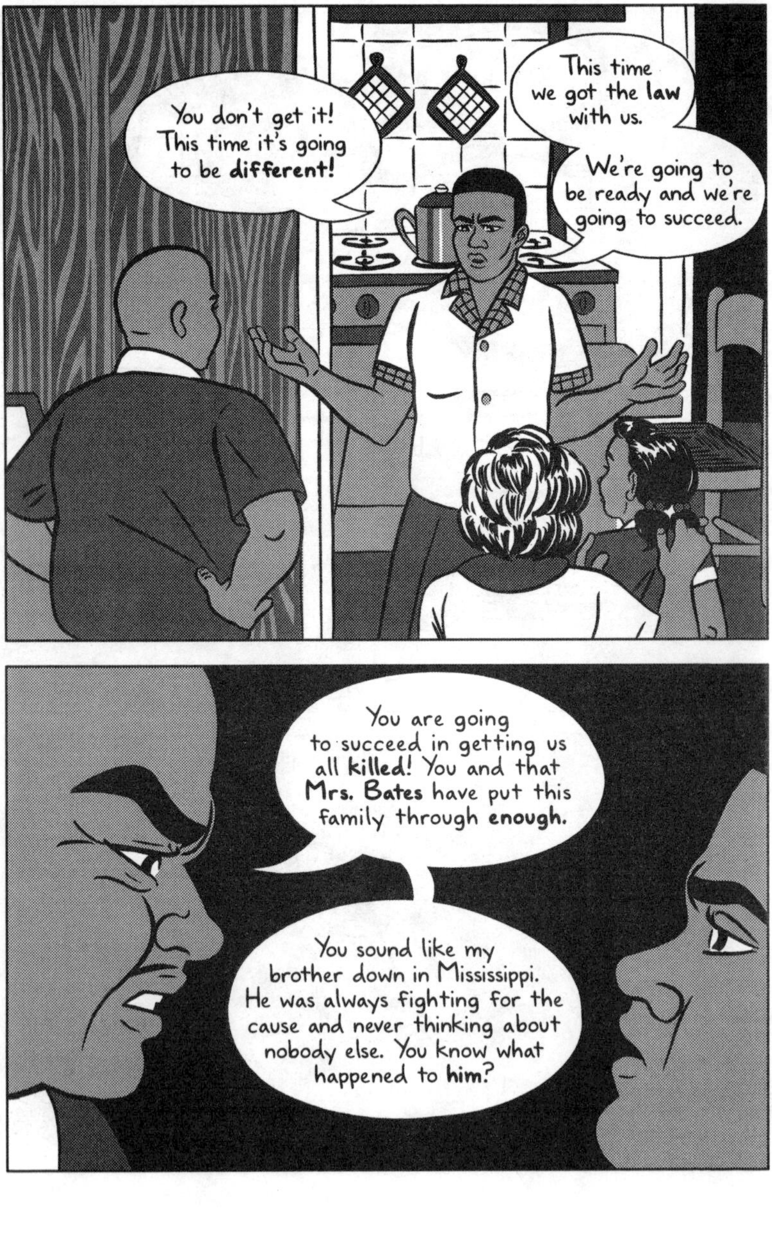
You don't get it! This time it's going to be **different!**
This time we got the **law** with us.
We're going to be ready and we're going to succeed.
You are going to succeed in getting us all **killed!** You and that **Mrs. Bates** have put this family through **enough.**
You sound like my brother down in Mississippi. He was always fighting for the cause and never thinking about nobody else. You know what happened to **him?**

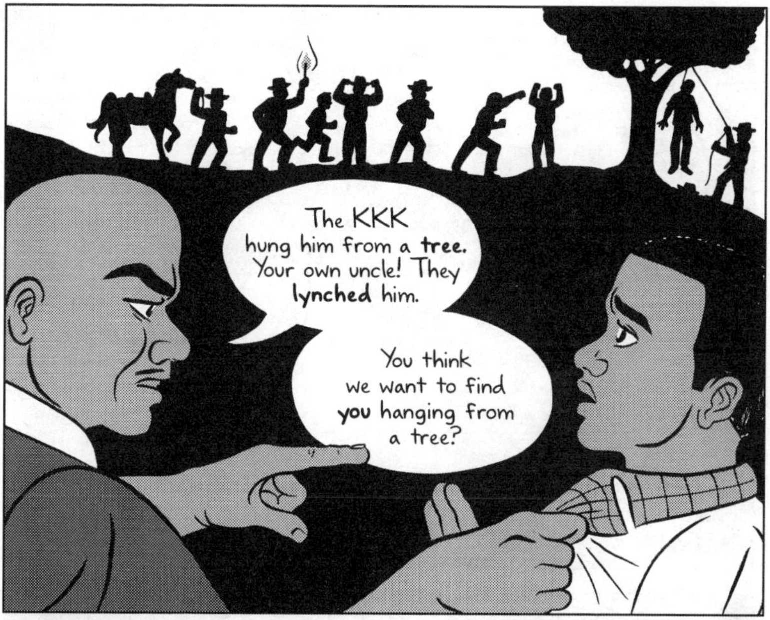
The KKK hung him from a **tree.** Your own uncle! They **lynched** him.
You think we want to find **you** hanging from a tree?

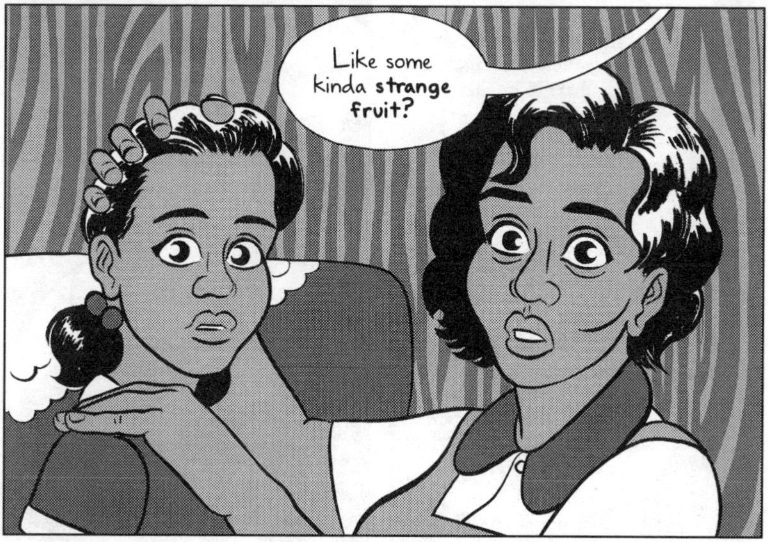
Like some kinda **strange fruit?**

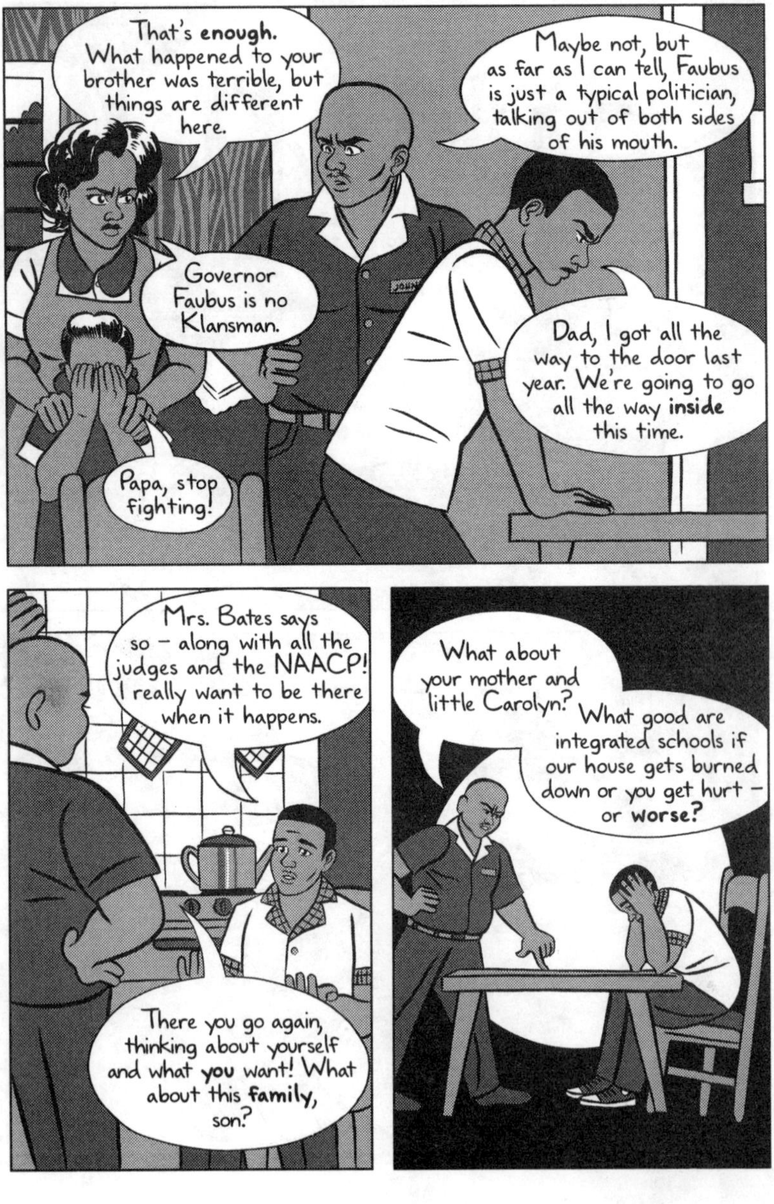
That's **enough.** What happened to your brother was terrible, but things are different here.
Maybe not, but as far as I can tell, Faubus is just a typical politician, talking out of both sides of his mouth.
Governor Faubus is no Klansman.
Dad, I got all the way to the door last year. We're going to go all the way **inside** this time.
Papa, stop fighting!
Mrs. Bates says so – along with all the judges and the NAACP! I really want to be there when it happens.
There you go again, thinking about yourself and what **you** want! What about this **family,** son?
What about your mother and little Carolyn?
What good are integrated schools if our house gets burned down or you get hurt – or **worse?**

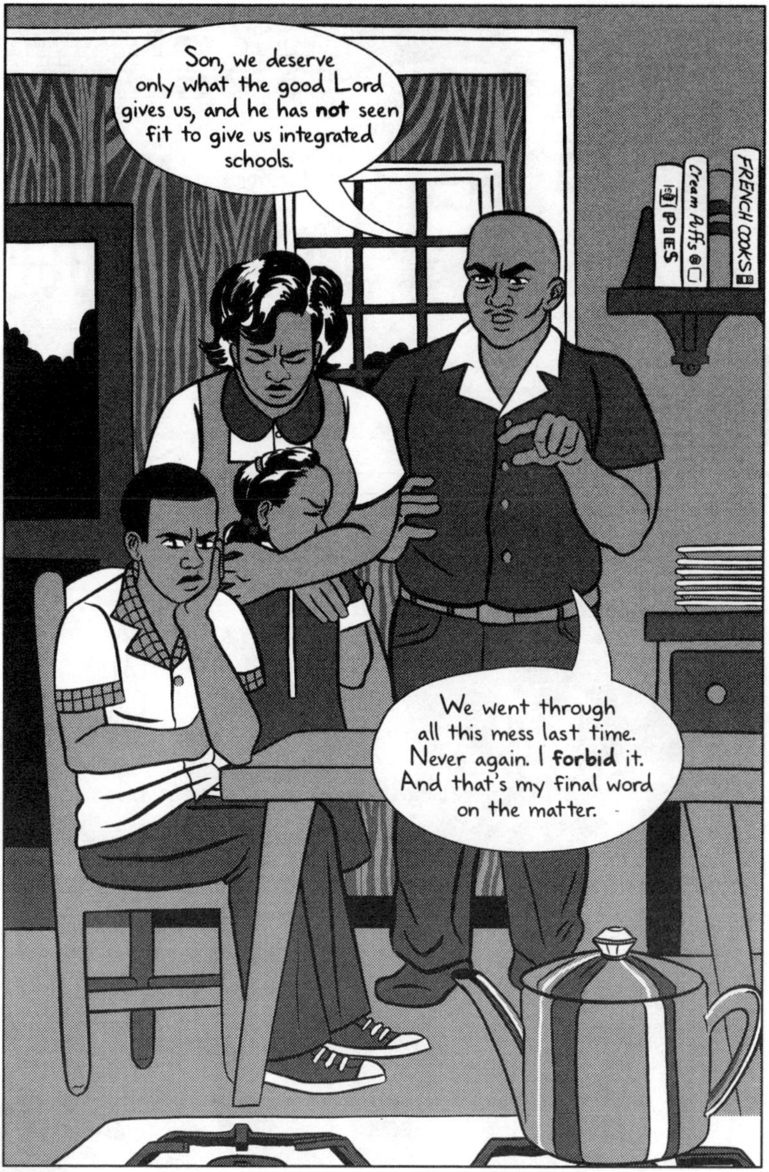
Son, we deserve only what the good Lord gives us, and he has **not** seen fit to give us integrated schools.
FRENCH COOKS
Cream Puffs
PIES
We went through all this mess last time. Never again. I **forbid** it. And that's my final word on the matter.

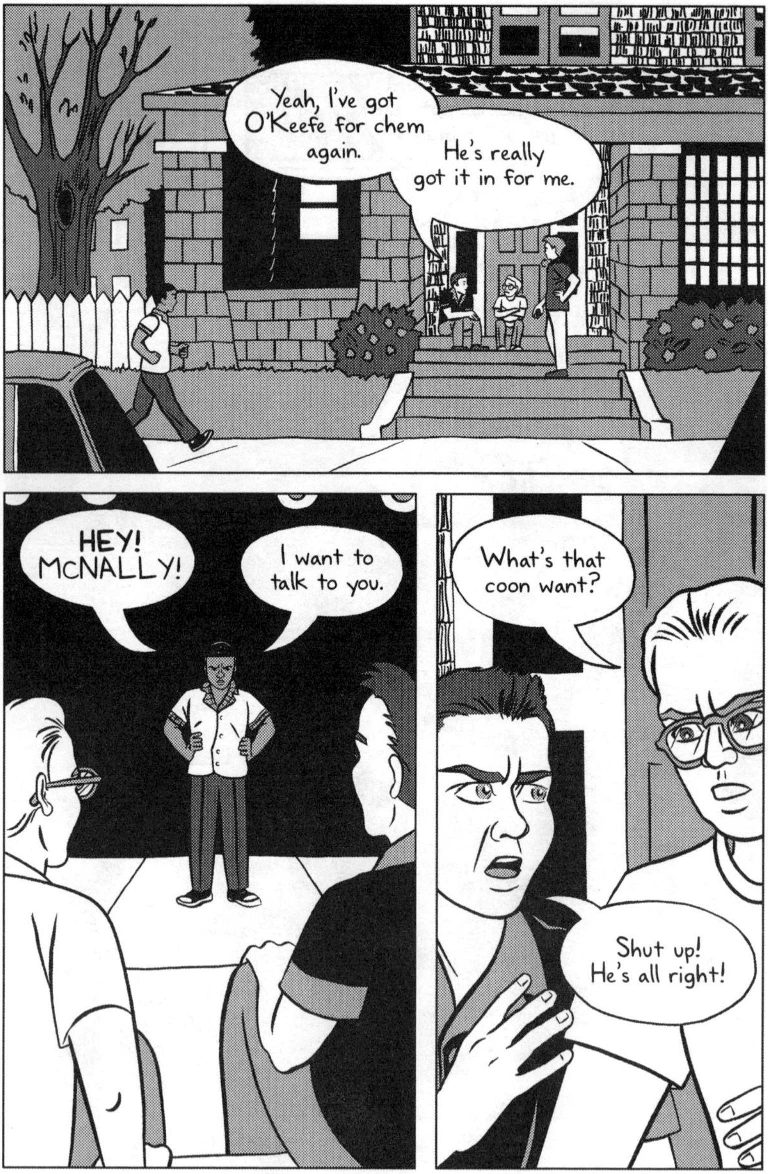
Yeah, I've got O'Keefe for chem again.
He's really got it in for me.
HEY! MCNALLY!
I want to talk to you.
What's that coon want?
Shut up! He's all right!

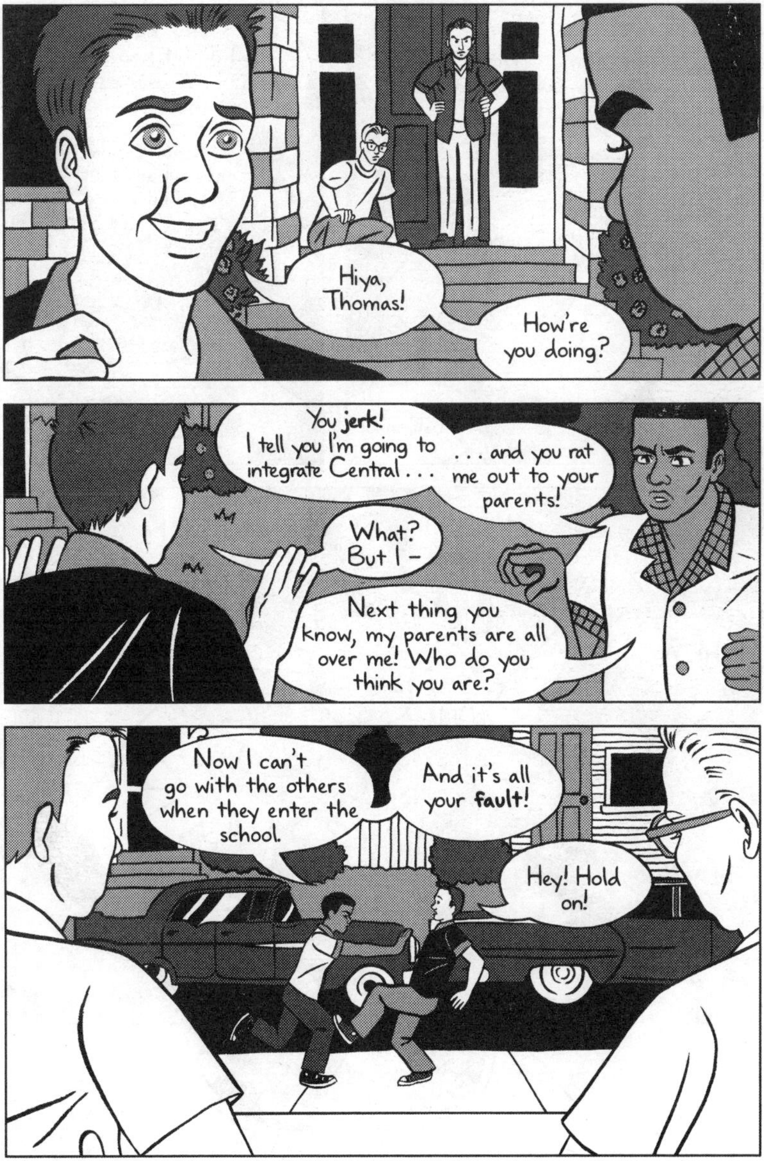
Hiya, Thomas!
How're you doing?
You **jerk**! I tell you I'm going to integrate Central . . .
. . . and you rat me out to your parents!
What? But I –
Next thing you know, my parents are all over me! Who do you think you are?
Now I can't go with the others when they enter the school.
And it's all your **fault**!
Hey! Hold on!

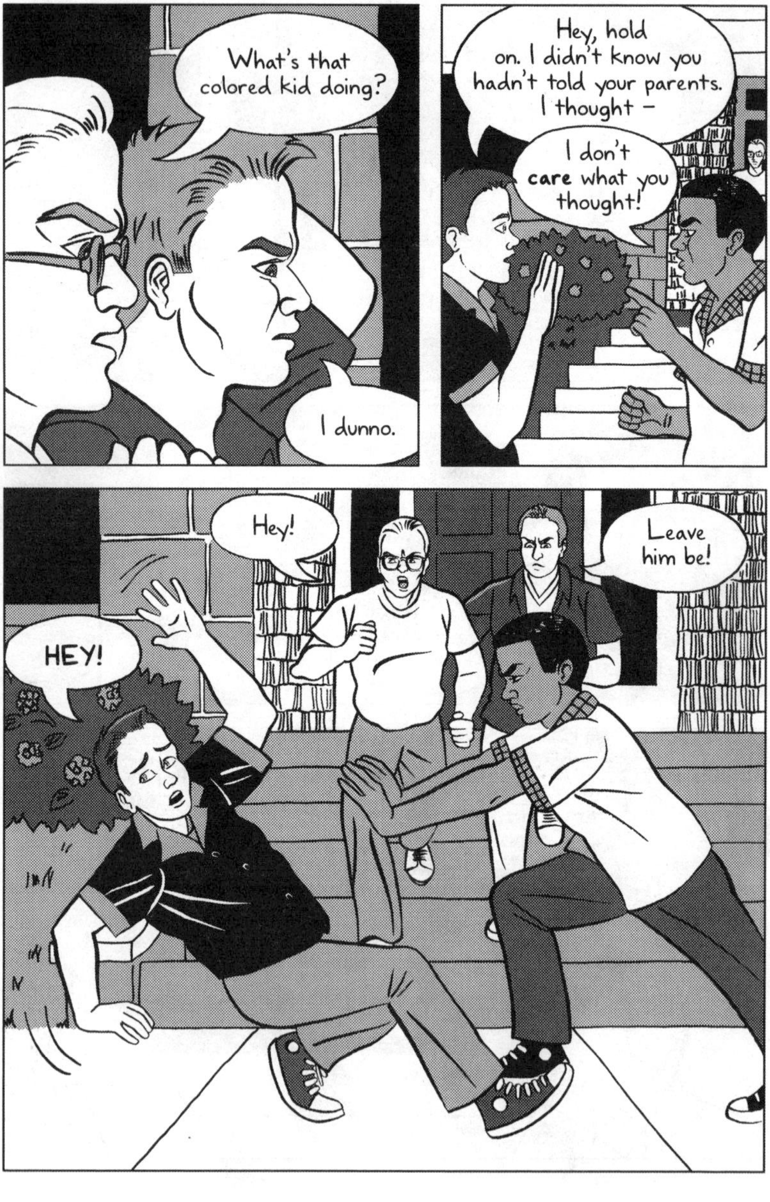
What's that colored kid doing?
I dunno.
Hey, hold on. I didn't know you hadn't told your parents. I thought –
I don't **care** what you thought!
Hey!
Leave him be!
HEY!

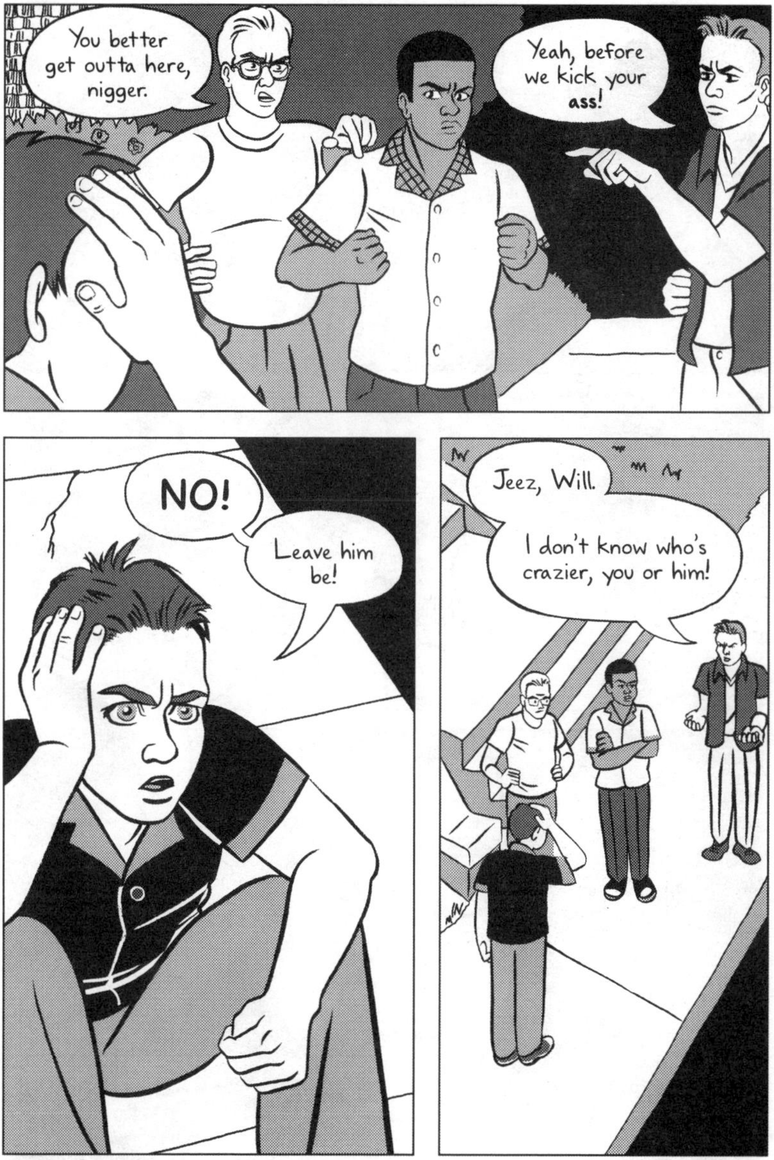
You better get outta here, nigger.
Yeah, before we kick your ass!
NO!
Leave him be!
Jeez, Will.
I don't know who's crazier, you or him!

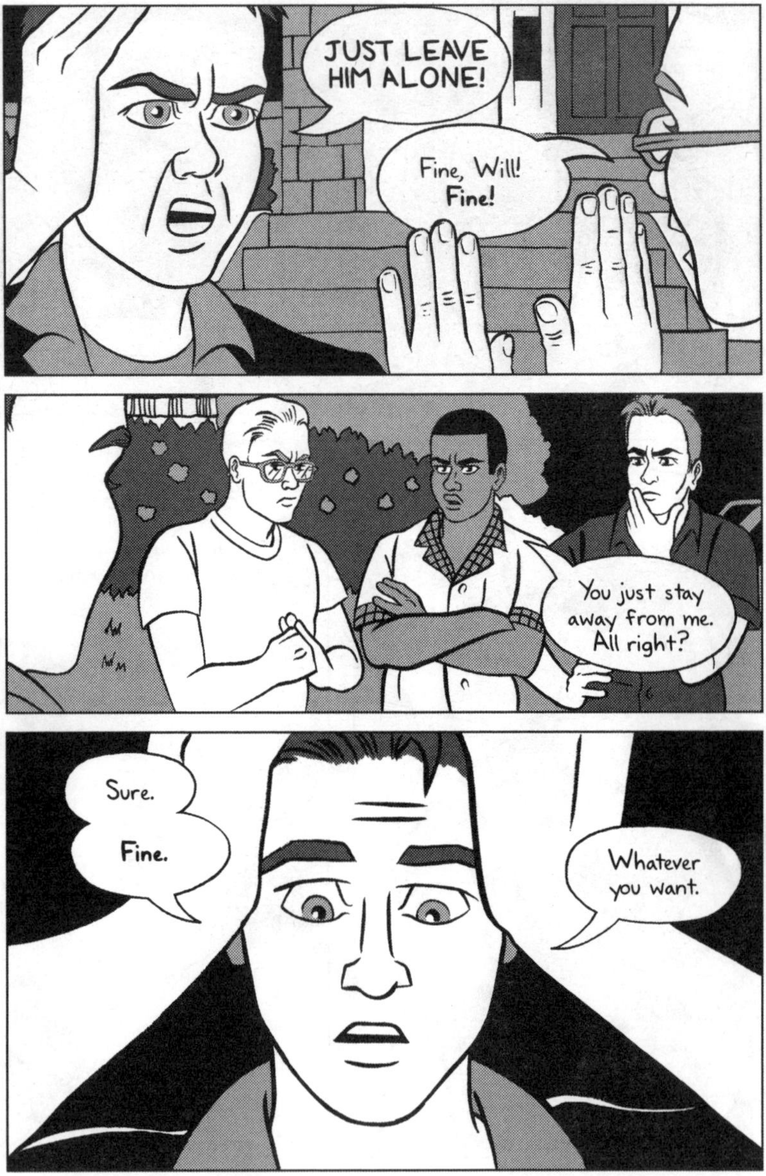
JUST LEAVE HIM ALONE!
Fine, Will! Fine!
You just stay away from me. All right?
Sure.
Fine.
Whatever you want.

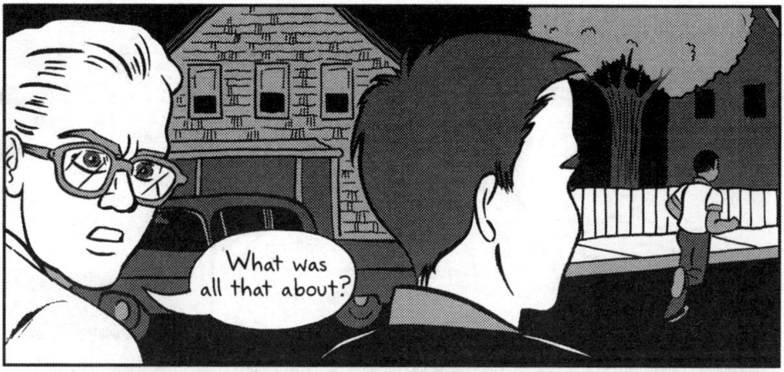
What was all that about?

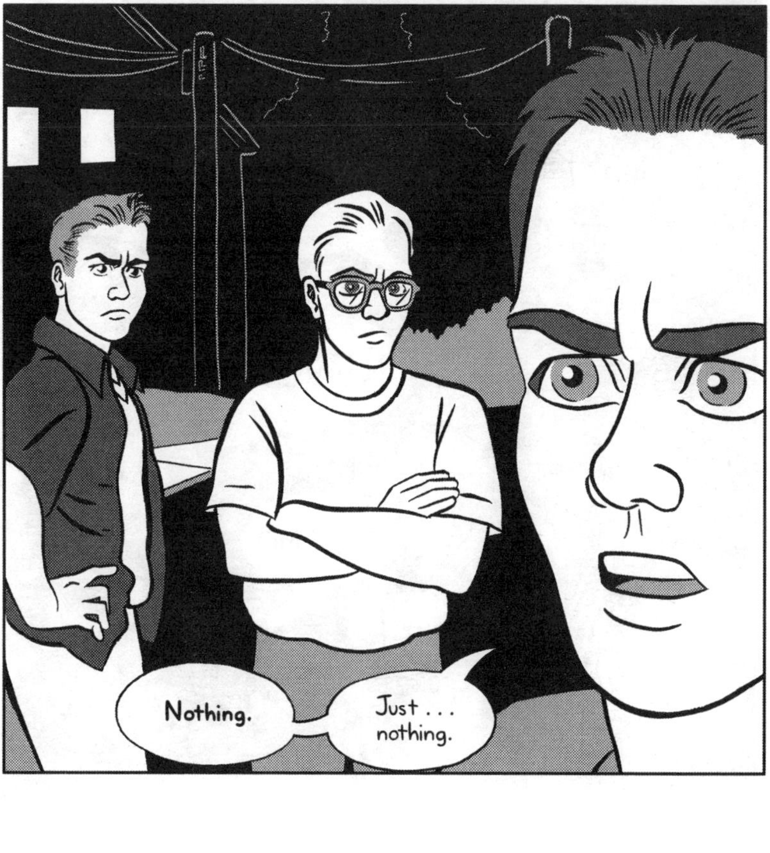
Nothing.
Just . . . nothing.

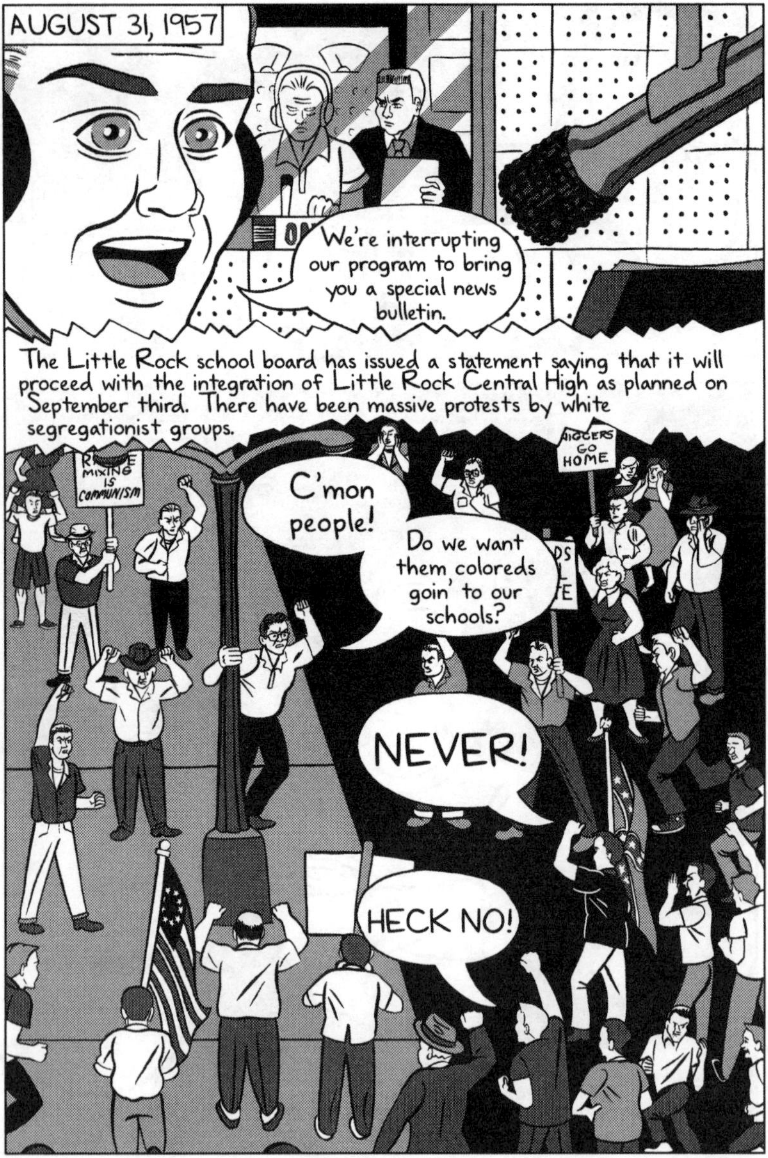
AUGUST 31, 1957
We're interrupting our program to bring you a special news bulletin.
The Little Rock school board has issued a statement saying that it will proceed with the integration of Little Rock Central High as planned on September third. There have been massive protests by white segregationist groups.
C'mon people!
Do we want them coloreds goin' to our schools?
NEVER!
HECK NO!

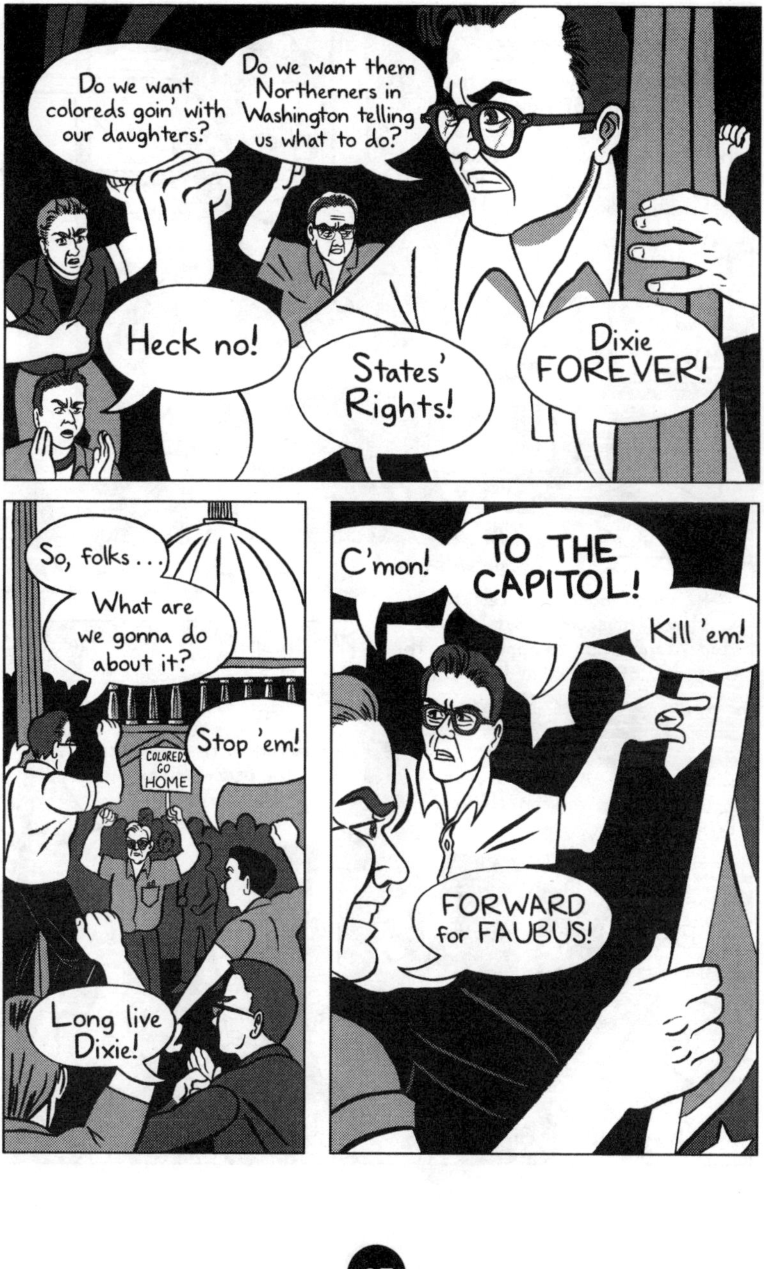

Do we want coloreds goin' with our daughters?
Do we want them Northerners in Washington telling us what to do?
Heck no!
States' Rights!
Dixie FOREVER!
So, folks . . .
What are we gonna do about it?
COLOREDS GO HOME
Stop 'em!
Long live Dixie!
C'mon!
TO THE CAPITOL!
Kill 'em!
FORWARD for FAUBUS!

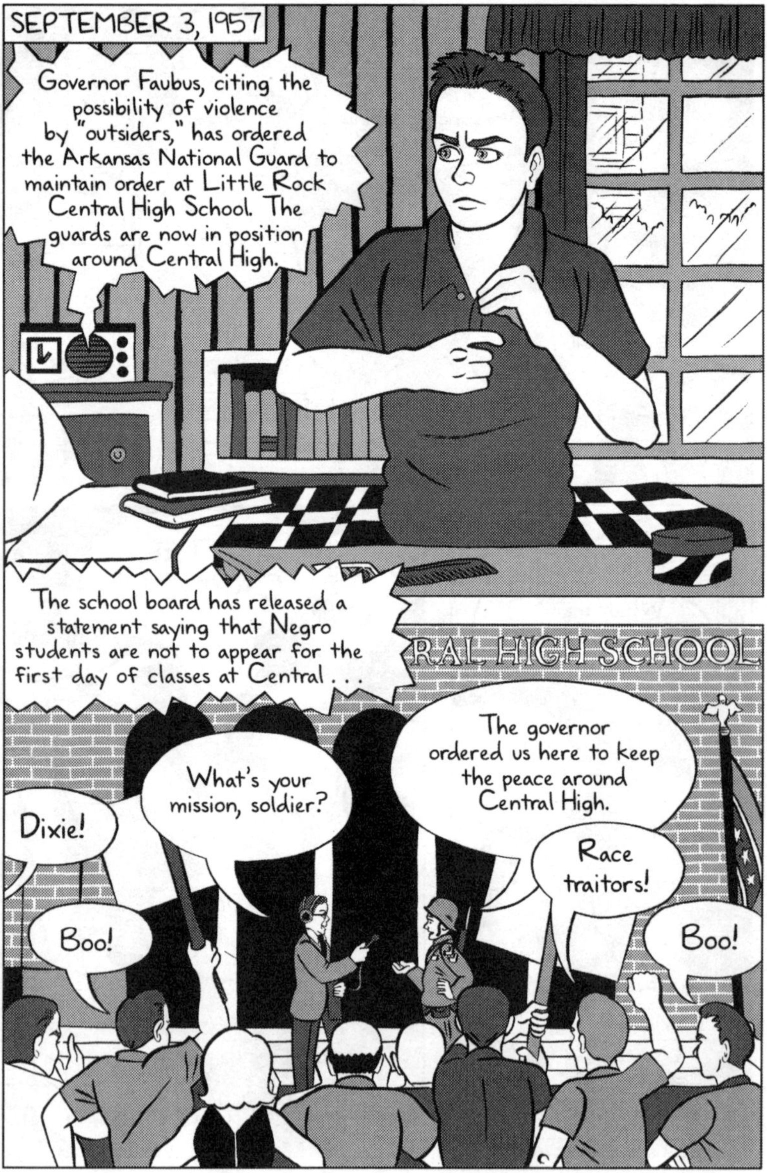
SEPTEMBER 3, 1957
Governor Faubus, citing the possibility of violence by "outsiders," has ordered the Arkansas National Guard to maintain order at Little Rock Central High School. The guards are now in position around Central High.
The school board has released a statement saying that Negro students are not to appear for the first day of classes at Central . . .
RAL HIGH SCHOOL
What's your mission, soldier?
The governor ordered us here to keep the peace around Central High.
Dixie!
Race traitors!
Boo!
Boo!

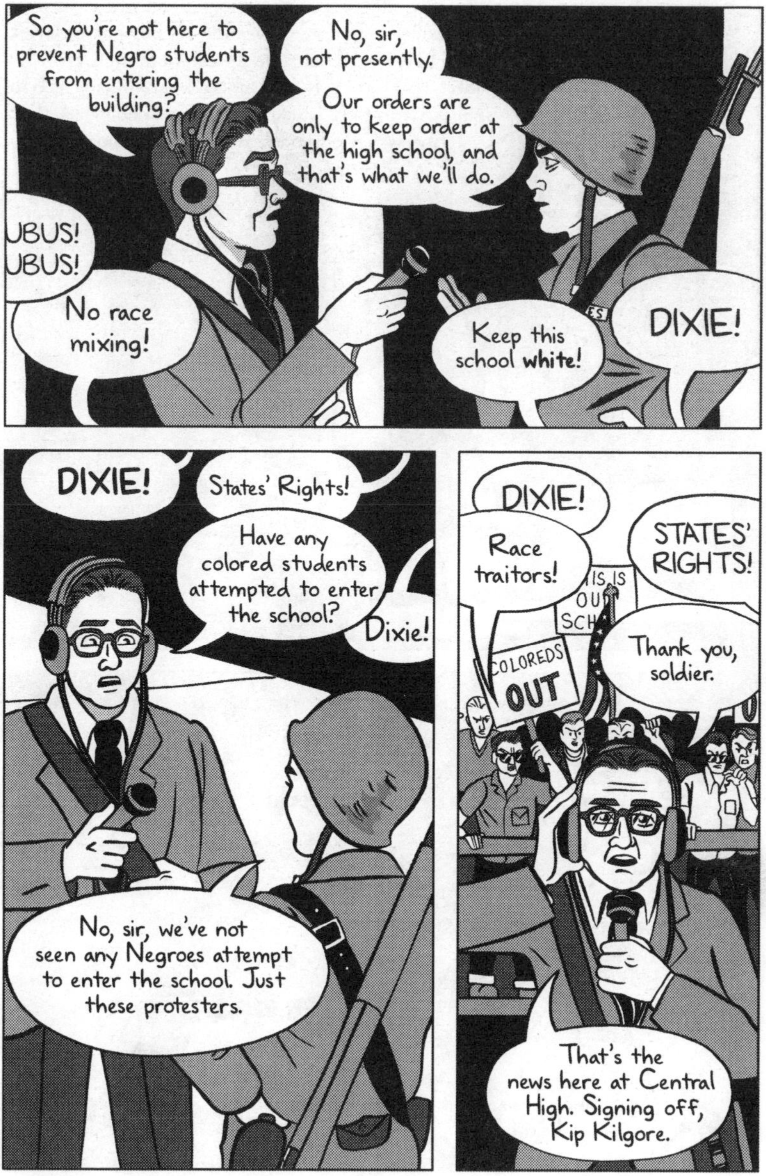

So you're not here to prevent Negro students from entering the building?
No, sir, not presently.
Our orders are only to keep order at the high school, and that's what we'll do.
UBUS!
UBUS!
No race mixing!
Keep this school **white**!
DIXIE!
DIXIE!
States' Rights!
Have any colored students attempted to enter the school?
Dixie!
No, sir, we've not seen any Negroes attempt to enter the school. Just these protesters.
DIXIE!
Race traitors!
STATES' RIGHTS!
COLOREDS OUT
Thank you, soldier.
That's the news here at Central High. Signing off, Kip Kilgore.

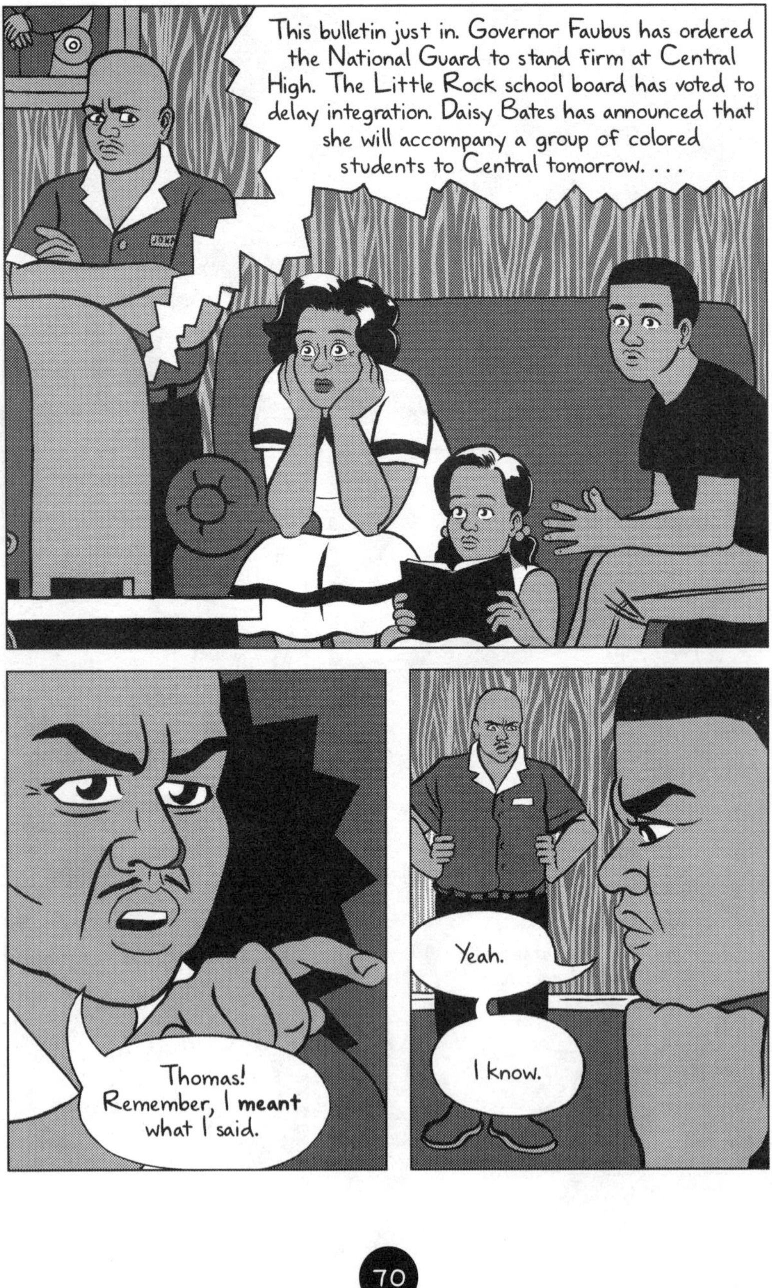
This bulletin just in. Governor Faubus has ordered the National Guard to stand firm at Central High. The Little Rock school board has voted to delay integration. Daisy Bates has announced that she will accompany a group of colored students to Central tomorrow. . . .
Thomas! Remember, I **meant** what I said.
Yeah.
I know.

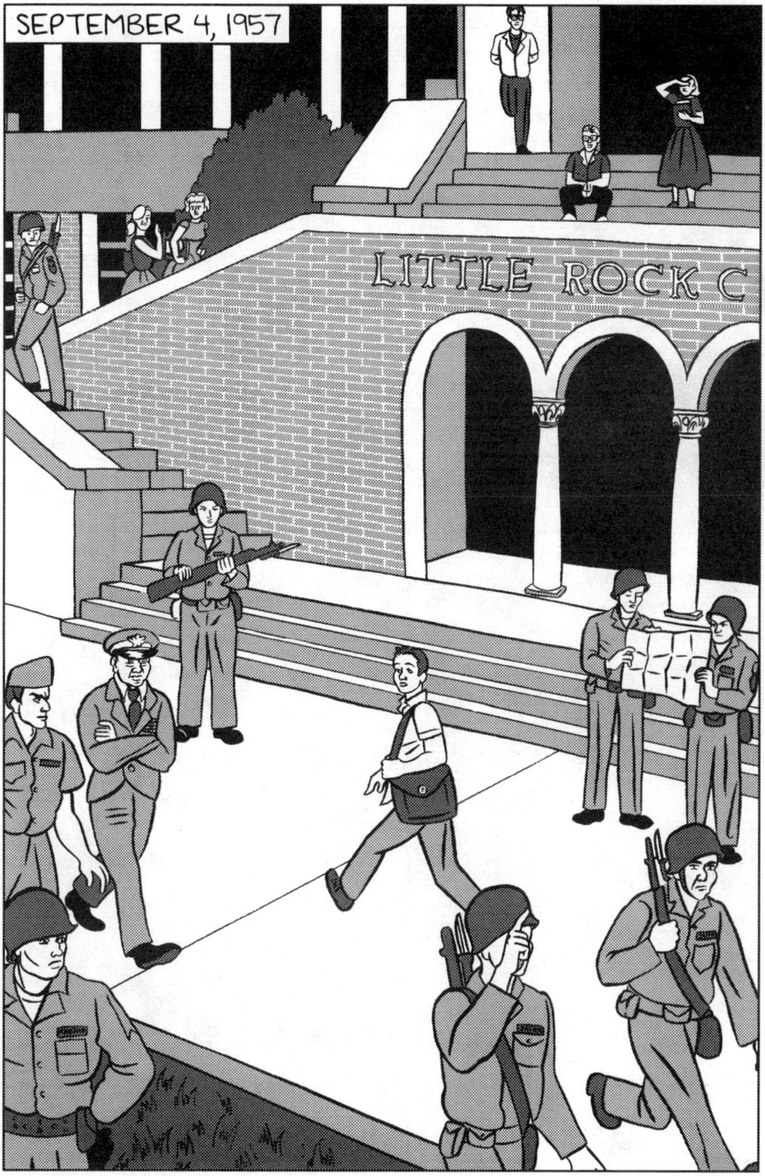
SEPTEMBER 4, 1957
LITTLE ROCK C

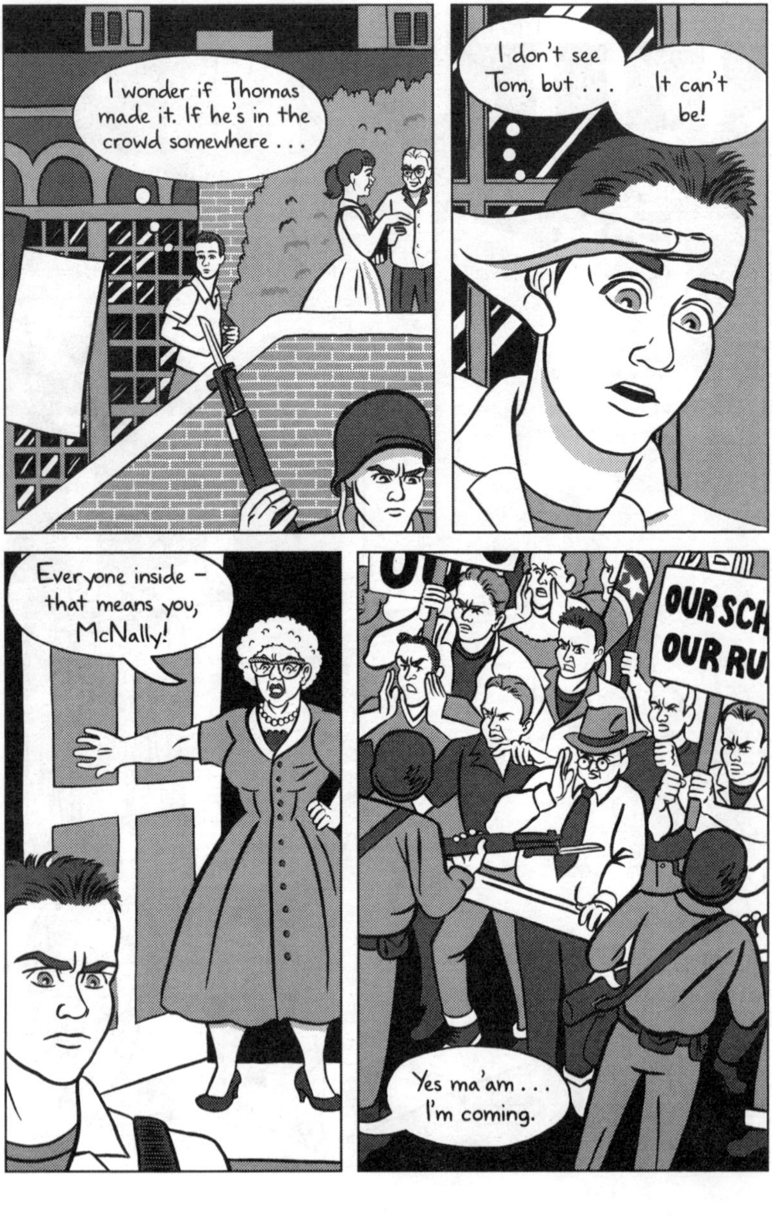
I wonder if Thomas made it. If he's in the crowd somewhere . . .
I don't see Tom, but . . .
It can't be!
Everyone inside – that means you, McNally!
OUR SCH
OUR RU
Yes ma'am . . . I'm coming.

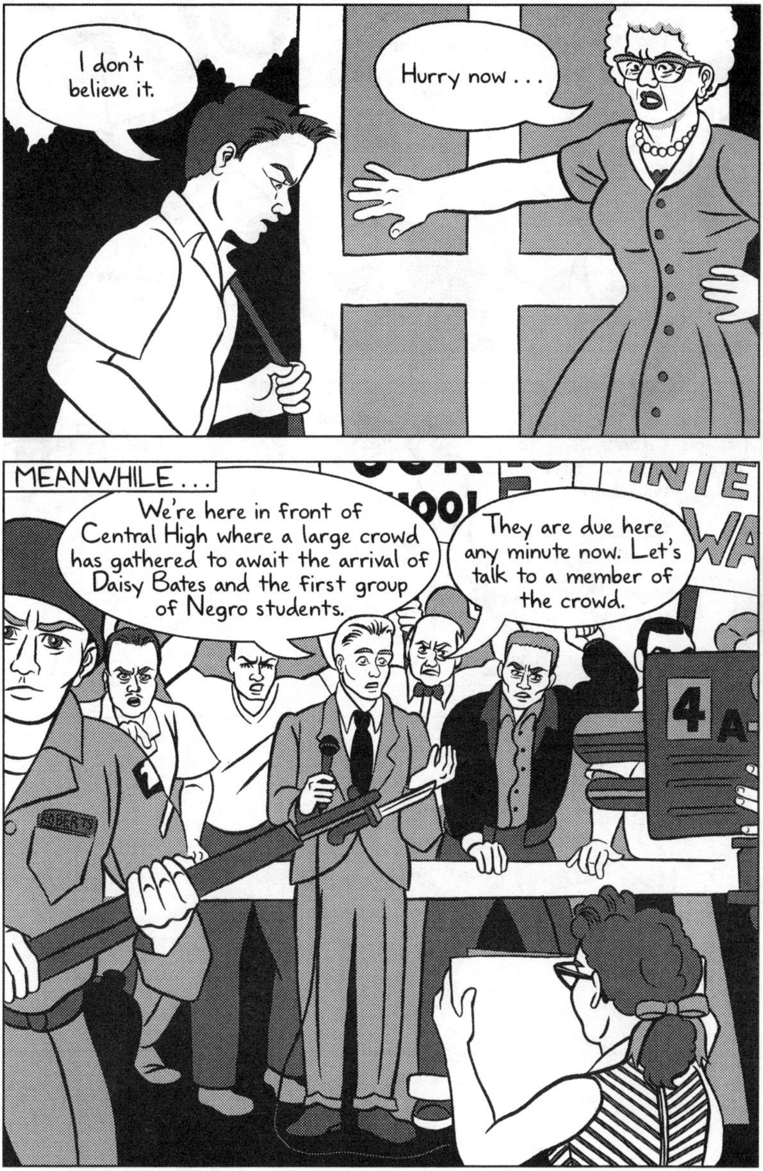
I don't believe it.
Hurry now . . .
MEANWHILE . . .
We're here in front of Central High where a large crowd has gathered to await the arrival of Daisy Bates and the first group of Negro students.
They are due here any minute now. Let's talk to a member of the crowd.

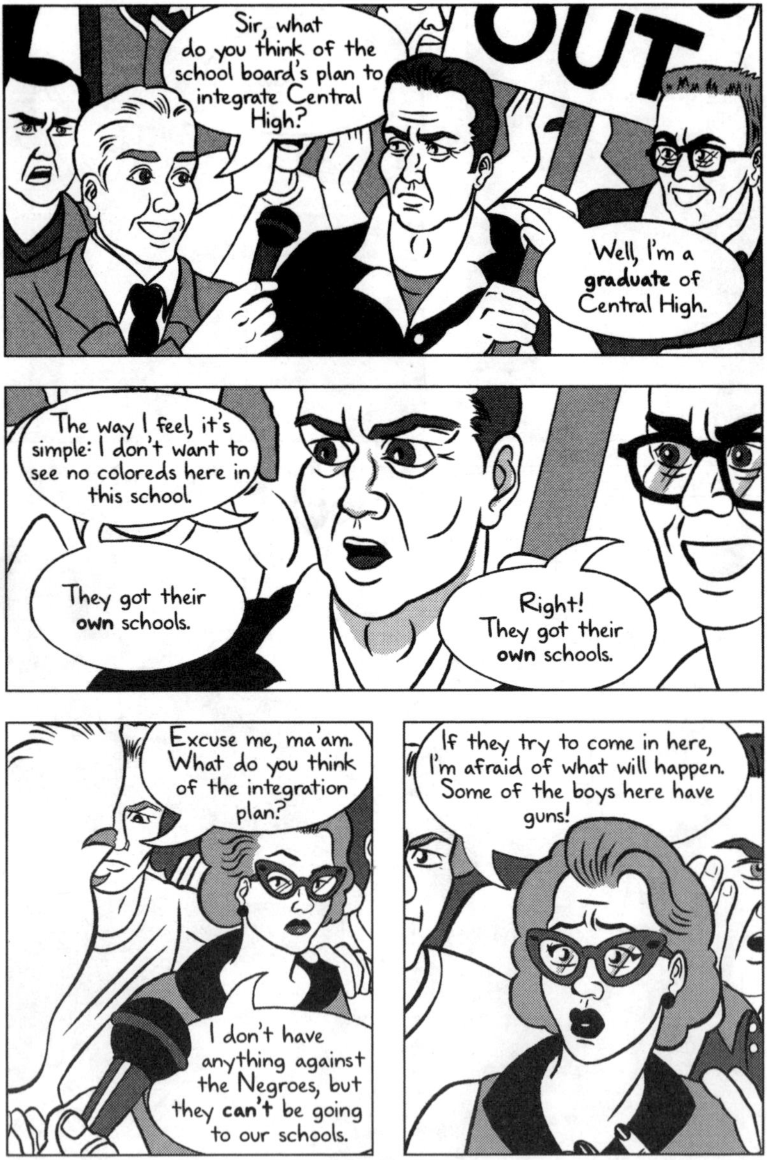
Sir, what do you think of the school board's plan to integrate Central High?
Well, I'm a **graduate** of Central High.
OUT
The way I feel, it's simple: I don't want to see no coloreds here in this school.
They got their **own** schools.
Right! They got their **own** schools.
Excuse me, ma'am. What do you think of the integration plan?
I don't have anything against the Negroes, but they **can't** be going to our schools.
If they try to come in here, I'm afraid of what will happen. Some of the boys here have guns!

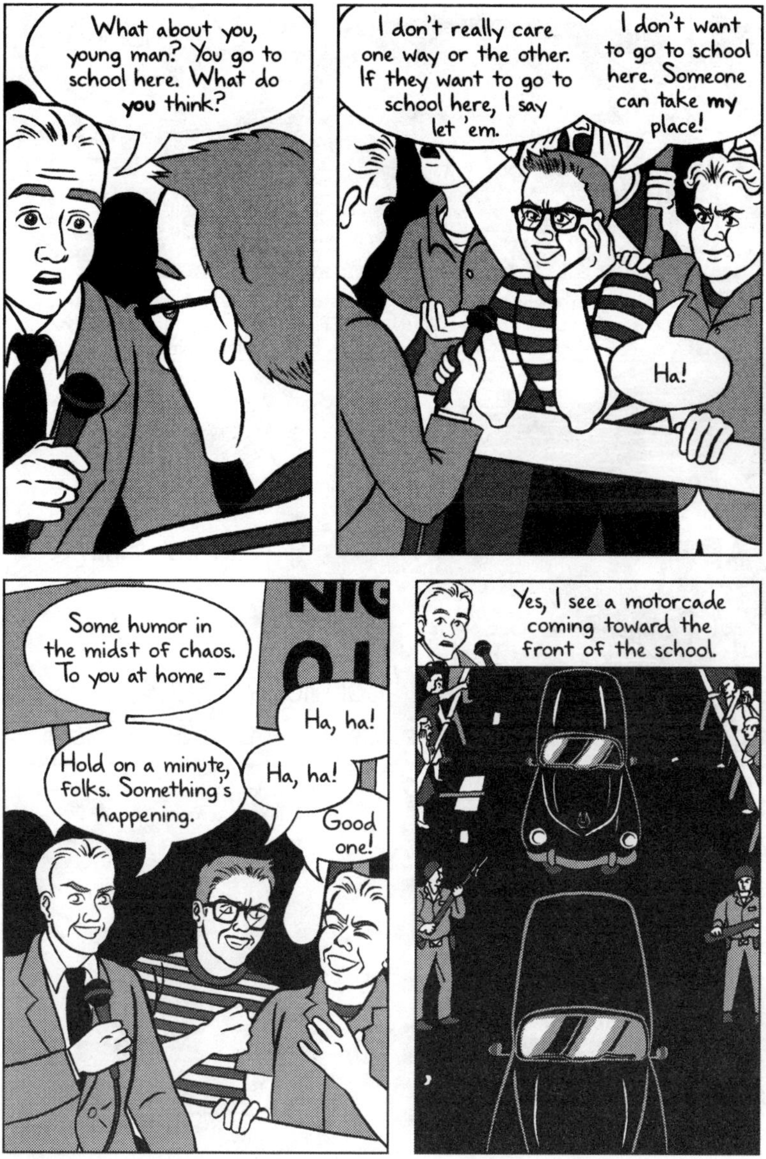
What about you, young man? You go to school here. What do you think?
I don't really care one way or the other. If they want to go to school here, I say let 'em.
I don't want to go to school here. Someone can take my place!
Ha!
Some humor in the midst of chaos. To you at home –
Hold on a minute, folks. Something's happening.
Ha, ha!
Ha, ha!
Good one!
Yes, I see a motorcade coming toward the front of the school.

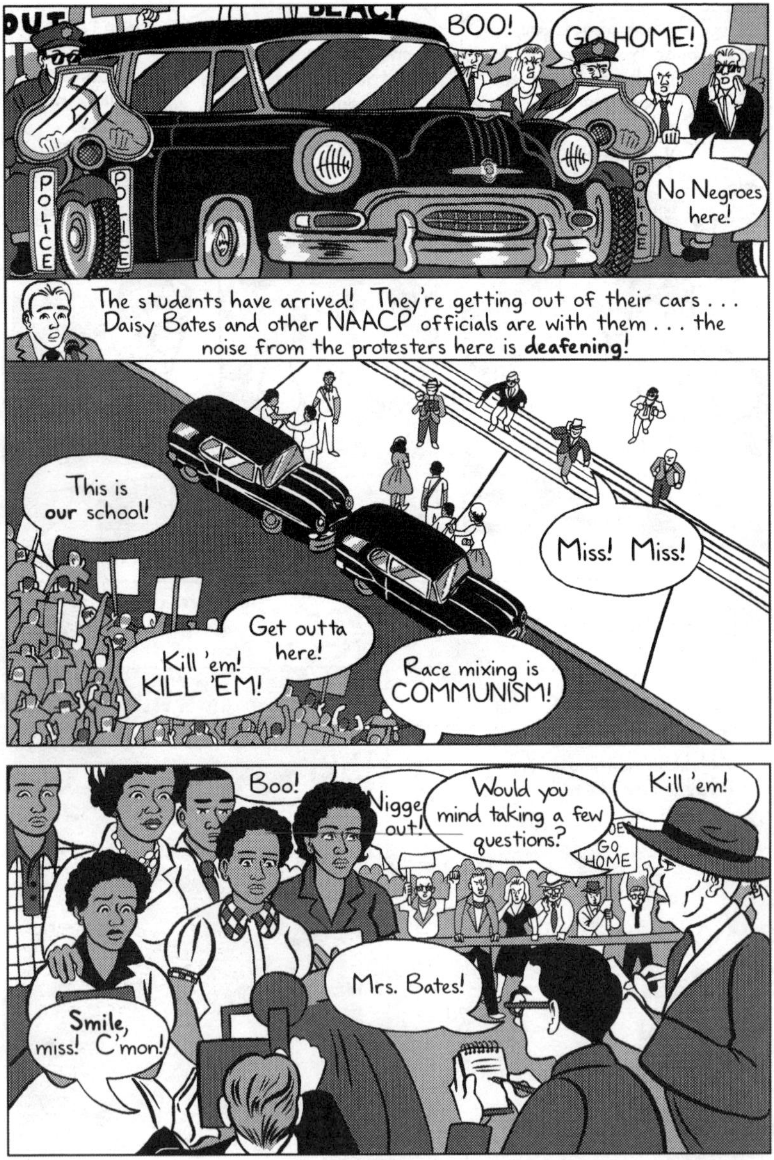
BOO!
GO HOME!
No Negroes here!
The students have arrived! They're getting out of their cars . . . Daisy Bates and other NAACP officials are with them . . . the noise from the protesters here is **deafening**!
This is **our** school!
Miss! Miss!
Get outta here!
Kill 'em! KILL 'EM!
Race mixing is COMMUNISM!
Boo!
Nigge out!
Would you mind taking a few questions?
Kill 'em!
GO HOME
Mrs. Bates!
Smile, miss! C'mon!

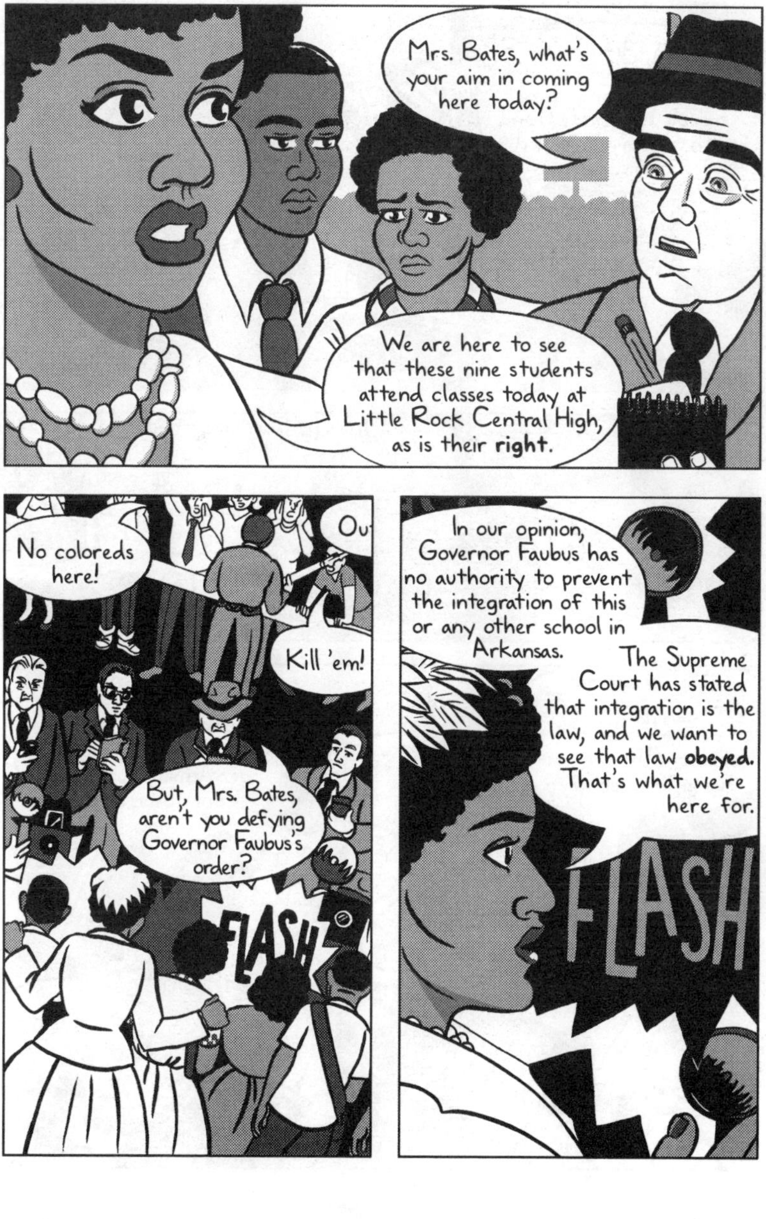
Mrs. Bates, what's your aim in coming here today?
We are here to see that these nine students attend classes today at Little Rock Central High, as is their **right**.
No coloreds here!
Ou
Kill 'em!
But, Mrs. Bates, aren't you defying Governor Faubus's order?
FLASH
In our opinion, Governor Faubus has no authority to prevent the integration of this or any other school in Arkansas.
The Supreme Court has stated that integration is the law, and we want to see that law **obeyed.** That's what we're here for.
FLASH

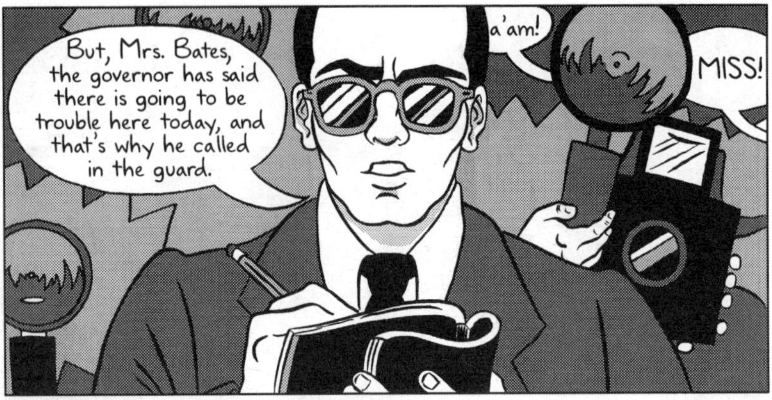
But, Mrs. Bates, the governor has said there is going to be trouble here today, and that's why he called in the guard.
a'am!
MISS!

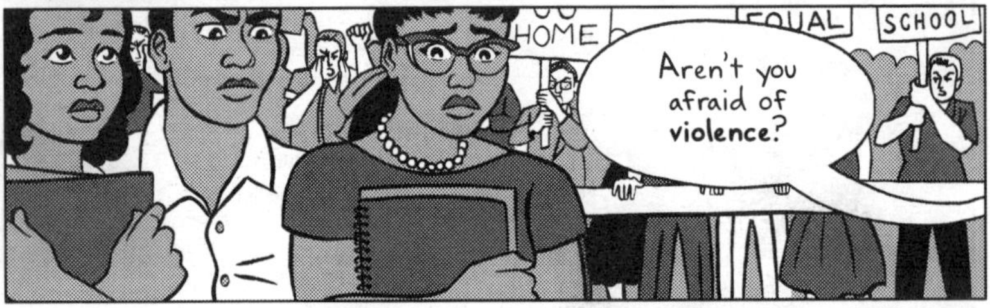
HOME
SCHOOL
Aren't you afraid of **violence**?

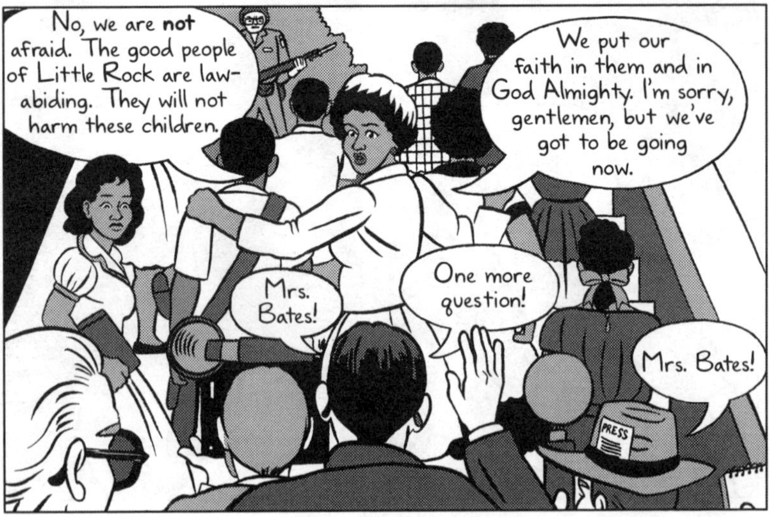
No, we are **not** afraid. The good people of Little Rock are law-abiding. They will not harm these children.
We put our faith in them and in God Almighty. I'm sorry, gentlemen, but we've got to be going now.
Mrs. Bates!
One more question!
Mrs. Bates!
PRESS

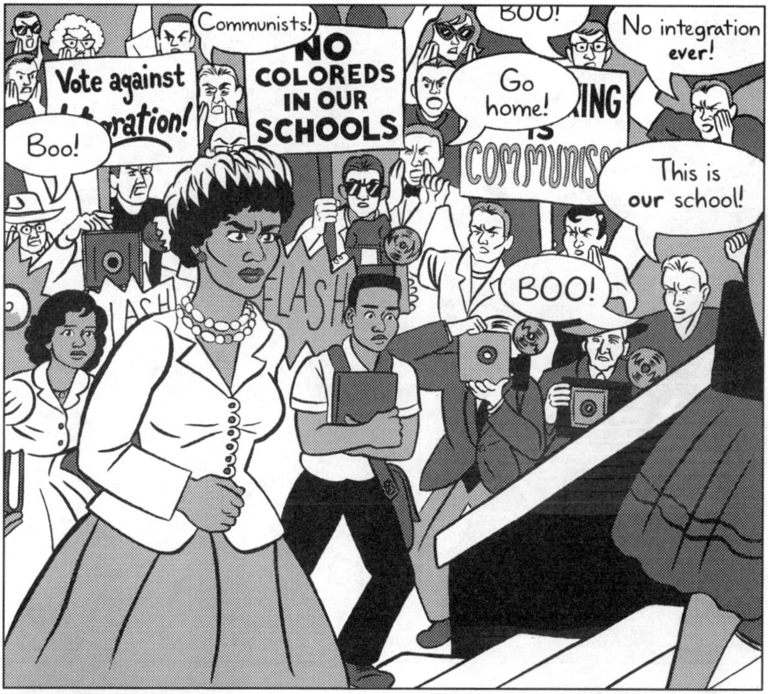
Communists!
NO COLOREDS IN OUR SCHOOLS
BOO!
No integration **ever**!
Vote against
Go home!
Boo!
This is **our** school!
FLASH
BOO!

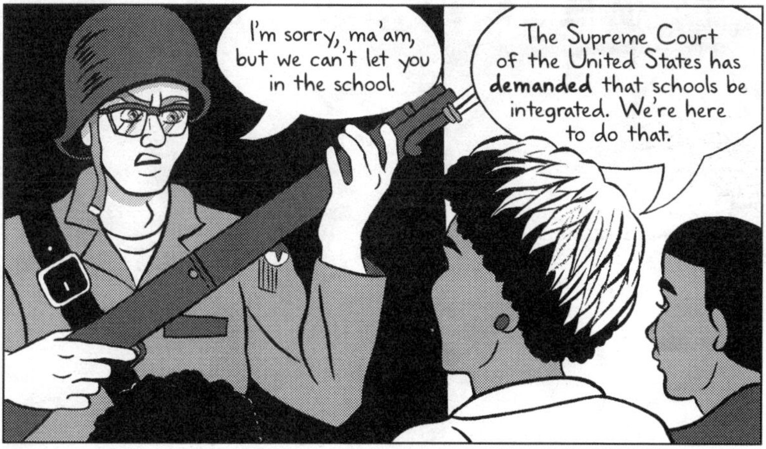
I'm sorry, ma'am, but we can't let you in the school.
The Supreme Court of the United States has **demanded** that schools be integrated. We're here to do that.

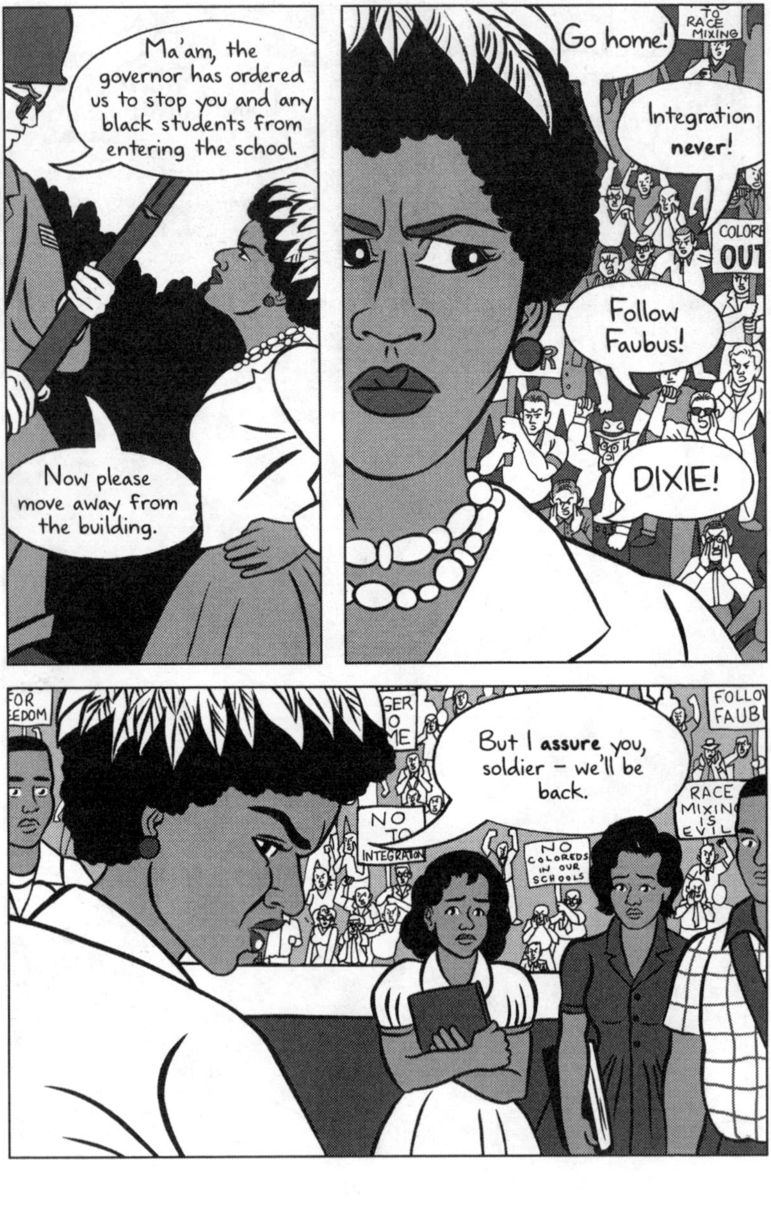
Ma'am, the governor has ordered us to stop you and any black students from entering the school.
Now please move away from the building.
Go home!
Integration **never!**
Follow Faubus!
DIXIE!
But I **assure** you, soldier – we'll be back.
NO TO INTEGRATION
NO COLOREDS IN OUR SCHOOLS
RACE MIXING IS EVIL

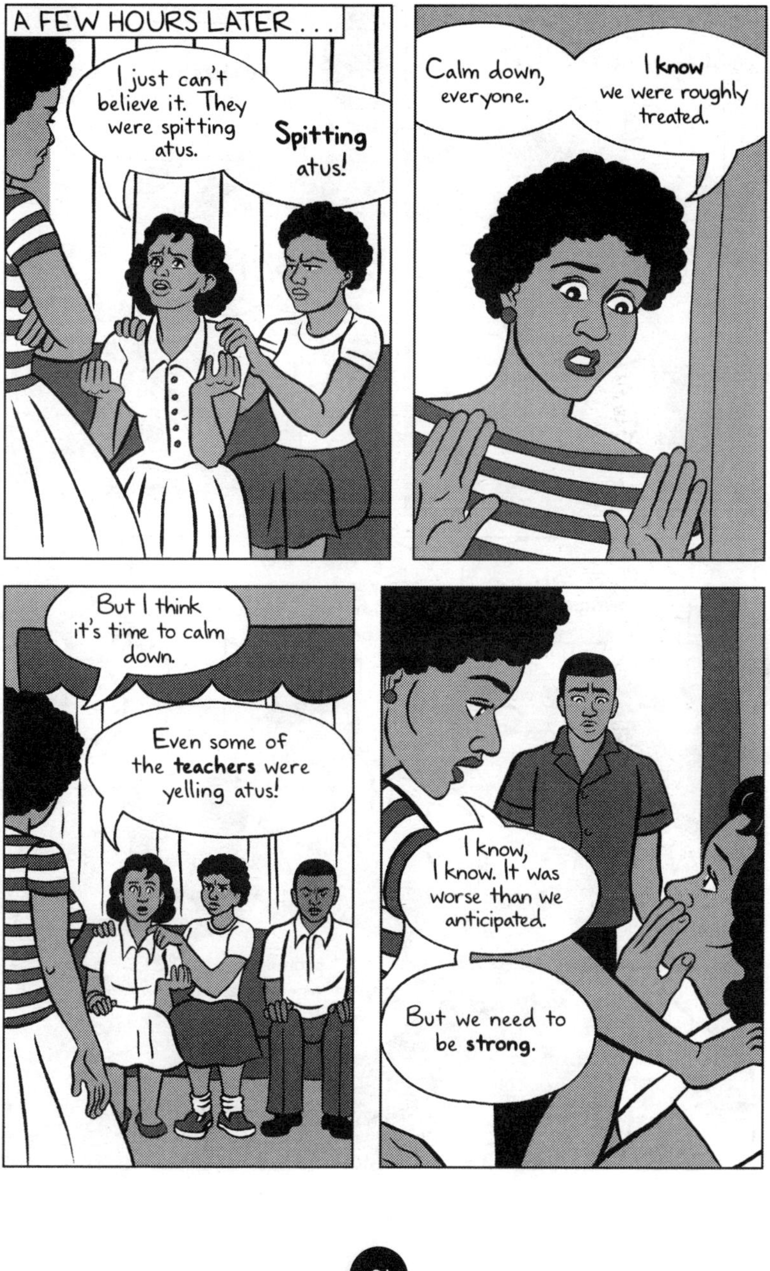
A FEW HOURS LATER . . .
I just can't believe it. They were spitting at us.
Spitting at us!
Calm down, everyone.
I **know** we were roughly treated.
But I think it's time to calm down.
Even some of the **teachers** were yelling at us!
I know, I know. It was worse than we anticipated.
But we need to be **strong**.

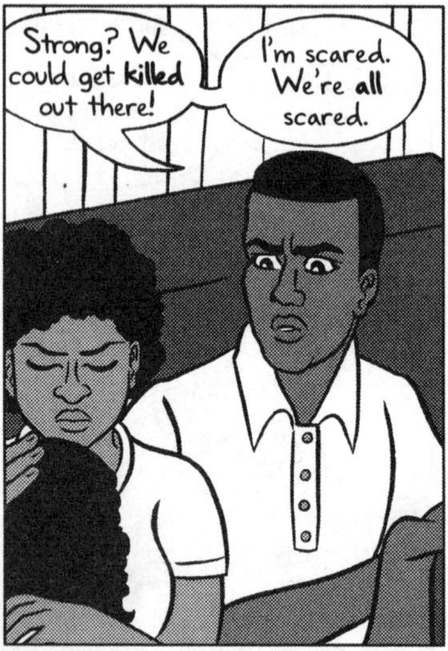
Strong? We could get **killed** out there!
I'm scared. We're **all** scared.

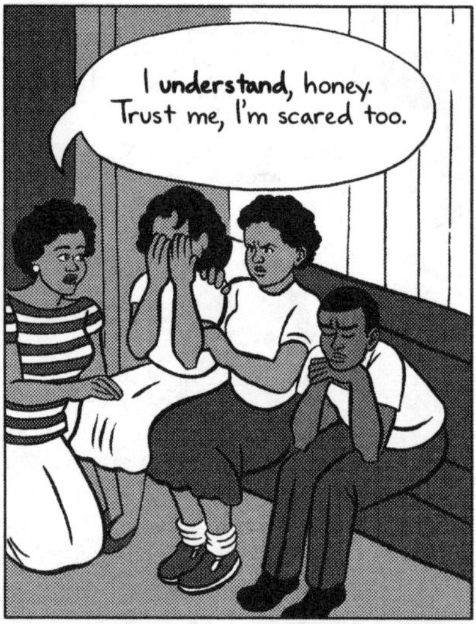
I **understand**, honey. Trust me, I'm scared too.

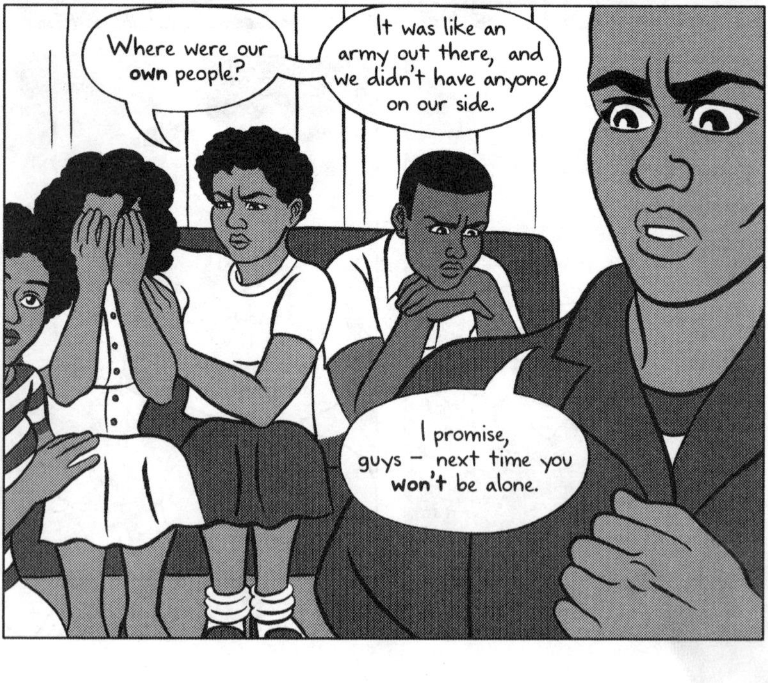
Where were our **own** people?
It was like an army out there, and we didn't have anyone on our side.
I promise, guys – next time you **won't** be alone.

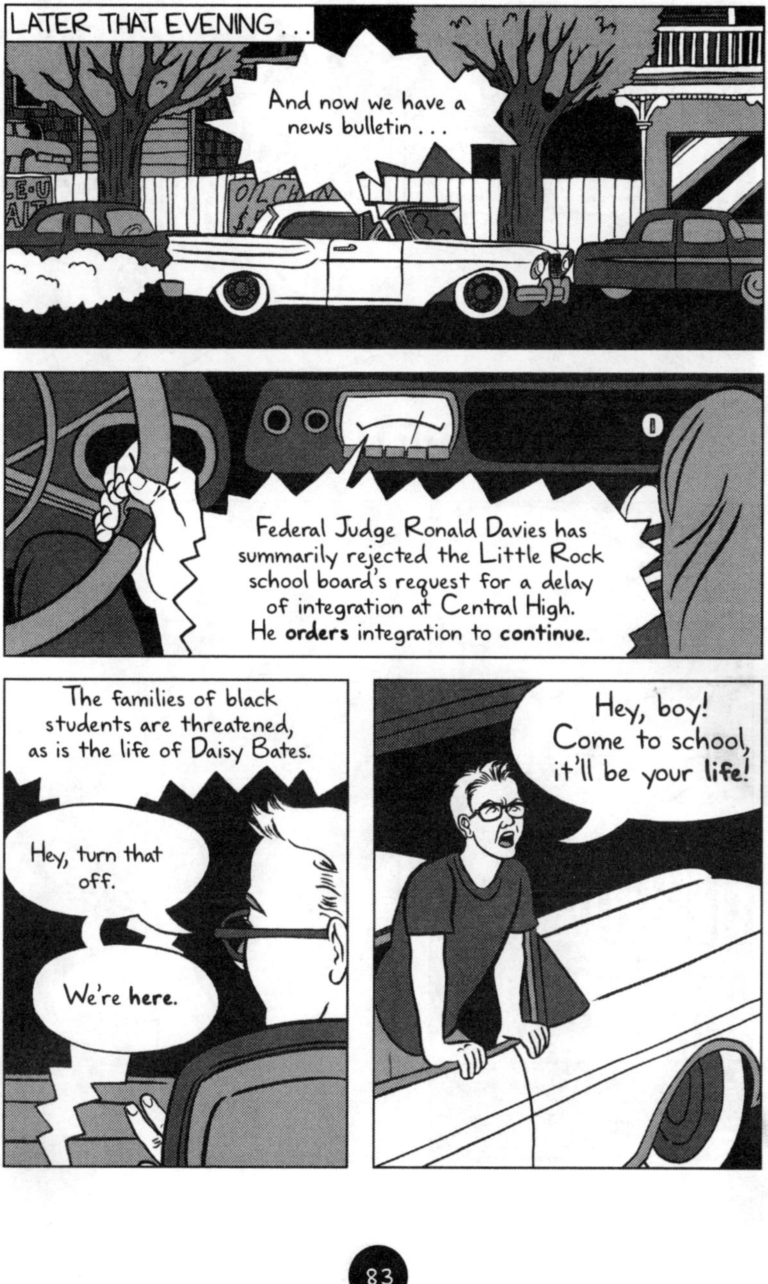
LATER THAT EVENING . . .
And now we have a news bulletin . . .
Federal Judge Ronald Davies has summarily rejected the Little Rock school board's request for a delay of integration at Central High. He **orders** integration to **continue**.
The families of black students are threatened, as is the life of Daisy Bates.
Hey, turn that off.
We're **here**.
Hey, boy! Come to school, it'll be your **life**!

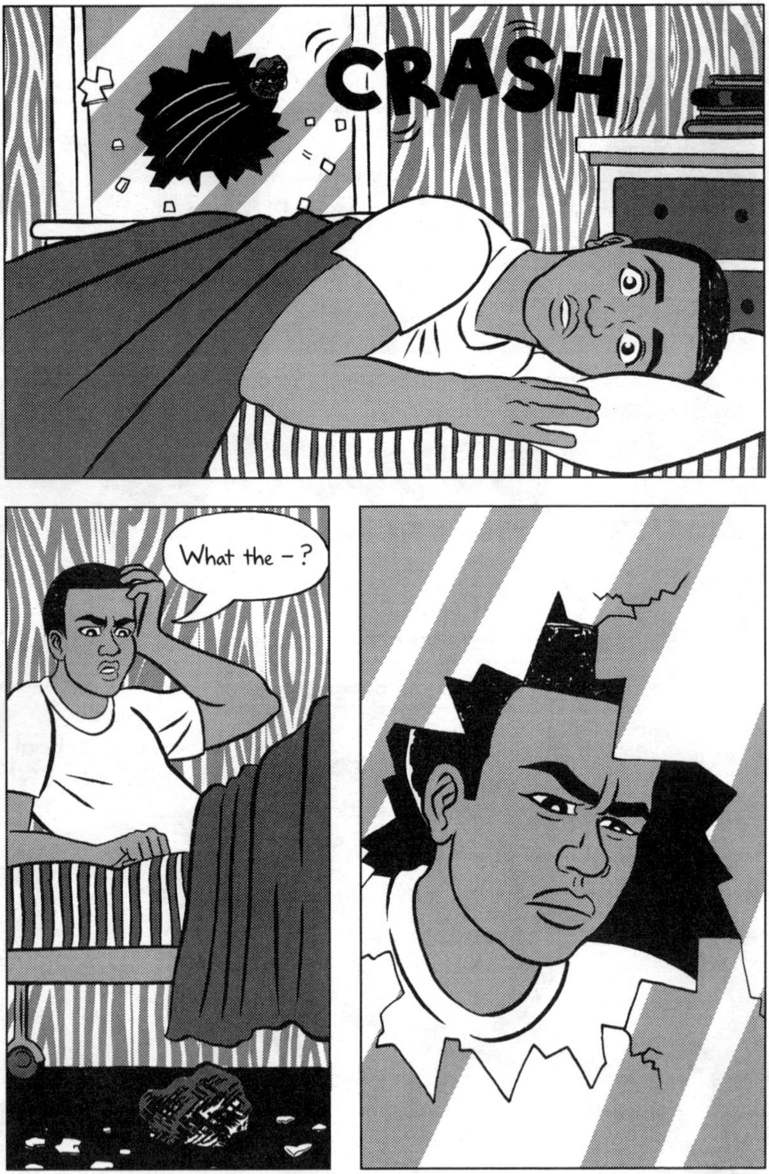
CRASH
What the -?

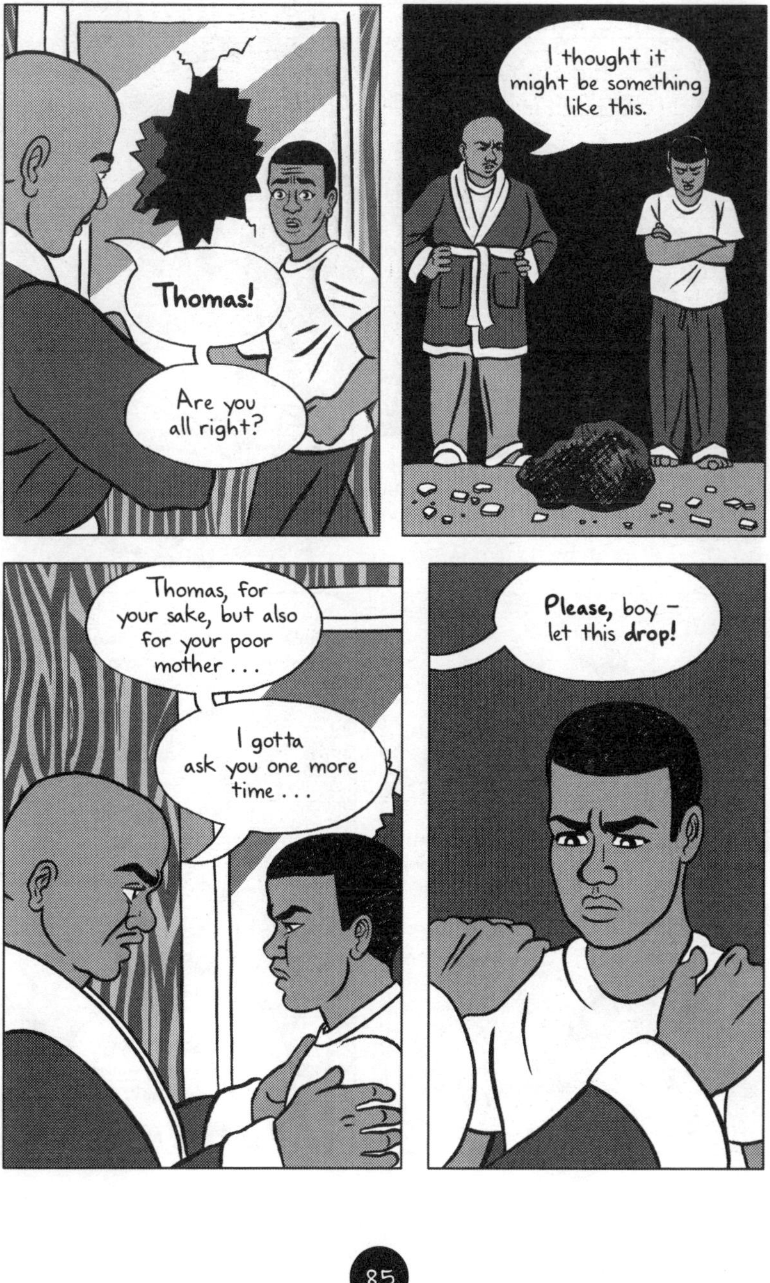

Thomas!
Are you all right?
I thought it might be something like this.
Thomas, for your sake, but also for your poor mother . . .
I gotta ask you one more time . . .
Please, boy – let this drop!

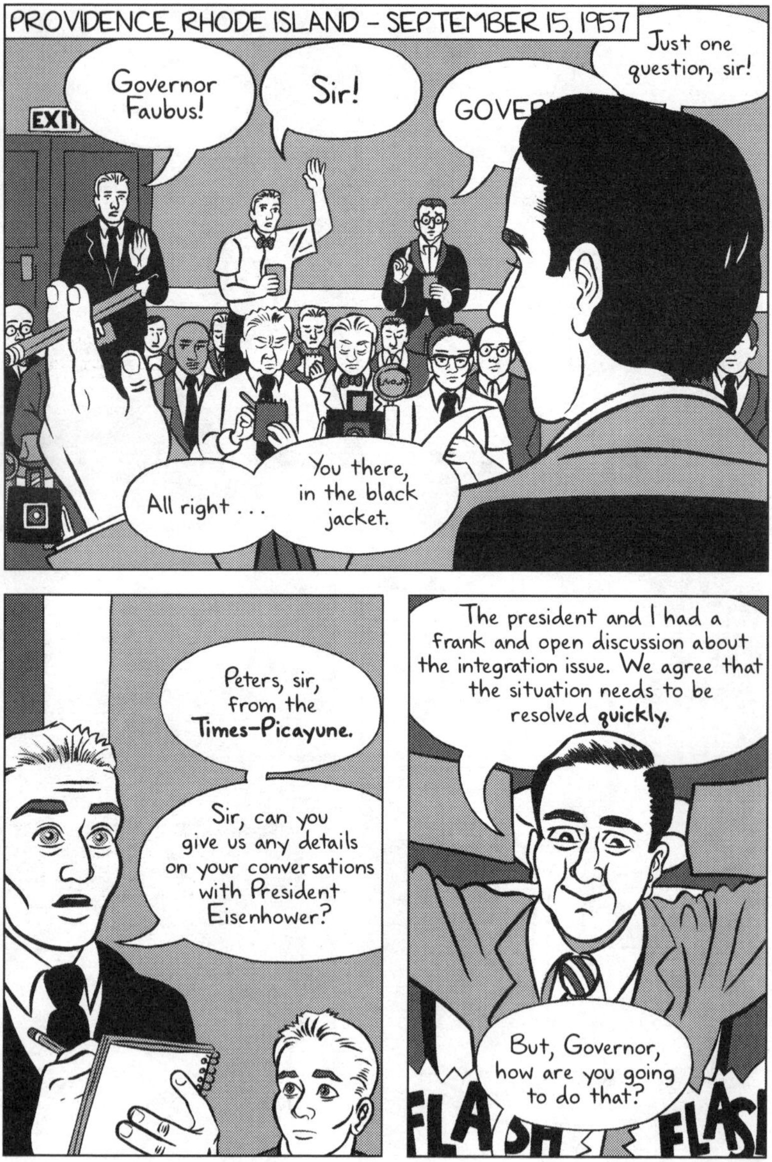
PROVIDENCE, RHODE ISLAND – SEPTEMBER 15, 1957
EXIT
Governor Faubus!
Sir!
GOVER
Just one question, sir!
All right . . .
You there, in the black jacket.
Peters, sir, from the **Times-Picayune.**
Sir, can you give us any details on your conversations with President Eisenhower?
The president and I had a frank and open discussion about the integration issue. We agree that the situation needs to be resolved **quickly.**
But, Governor, how are you going to do that?
FLASH
FLAS

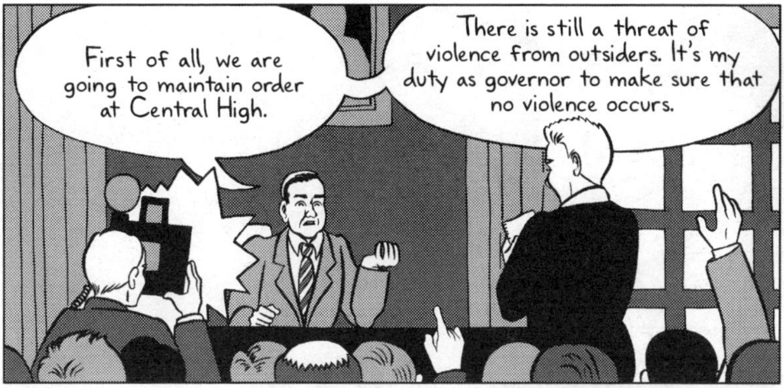
First of all, we are going to maintain order at Central High.
There is still a threat of violence from outsiders. It's my duty as governor to make sure that no violence occurs.

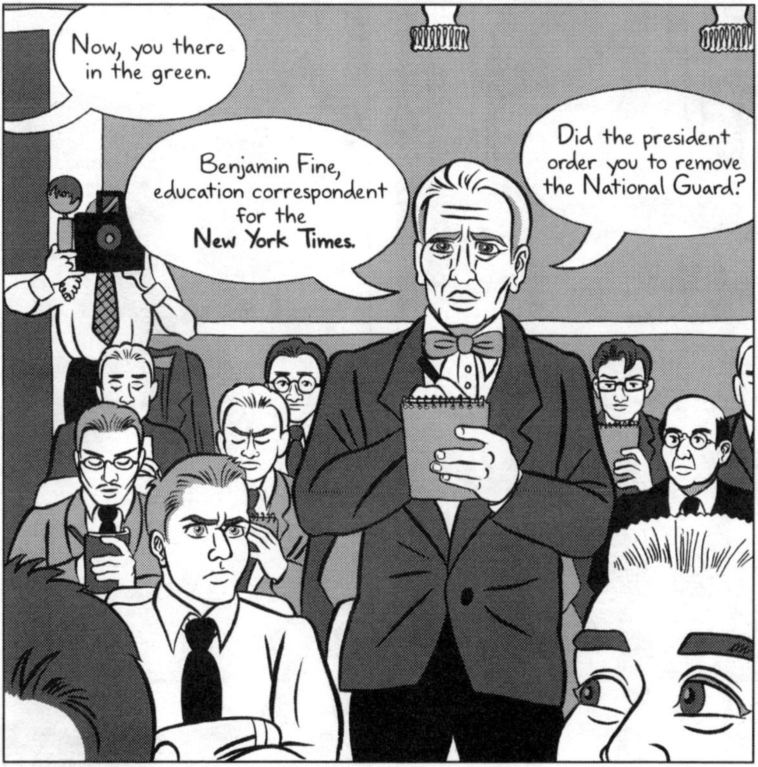
Now, you there in the green.
Benjamin Fine, education correspondent for the **New York Times.**
Did the president order you to remove the National Guard?

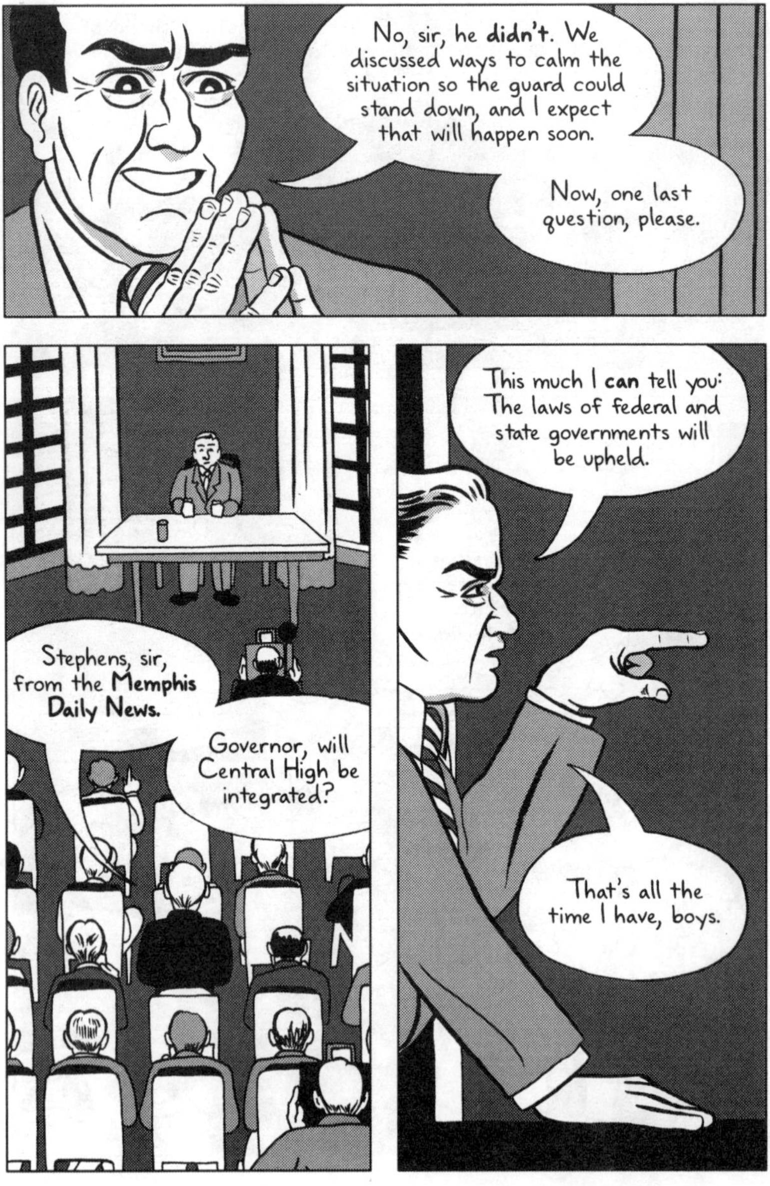
No, sir, he **didn't**. We discussed ways to calm the situation so the guard could stand down, and I expect that will happen soon.
Now, one last question, please.
Stephens, sir, from the **Memphis Daily News.**
Governor, will Central High be integrated?
This much I **can** tell you: The laws of federal and state governments will be upheld.
That's all the time I have, boys.

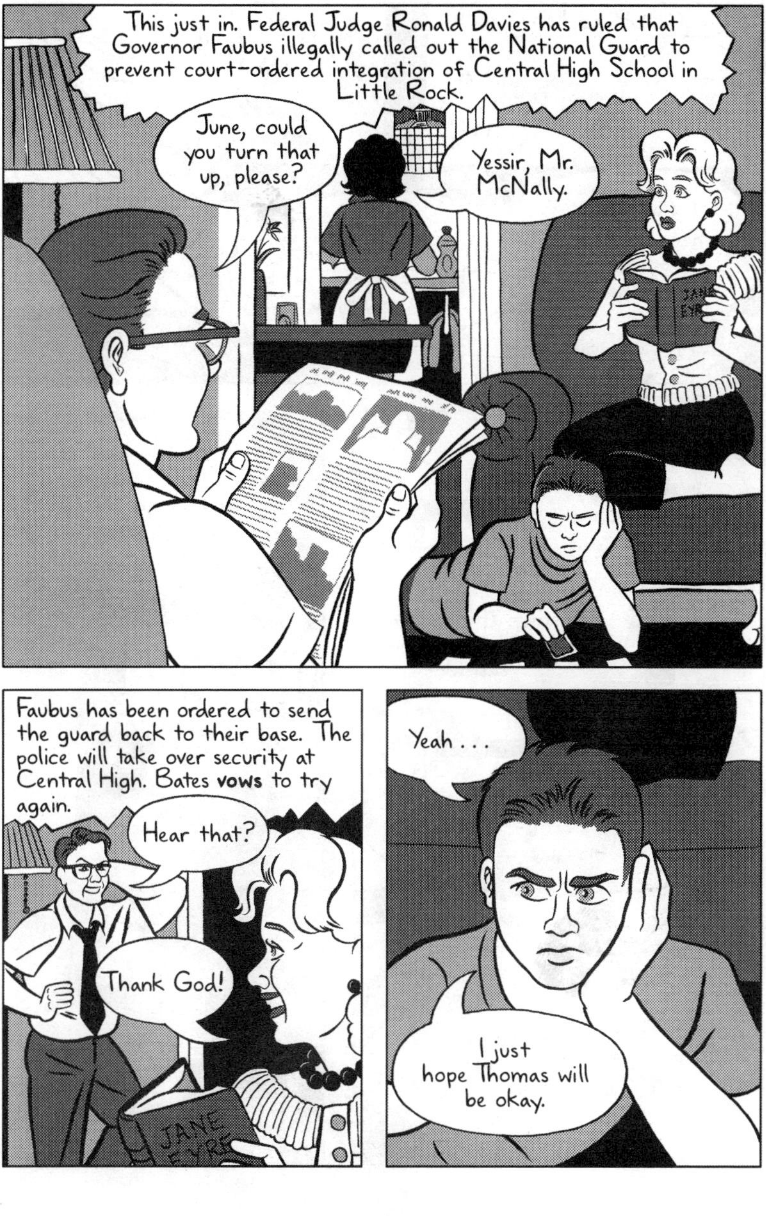
This just in. Federal Judge Ronald Davies has ruled that Governor Faubus illegally called out the National Guard to prevent court-ordered integration of Central High School in Little Rock.
June, could you turn that up, please?
Yessir, Mr. McNally.
JANE EYRE
Faubus has been ordered to send the guard back to their base. The police will take over security at Central High. Bates **vows** to try again.
Hear that?
Thank God!
JANE EYRE
Yeah . . .
I just hope Thomas will be okay.

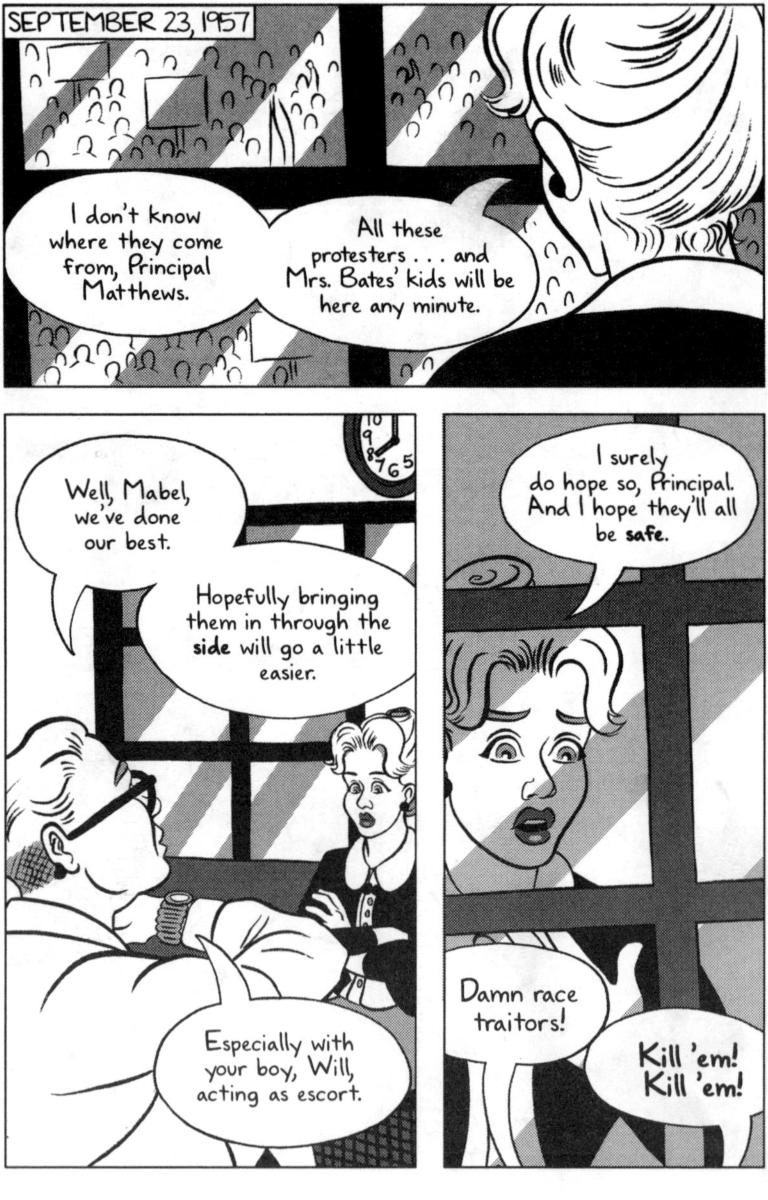
SEPTEMBER 23, 1957
I don't know where they come from, Principal Matthews.
All these protesters . . . and Mrs. Bates' kids will be here any minute.
Well, Mabel, we've done our best.
Hopefully bringing them in through the **side** will go a little easier.
Especially with your boy, Will, acting as escort.
I surely do hope so, Principal. And I hope they'll all be **safe**.
Damn race traitors!
Kill 'em! Kill 'em!

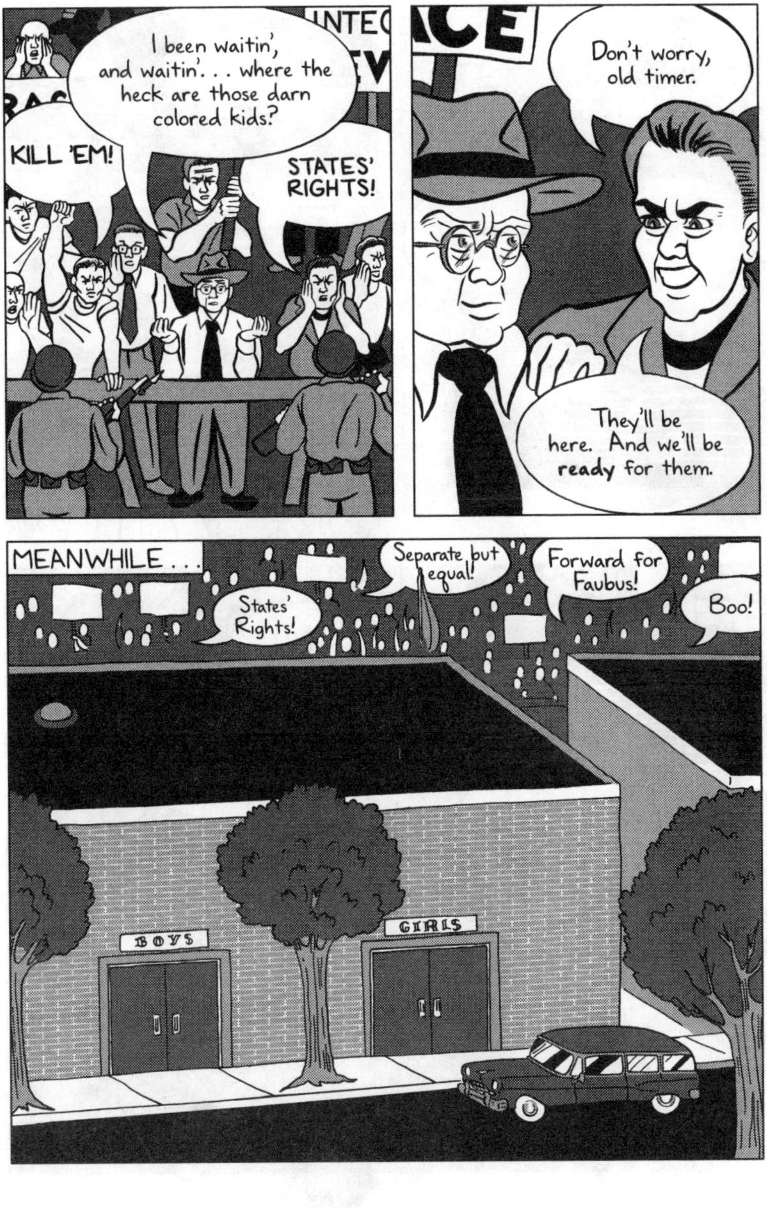
I been waitin', and waitin'. . . where the heck are those darn colored kids?
KILL 'EM!
STATES' RIGHTS!
Don't worry, old timer.
They'll be here. And we'll be **ready** for them.
MEANWHILE . . .
States' Rights!
Separate but equal!
Forward for Faubus!
Boo!
BOYS
GIRLS

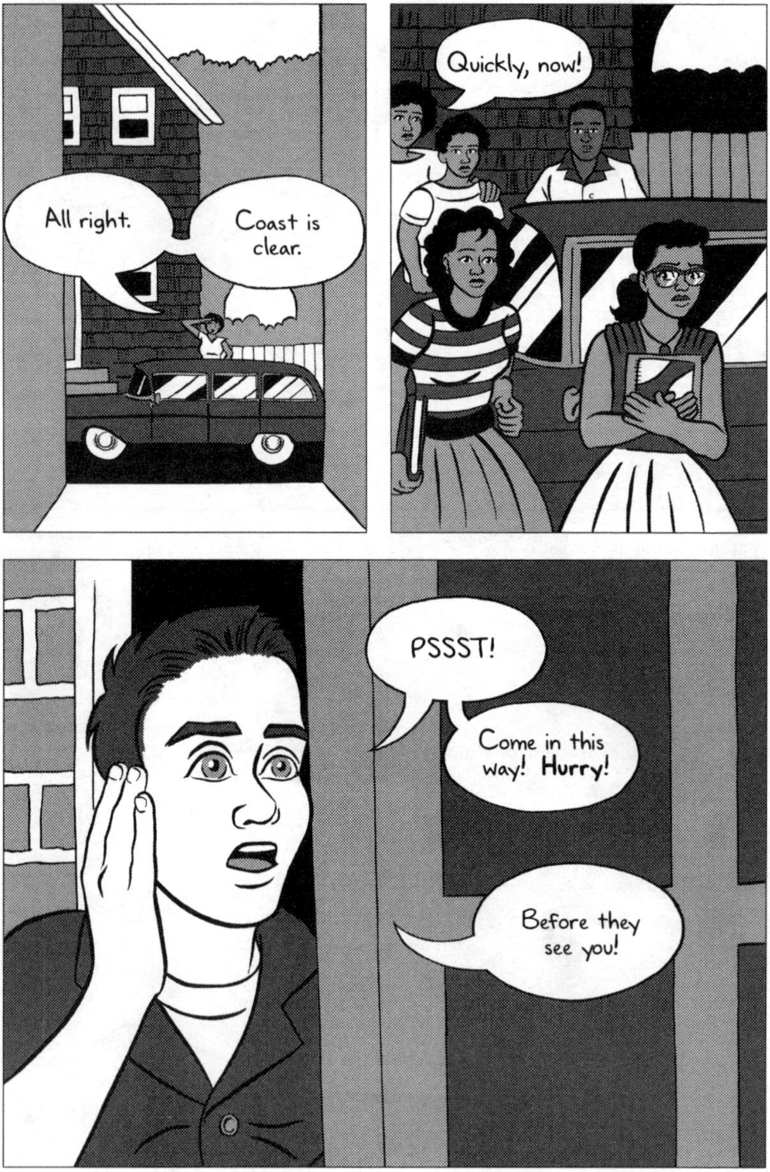
All right.
Coast is clear.
Quickly, now!
PSSST!
Come in this way! **Hurry!**
Before they see you!

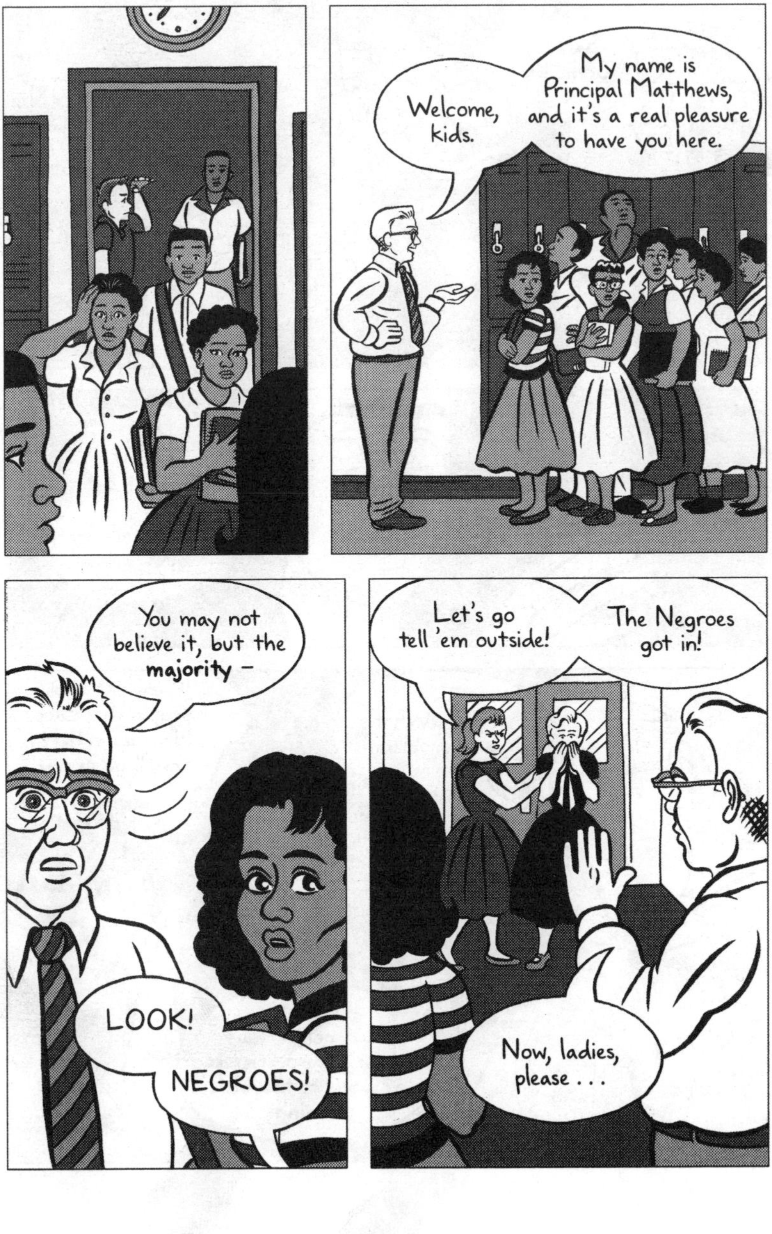
Welcome, kids.
My name is Principal Matthews, and it's a real pleasure to have you here.
You may not believe it, but the **majority** –
LOOK!
NEGROES!
Let's go tell 'em outside!
The Negroes got in!
Now, ladies, please . . .

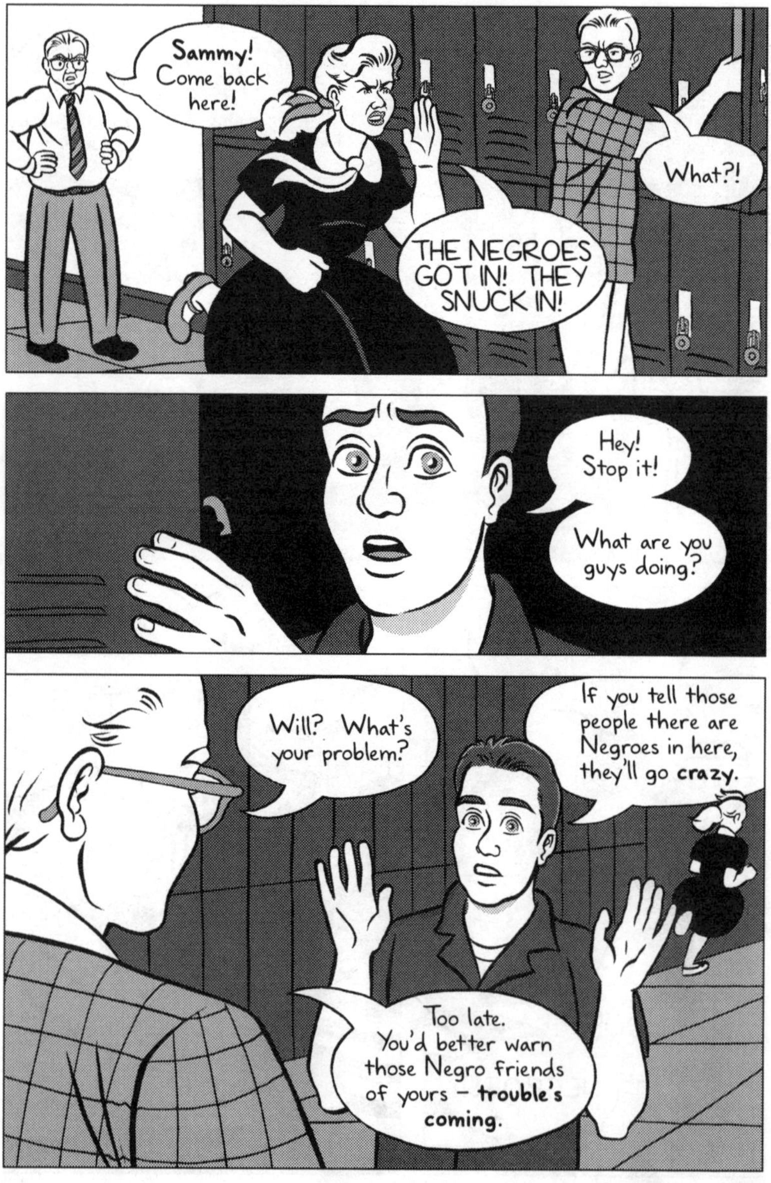
Sammy! Come back here!
THE NEGROES GOT IN! THEY SNUCK IN!
What?!
Hey! Stop it!
What are you guys doing?
Will? What's your problem?
If you tell those people there are Negroes in here, they'll go **crazy**.
Too late. You'd better warn those Negro friends of yours – **trouble's coming**.

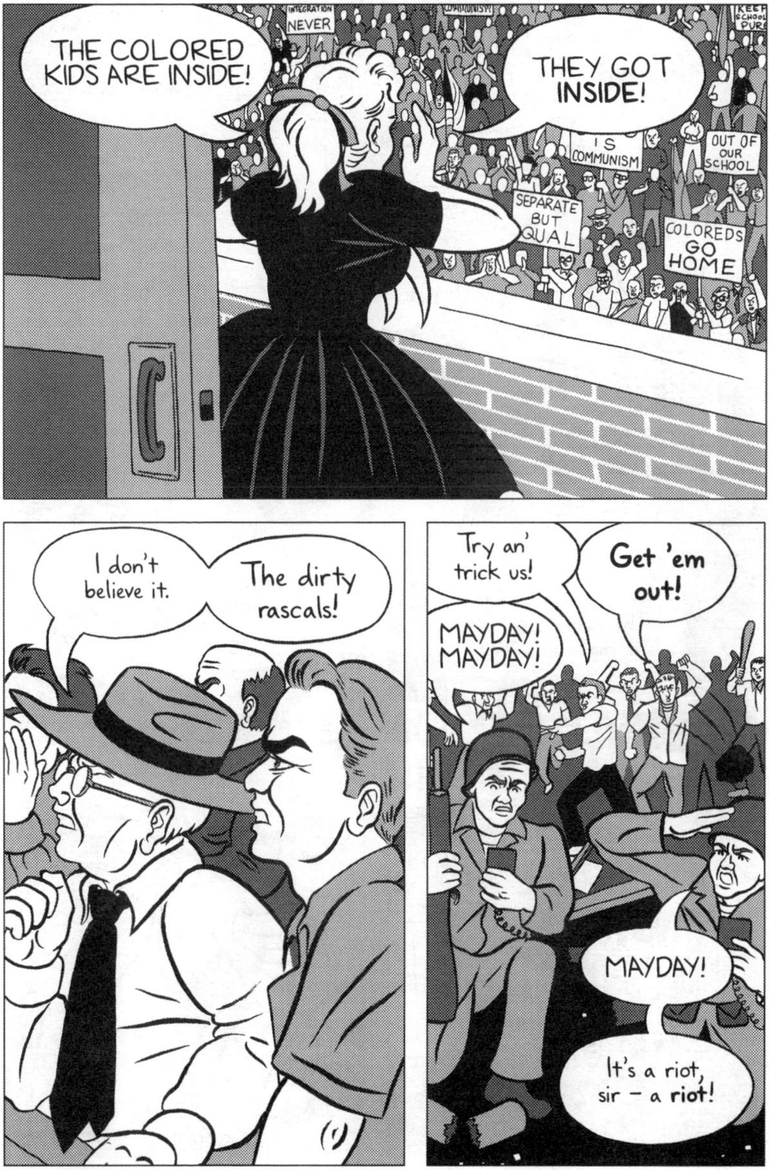
INTEGRATION NEVER
THE COLORED KIDS ARE INSIDE!
THEY GOT **INSIDE!**
IS COMMUNISM
OUT OF OUR SCHOOL
SEPARATE BUT QUAL
COLOREDS GO HOME
I don't believe it.
The dirty rascals!
Try an' trick us!
Get 'em out!
MAYDAY! MAYDAY!
MAYDAY!
It's a riot, sir – a **riot**!

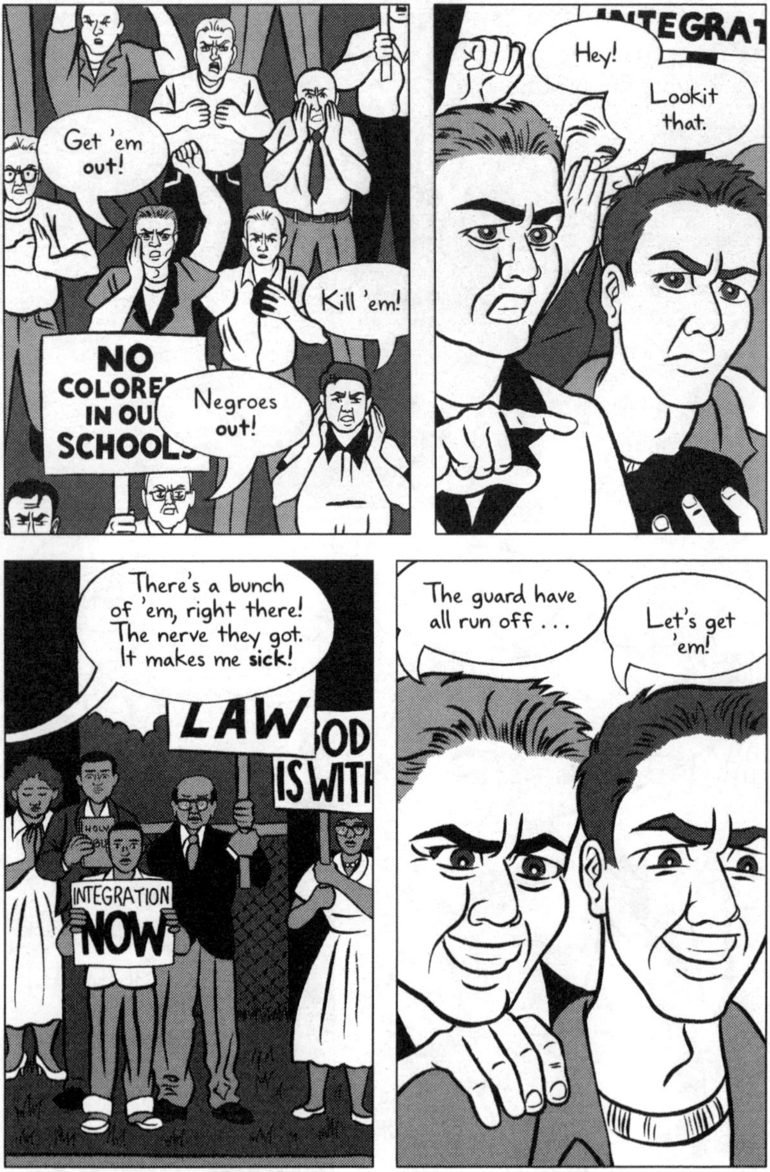
Get 'em out!
Kill 'em!
NO COLORE
IN OU
SCHOOL
Negroes out!
INTEGRAT
Hey!
Lookit that.
There's a bunch of 'em, right there! The nerve they got. It makes me sick!
LAW
OD
IS WIT
INTEGRATION NOW
The guard have all run off . . .
Let's get 'em!

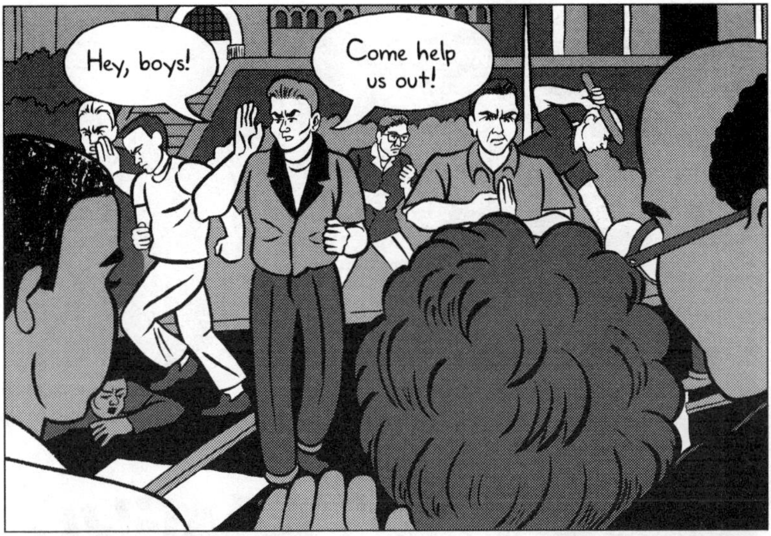
Hey, boys!
Come help us out!

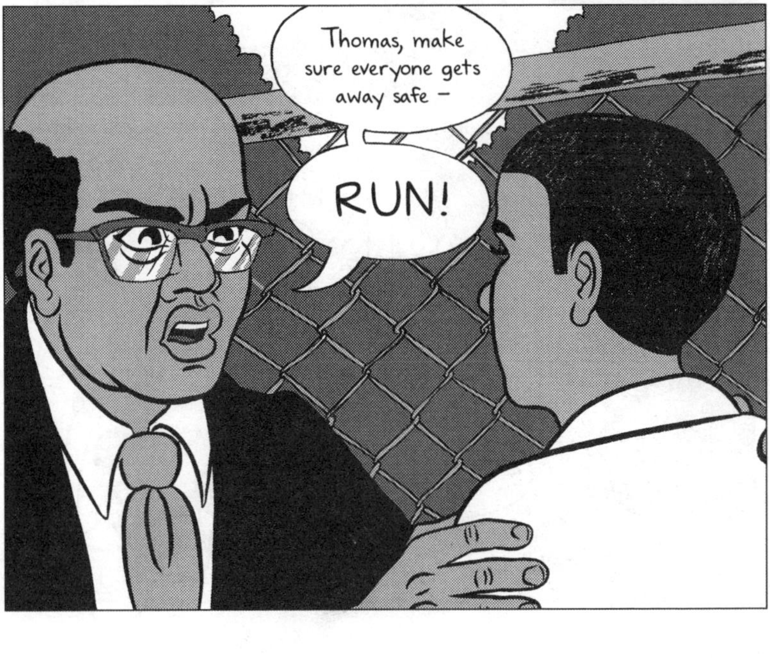
Thomas, make sure everyone gets away safe –
RUN!

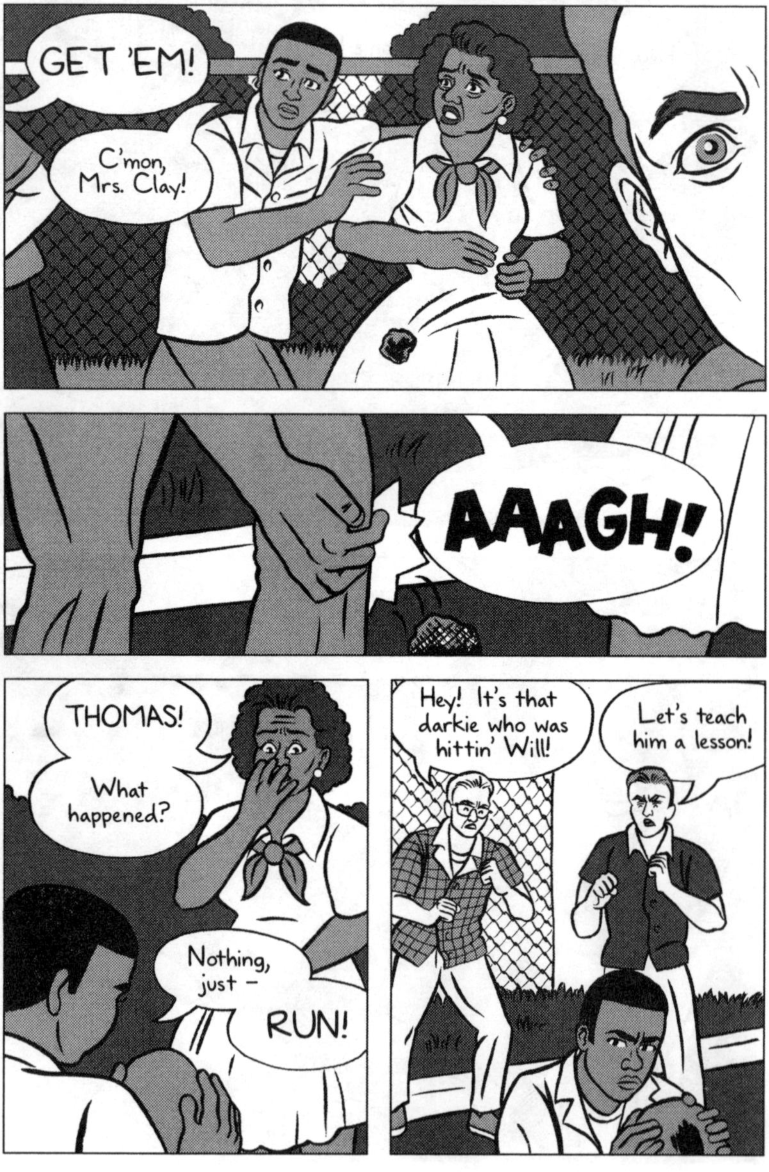
GET 'EM!
C'mon, Mrs. Clay!
AAAGH!
THOMAS!
What happened?
Nothing, just –
RUN!
Hey! It's that darkie who was hittin' Will!
Let's teach him a lesson!

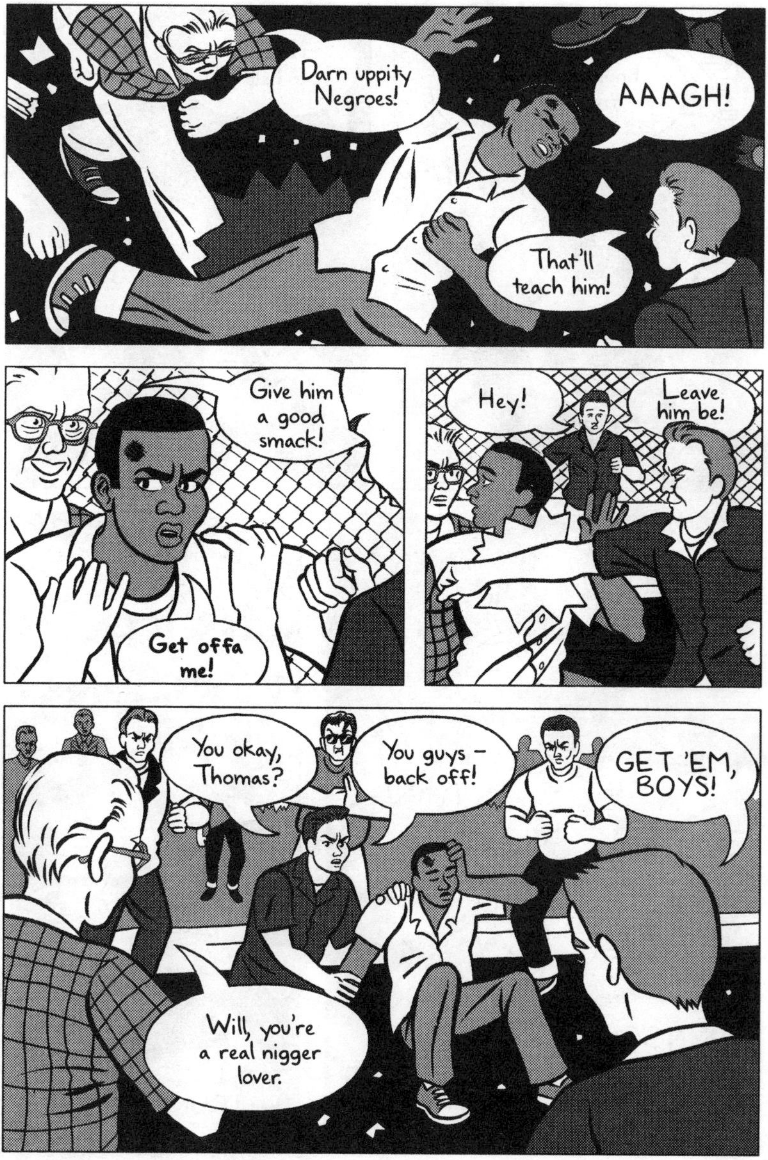
Darn uppity Negroes!
AAAGH!
That'll teach him!
Give him a good smack!
Get offa me!
Hey!
Leave him be!
You okay, Thomas?
You guys – back off!
GET 'EM, BOYS!
Will, you're a real nigger lover.

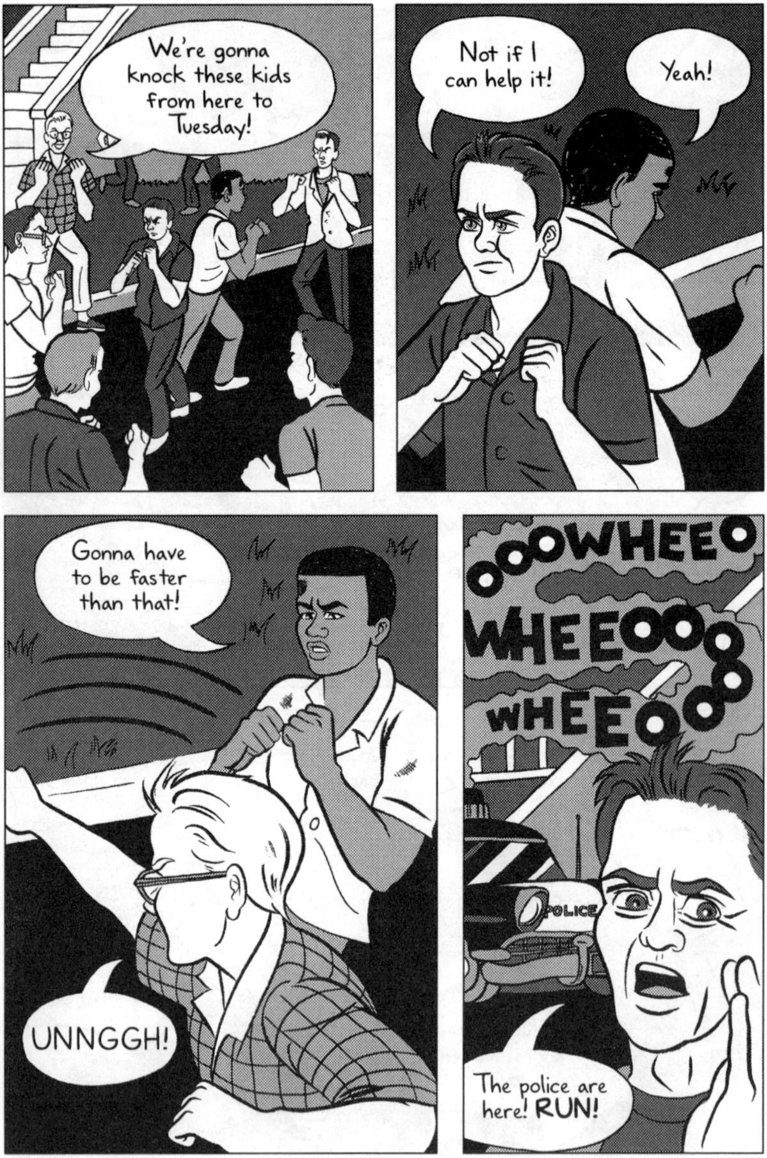

We're gonna knock these kids from here to Tuesday!
Not if I can help it!
Yeah!
Gonna have to be faster than that!
UNNGGH!
OOOWHEEO
WHEEOOO
WHEEOOO
POLICE
The police are here! RUN!

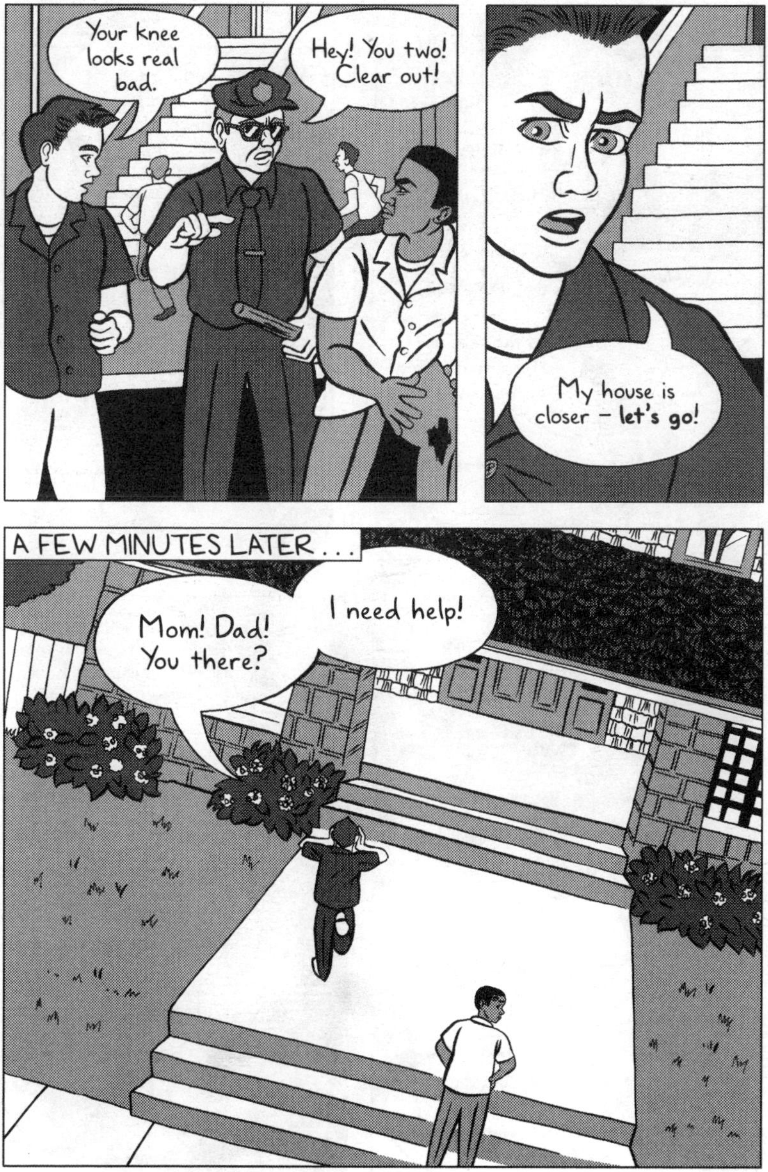
Your knee looks real bad.
Hey! You two! Clear out!
My house is closer – **let's go!**
A FEW MINUTES LATER . . .
Mom! Dad! You there?
I need help!

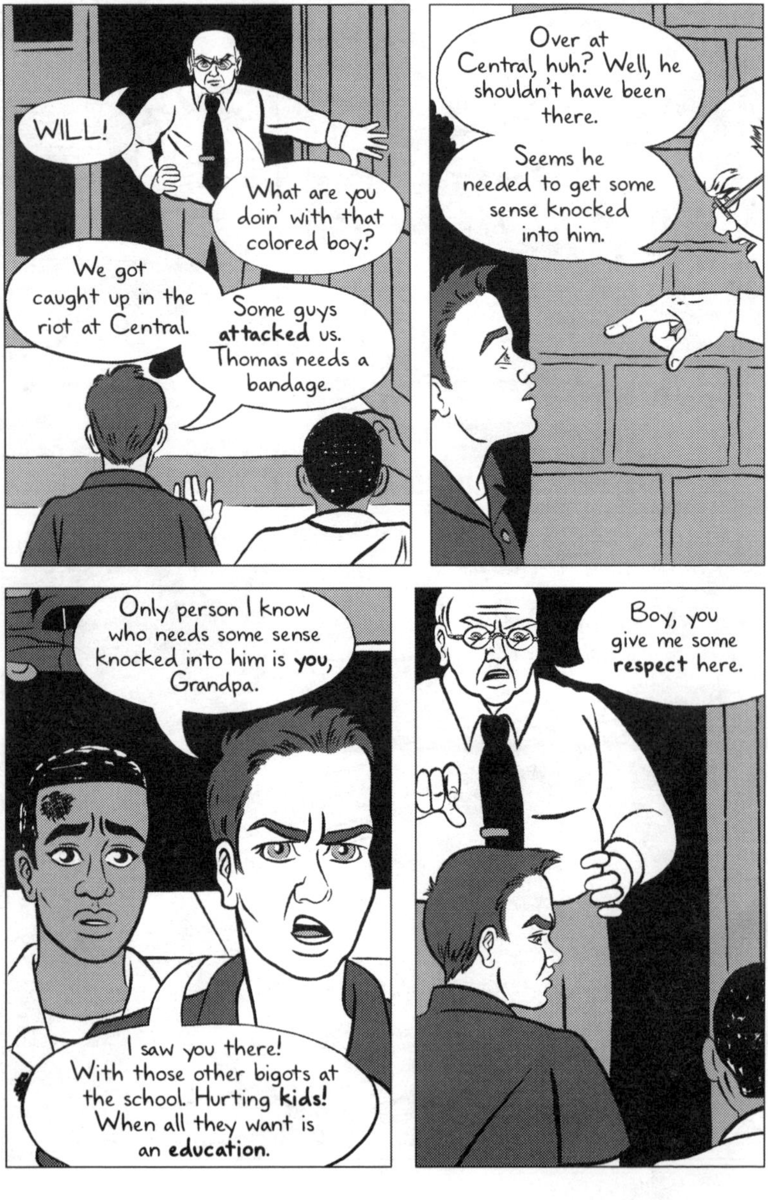
WILL!
What are you doin' with that colored boy?
We got caught up in the riot at Central.
Some guys **attacked** us. Thomas needs a bandage.
Over at Central, huh? Well, he shouldn't have been there.
Seems he needed to get some sense knocked into him.
Only person I know who needs some sense knocked into him is **you**, Grandpa.
I saw you there! With those other bigots at the school. Hurting **kids!** When all they want is an **education**.
Boy, you give me some **respect** here.

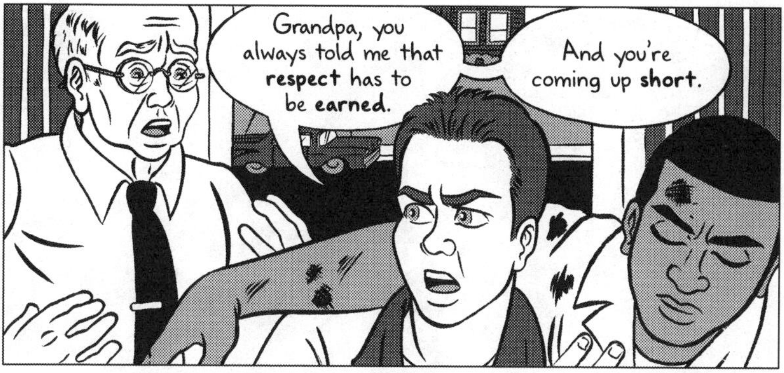
Grandpa, you always told me that **respect** has to be **earned**.
And you're coming up **short**.

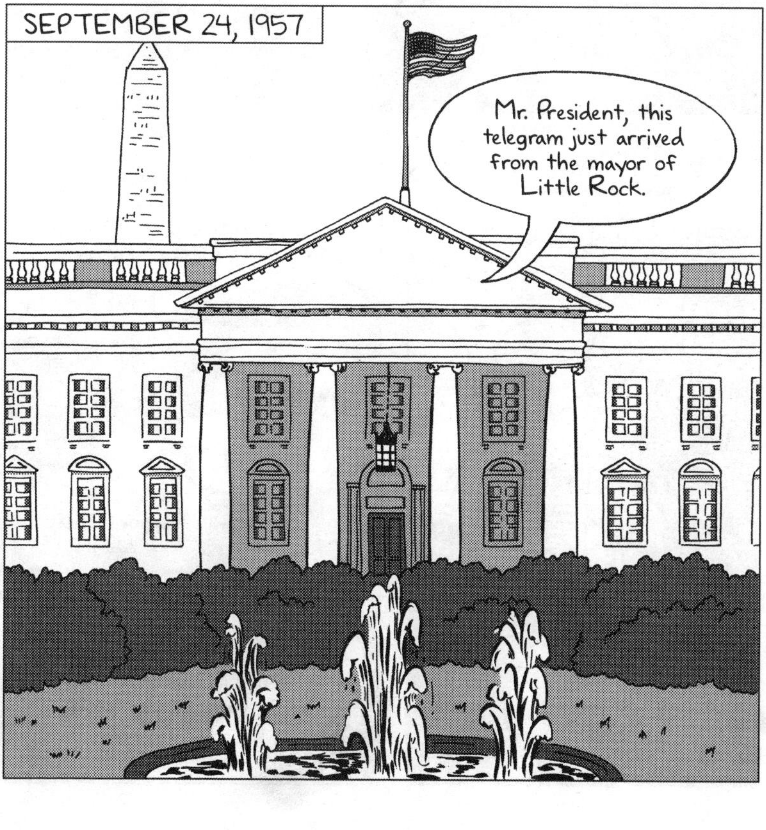
SEPTEMBER 24, 1957
Mr. President, this telegram just arrived from the mayor of Little Rock.

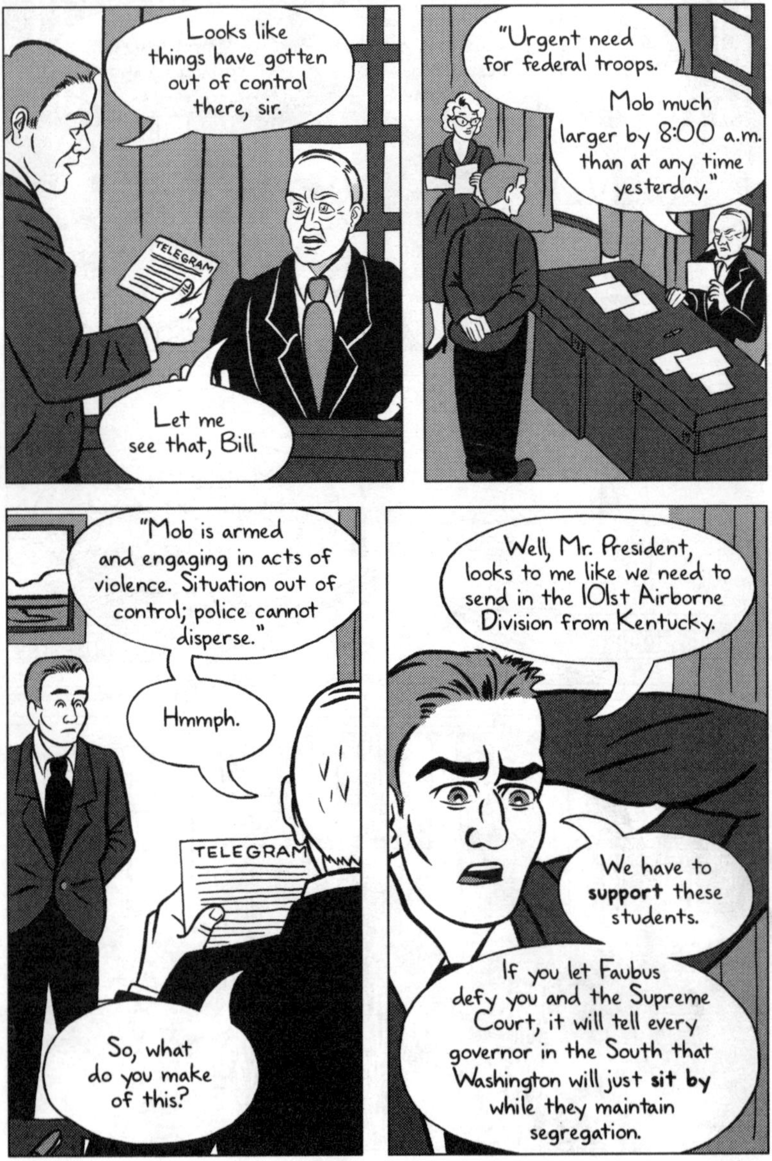
Looks like things have gotten out of control there, sir.
Let me see that, Bill.
TELEGRAM
"Urgent need for federal troops.
Mob much larger by 8:00 a.m. than at any time yesterday."
"Mob is armed and engaging in acts of violence. Situation out of control; police cannot disperse."
Hmmph.
TELEGRAM
So, what do you make of this?
Well, Mr. President, looks to me like we need to send in the 101st Airborne Division from Kentucky.
We have to **support** these students.
If you let Faubus defy you and the Supreme Court, it will tell every governor in the South that Washington will just **sit by** while they maintain segregation.

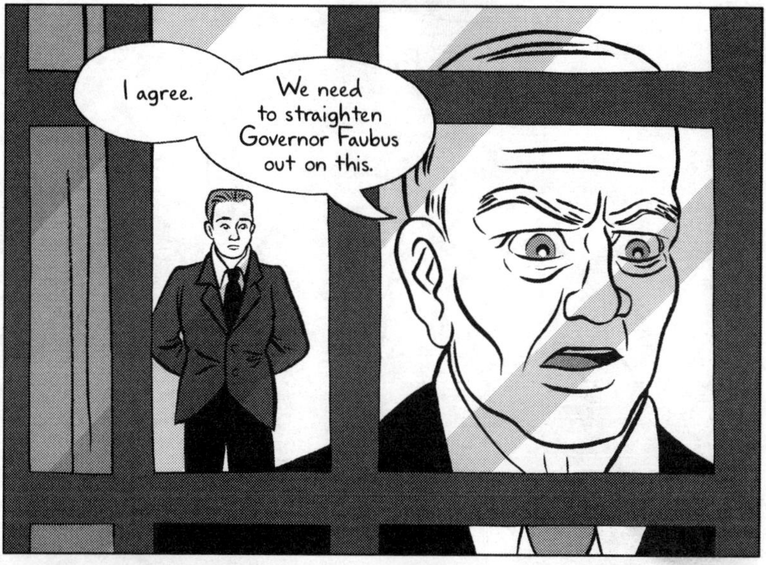
I agree.
We need to straighten Governor Faubus out on this.

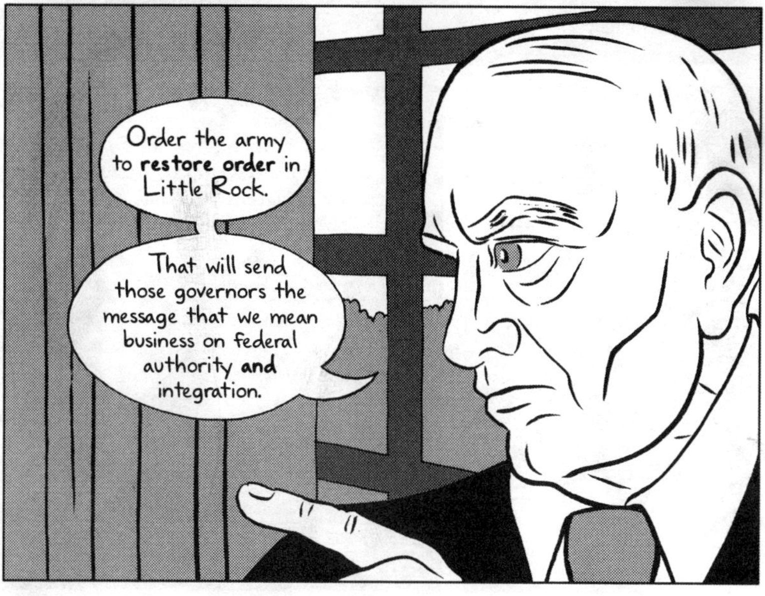
Order the army to **restore order** in Little Rock.
That will send those governors the message that we mean business on federal authority **and** integration.

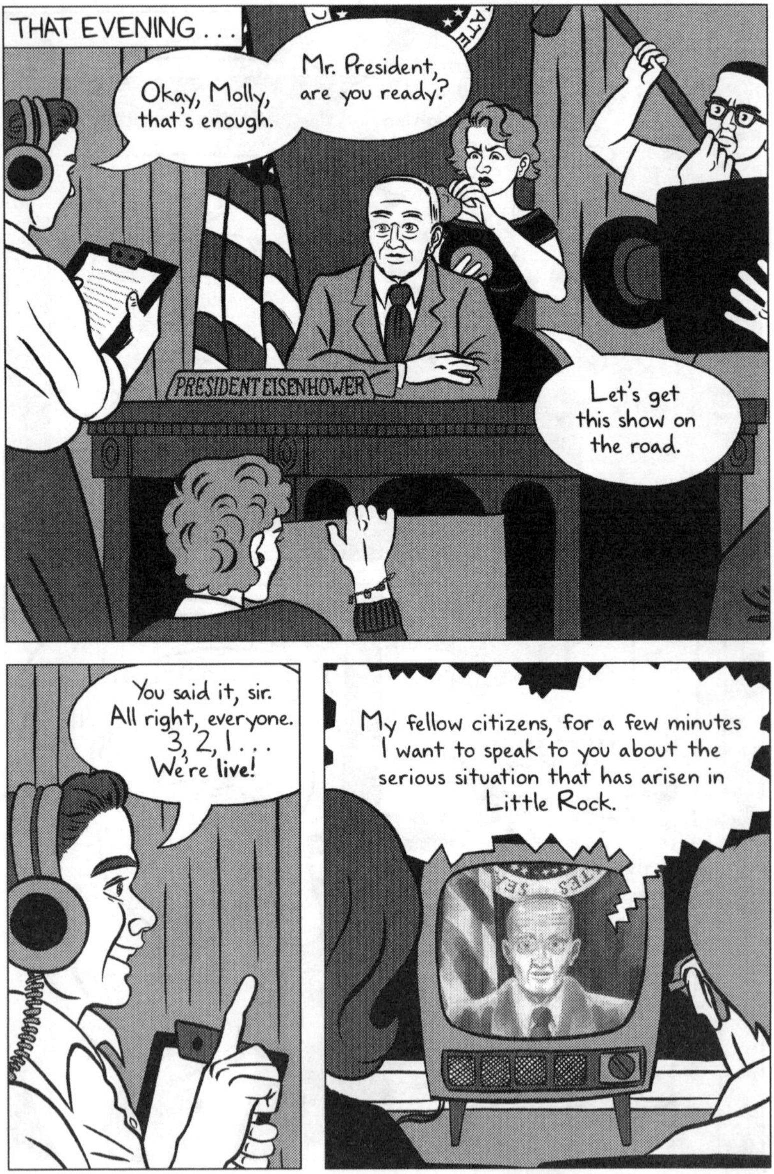
THAT EVENING . . .
Okay, Molly, that's enough.
Mr. President, are you ready?
PRESIDENT EISENHOWER
Let's get this show on the road.
You said it, sir. All right, everyone. 3, 2, 1 . . . We're live!
My fellow citizens, for a few minutes I want to speak to you about the serious situation that has arisen in Little Rock.

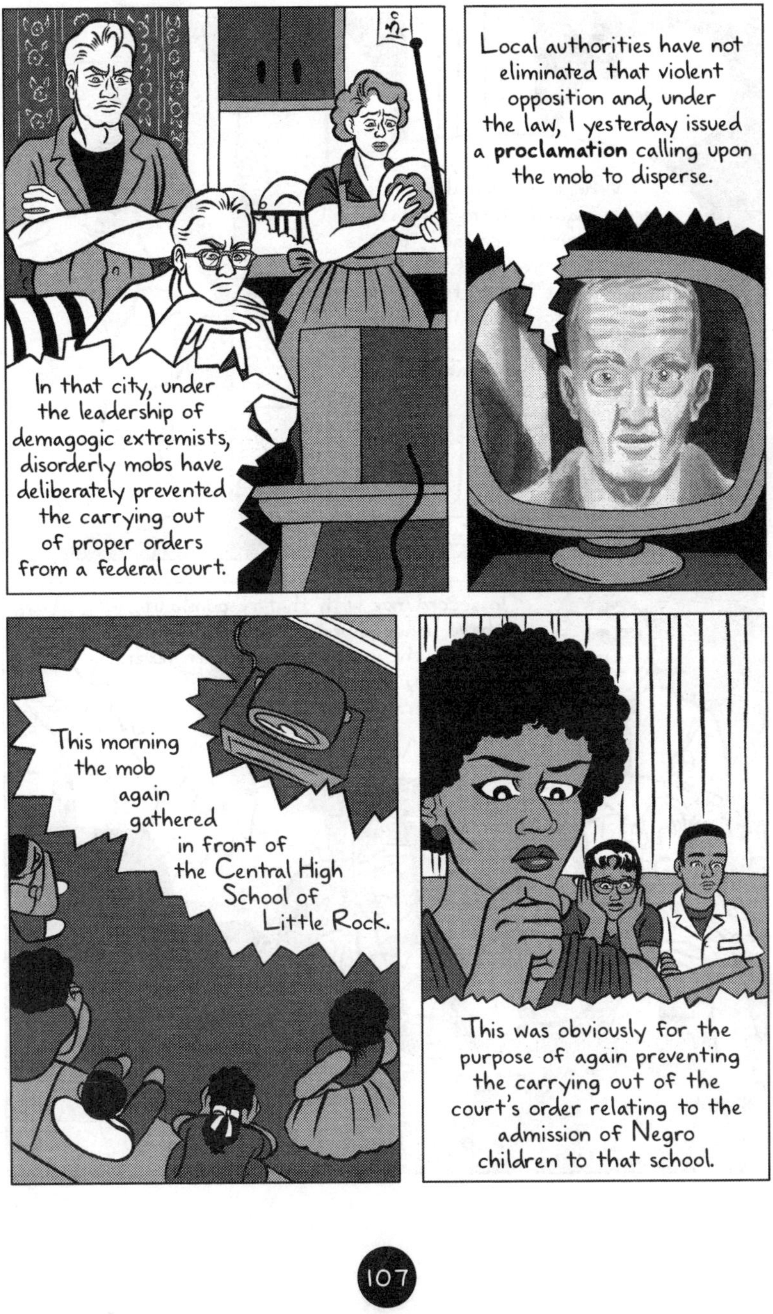
In that city, under the leadership of demagogic extremists, disorderly mobs have deliberately prevented the carrying out of proper orders from a federal court.
Local authorities have not eliminated that violent opposition and, under the law, I yesterday issued a **proclamation** calling upon the mob to disperse.
This morning the mob again gathered in front of the Central High School of Little Rock.
This was obviously for the purpose of again preventing the carrying out of the court's order relating to the admission of Negro children to that school.

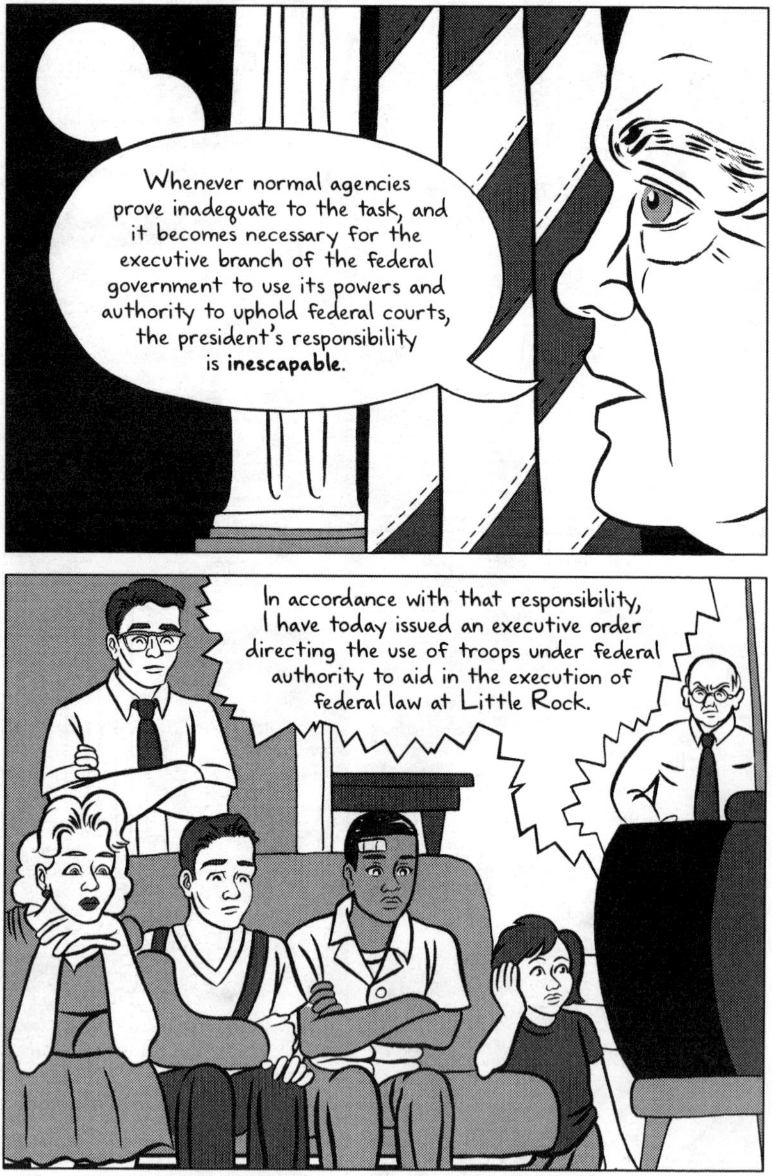
Whenever normal agencies prove inadequate to the task, and it becomes necessary for the executive branch of the federal government to use its powers and authority to uphold federal courts, the president's responsibility is **inescapable**.
In accordance with that responsibility, I have today issued an executive order directing the use of troops under federal authority to aid in the execution of federal law at Little Rock.

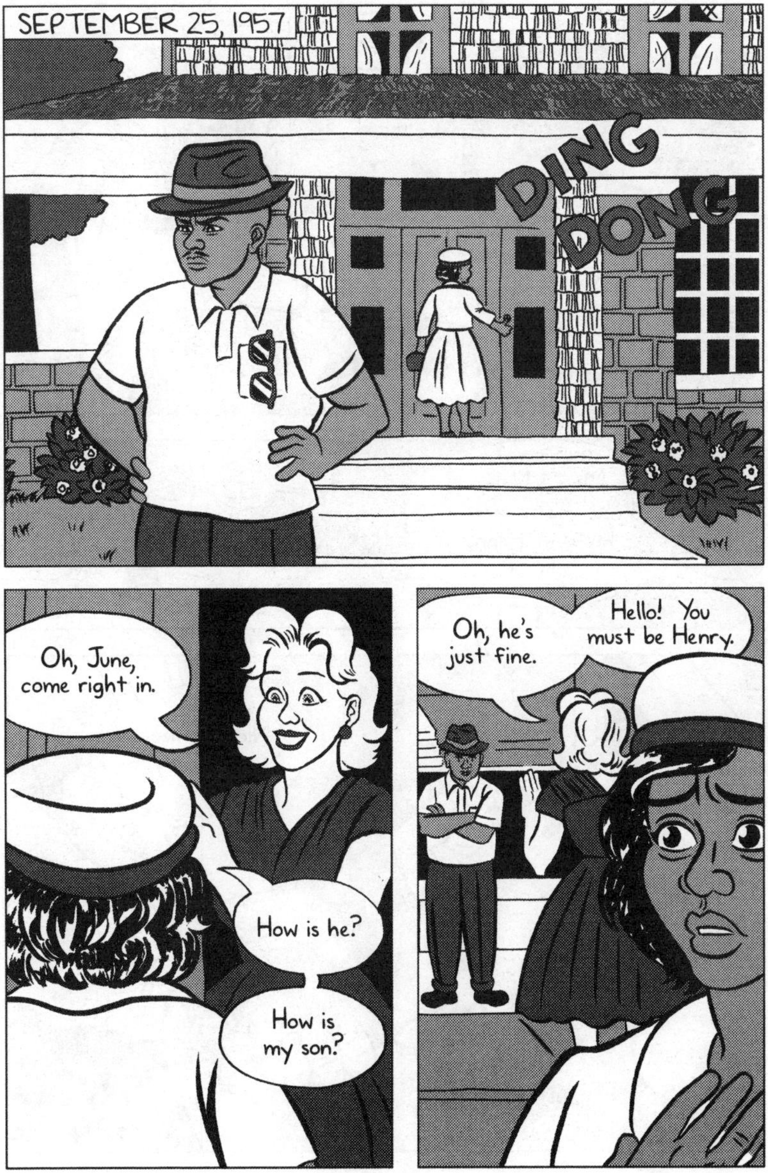
SEPTEMBER 25, 1957
DING
DONG
Oh, June, come right in.
How is he?
How is my son?
Oh, he's just fine.
Hello! You must be Henry.

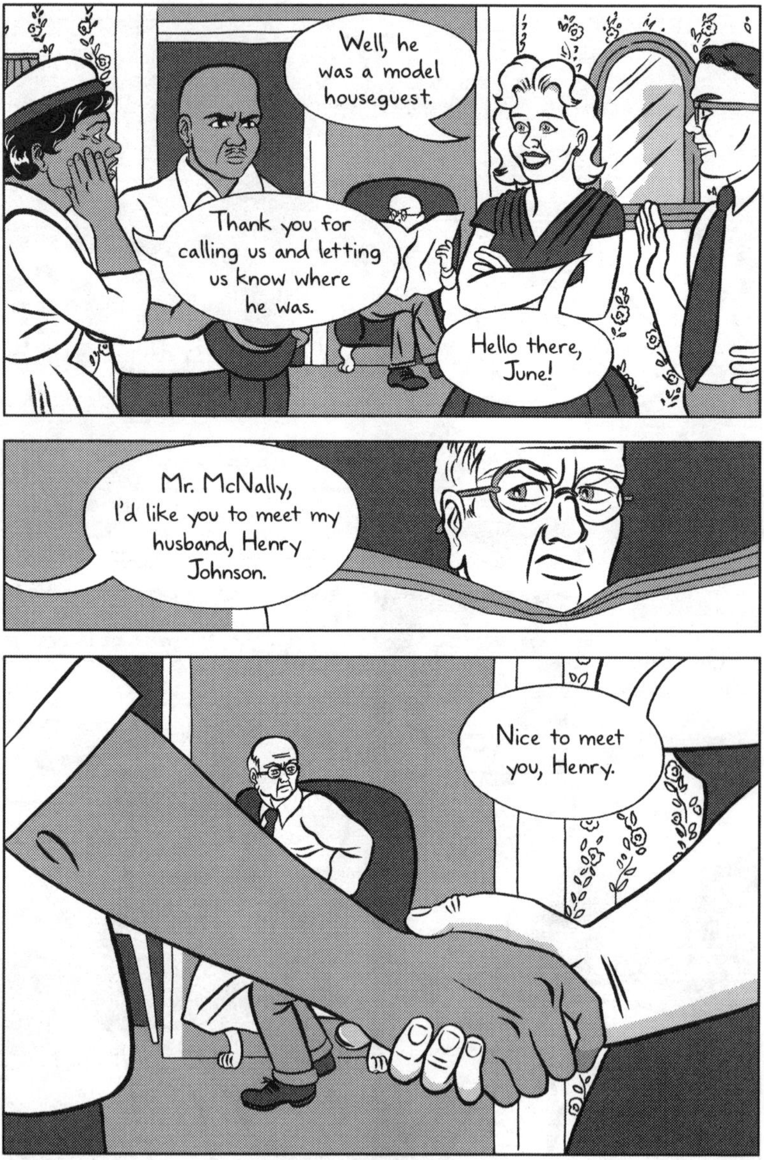

Well, he was a model houseguest.
Thank you for calling us and letting us know where he was.
Hello there, June!
Mr. McNally, I'd like you to meet my husband, Henry Johnson.
Nice to meet you, Henry.

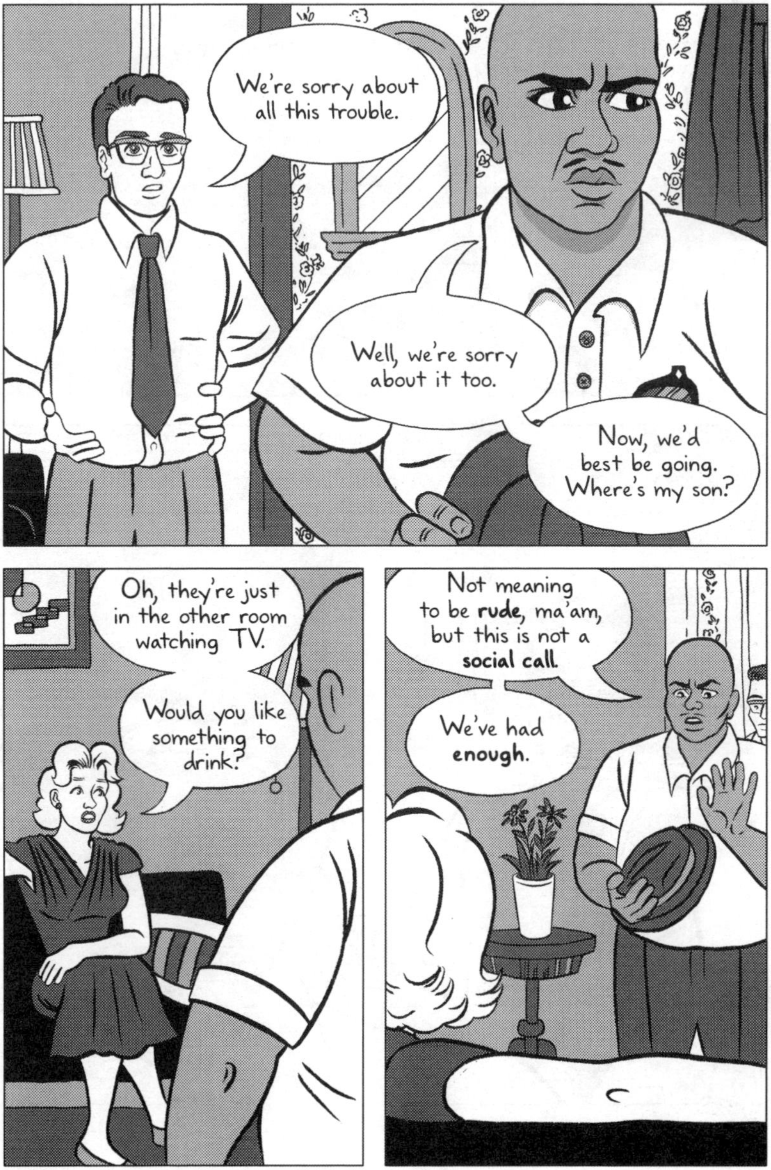
We're sorry about all this trouble.
Well, we're sorry about it too.
Now, we'd best be going. Where's my son?
Oh, they're just in the other room watching TV.
Would you like something to drink?
Not meaning to be **rude**, ma'am, but this is not a **social call**.
We've had **enough**.

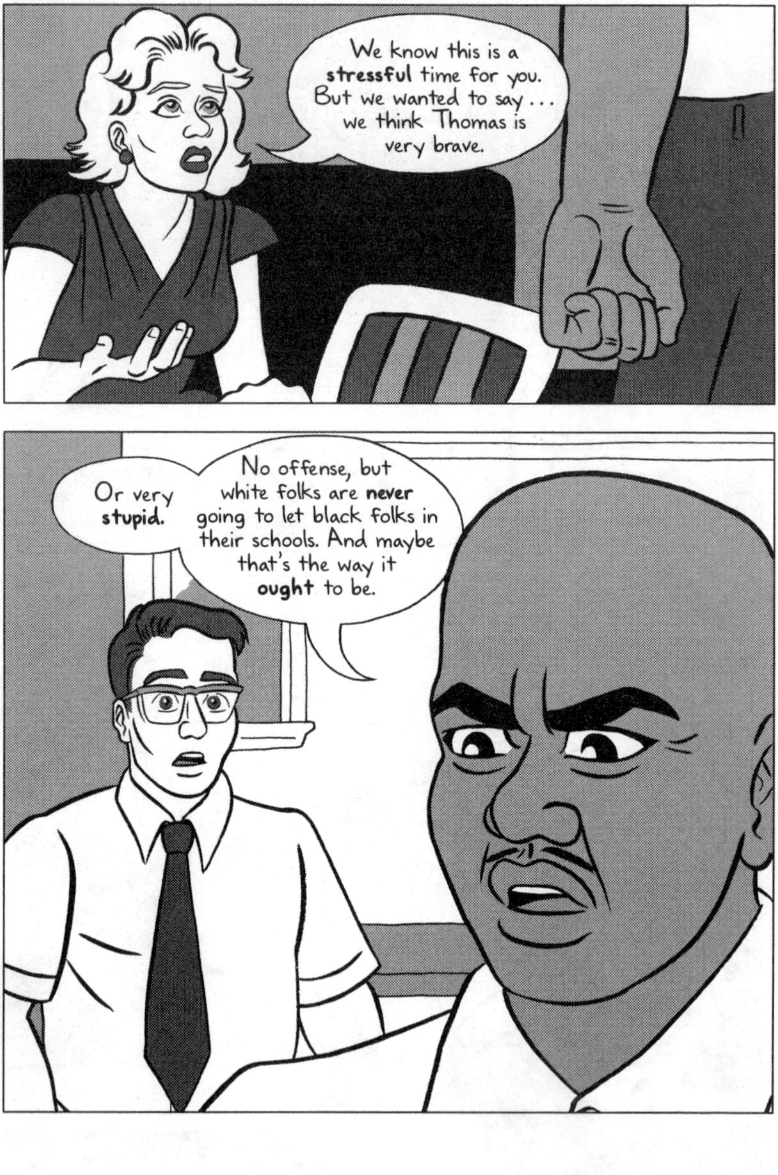
We know this is a **stressful** time for you. But we wanted to say . . . we think Thomas is very brave.
Or very **stupid.**
No offense, but white folks are **never** going to let black folks in their schools. And maybe that's the way it **ought** to be.

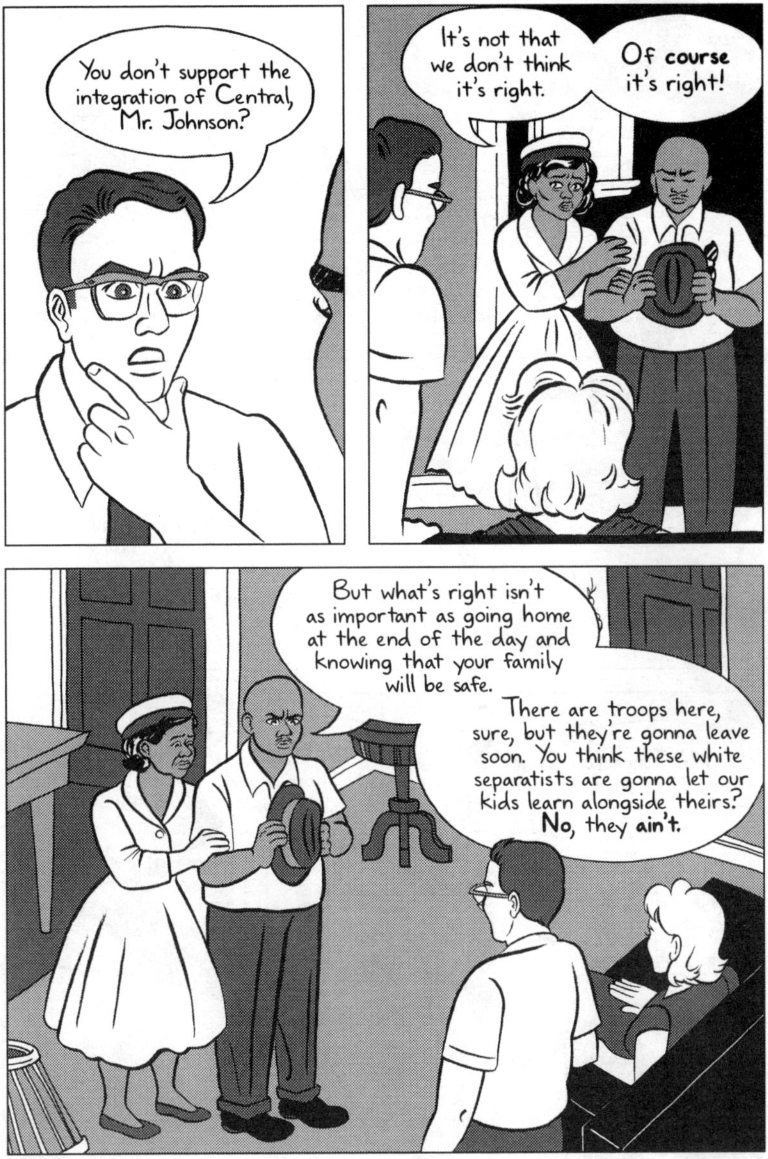
You don't support the integration of Central, Mr. Johnson?
It's not that we don't think it's right.
Of **course** it's right!
But what's right isn't as important as going home at the end of the day and knowing that your family will be safe.
There are troops here, sure, but they're gonna leave soon. You think these white separatists are gonna let our kids learn alongside theirs? **No**, they **ain't**.

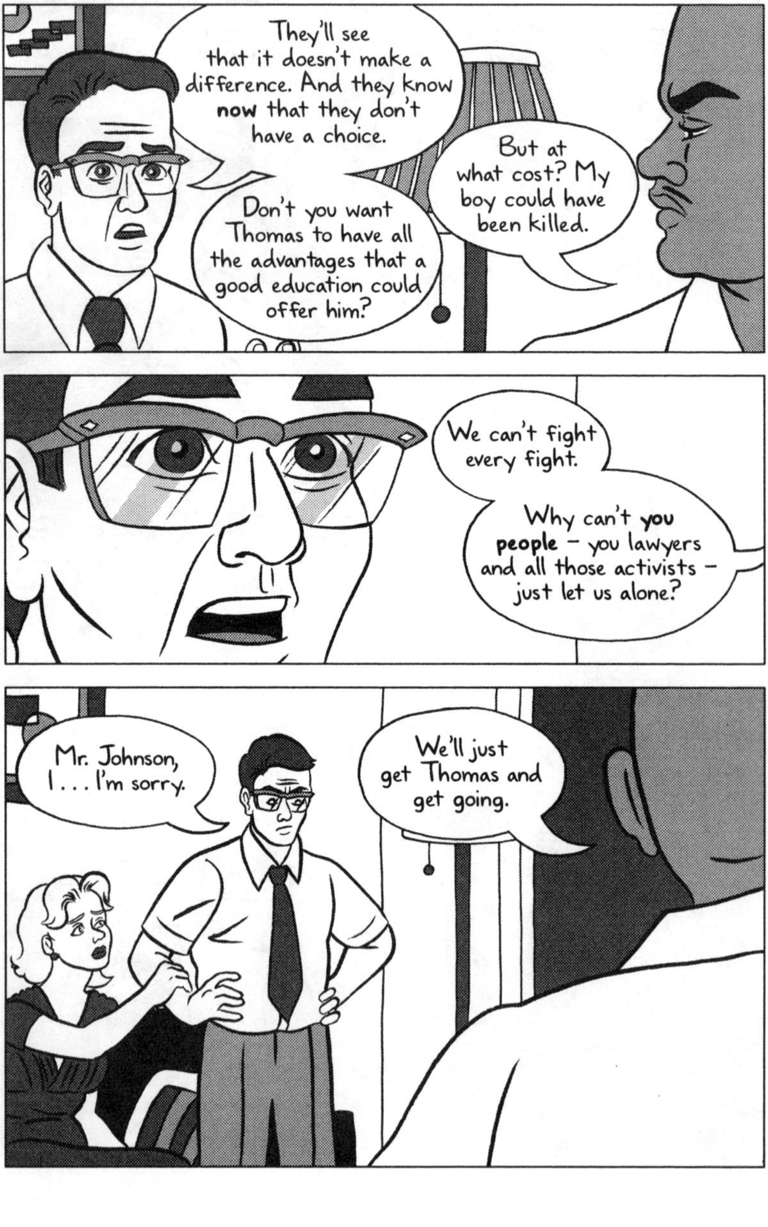
They'll see that it doesn't make a difference. And they know **now** that they don't have a choice.
Don't you want Thomas to have all the advantages that a good education could offer him?
But at what cost? My boy could have been killed.
We can't fight every fight.
Why can't **you people** – you lawyers and all those activists – just let us alone?
Mr. Johnson, I . . . I'm sorry.
We'll just get Thomas and get going.

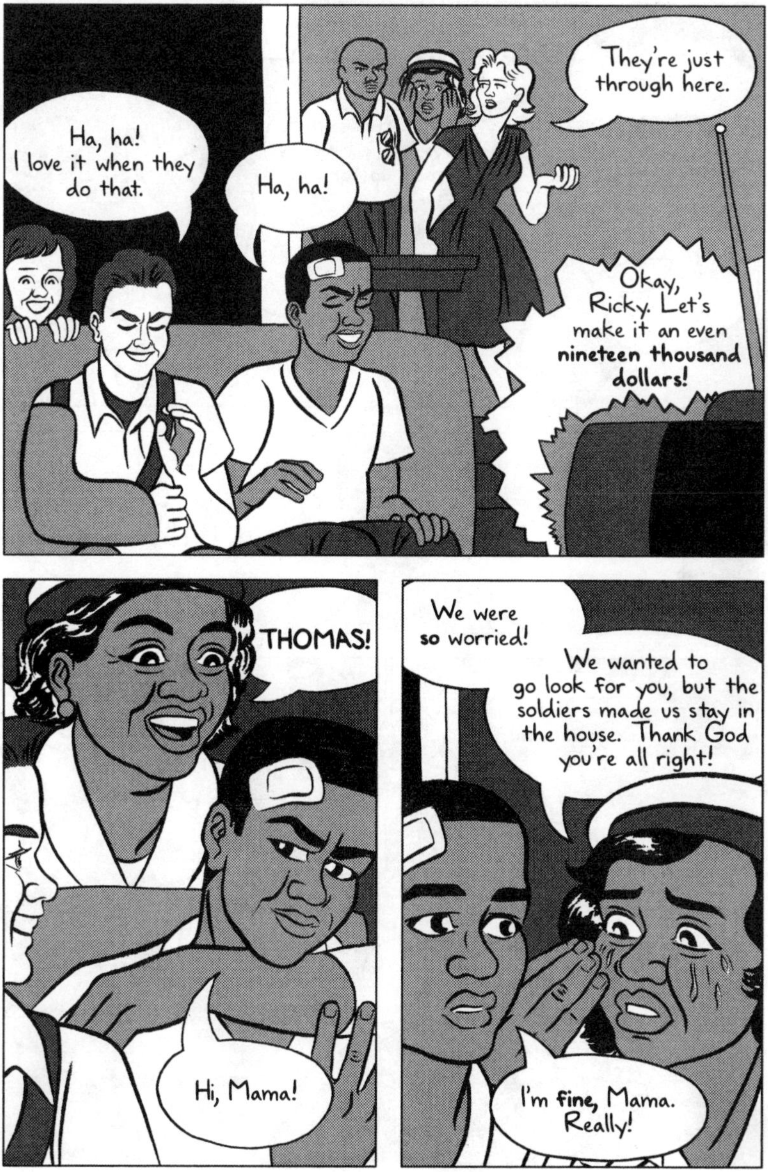
They're just through here.
Ha, ha! I love it when they do that.
Ha, ha!
Okay, Ricky. Let's make it an even **nineteen thousand dollars!**
THOMAS!
Hi, Mama!
We were **so** worried!
We wanted to go look for you, but the soldiers made us stay in the house. Thank God you're all right!
I'm **fine,** Mama. Really!

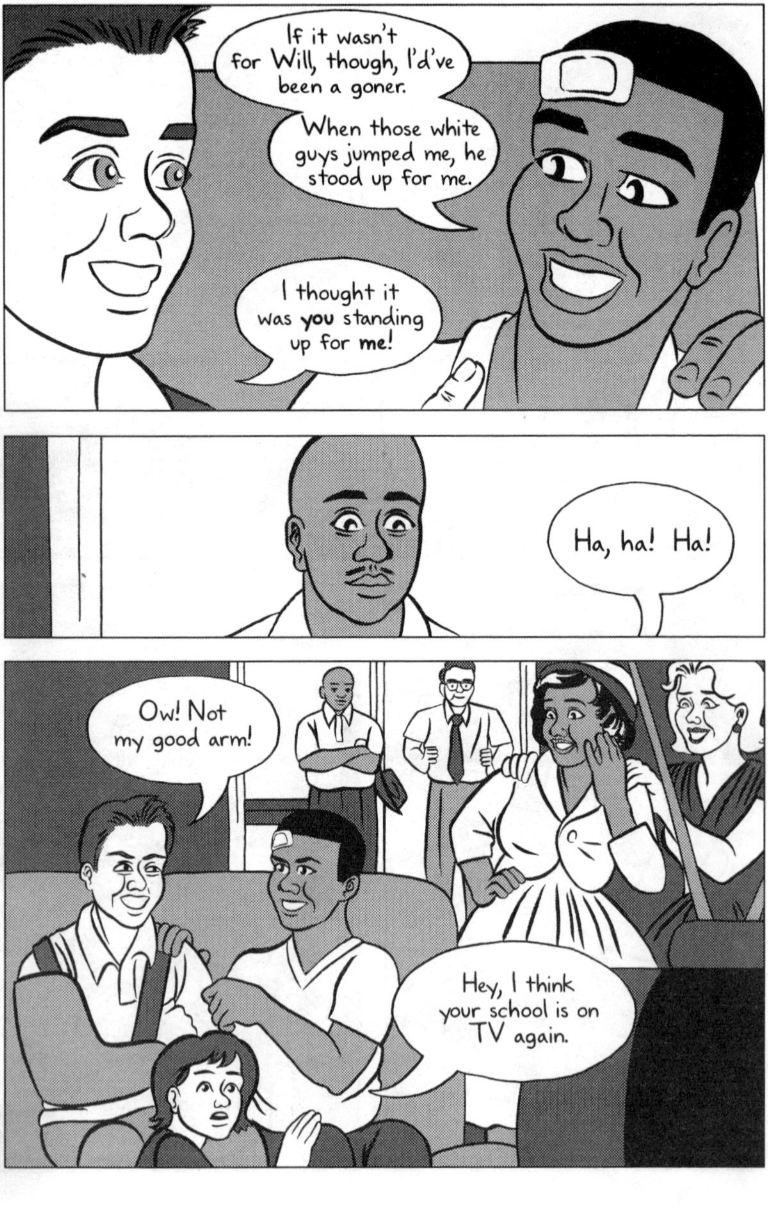
If it wasn't for Will, though, I'd've been a goner.
When those white guys jumped me, he stood up for me.
I thought it was **you** standing up for **me**!
Ha, ha! Ha!
Ow! Not my good arm!
Hey, I think your school is on TV again.

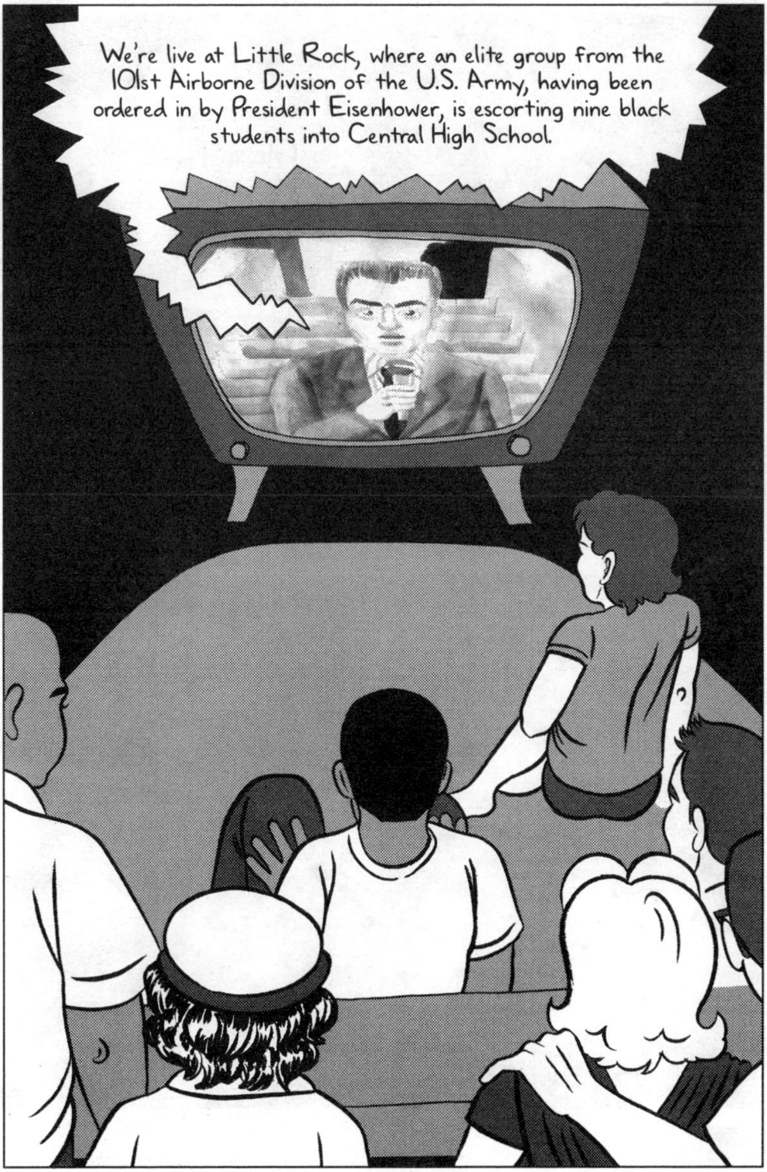
We're live at Little Rock, where an elite group from the 101st Airborne Division of the U.S. Army, having been ordered in by President Eisenhower, is escorting nine black students into Central High School.

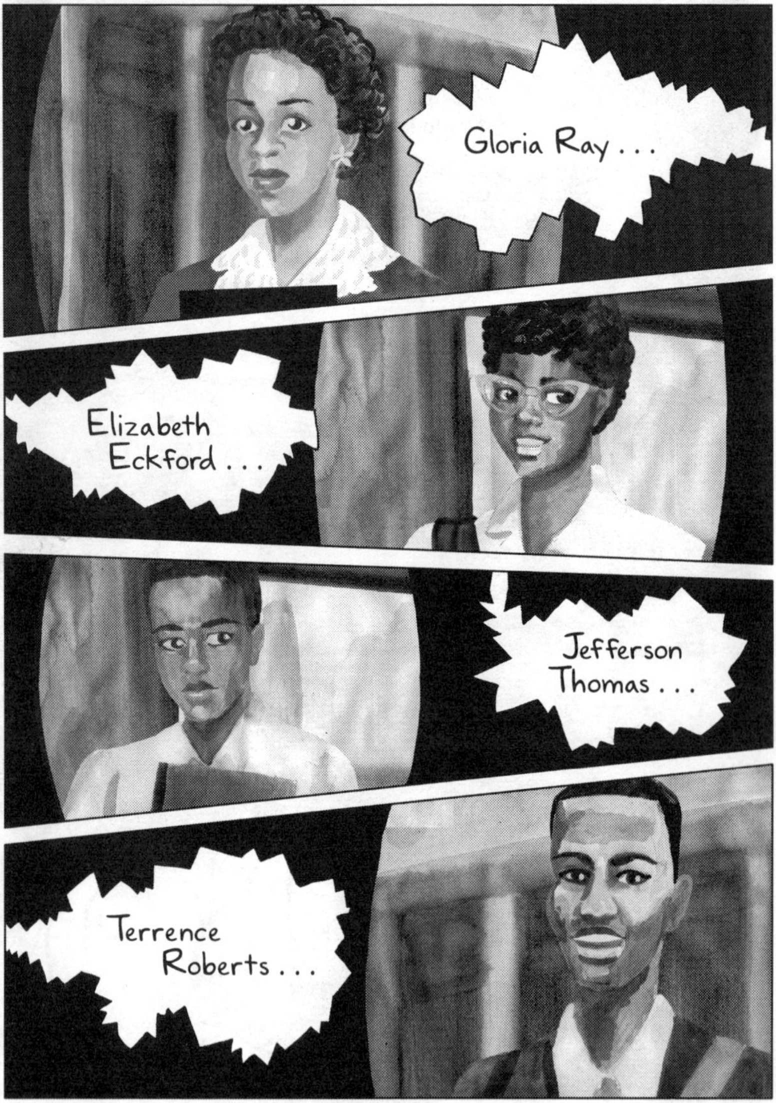
Gloria Ray . . .
Elizabeth Eckford . . .
Jefferson Thomas . . .
Terrence Roberts . . .

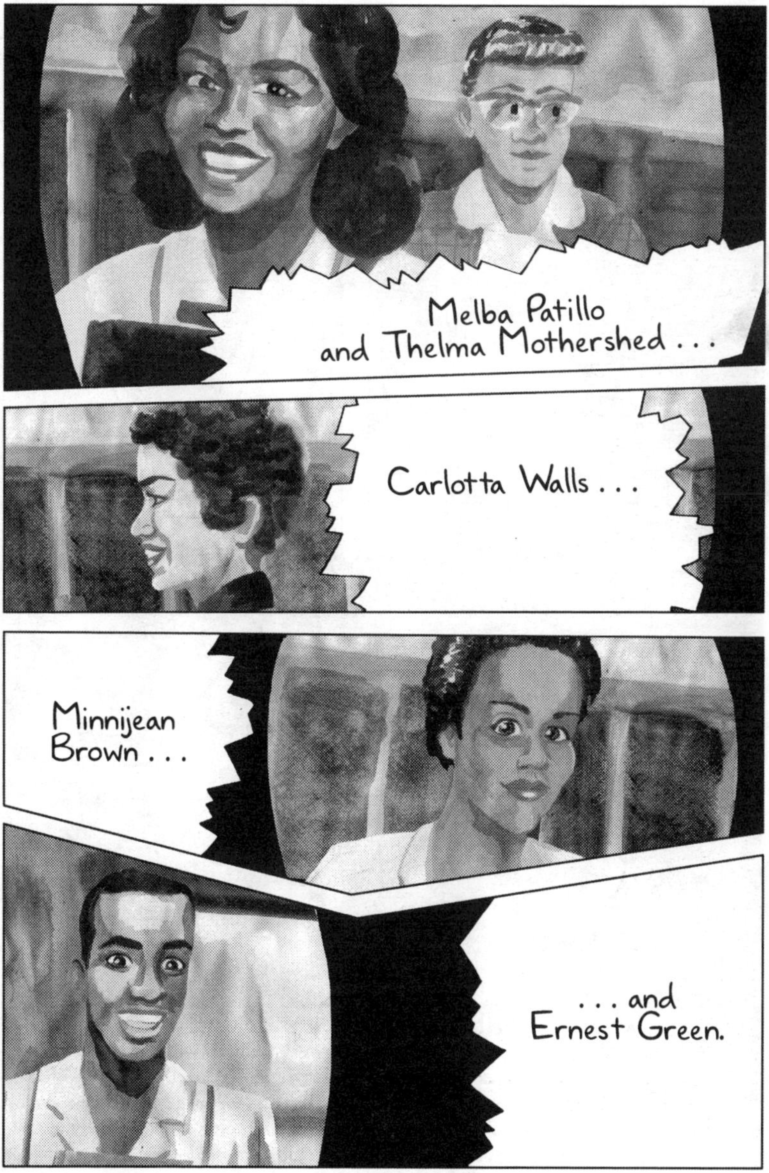
Melba Patillo
and Thelma Mothershed . . .
Carlotta Walls . . .
Minnijean
Brown . . .
. . . and
Ernest Green.

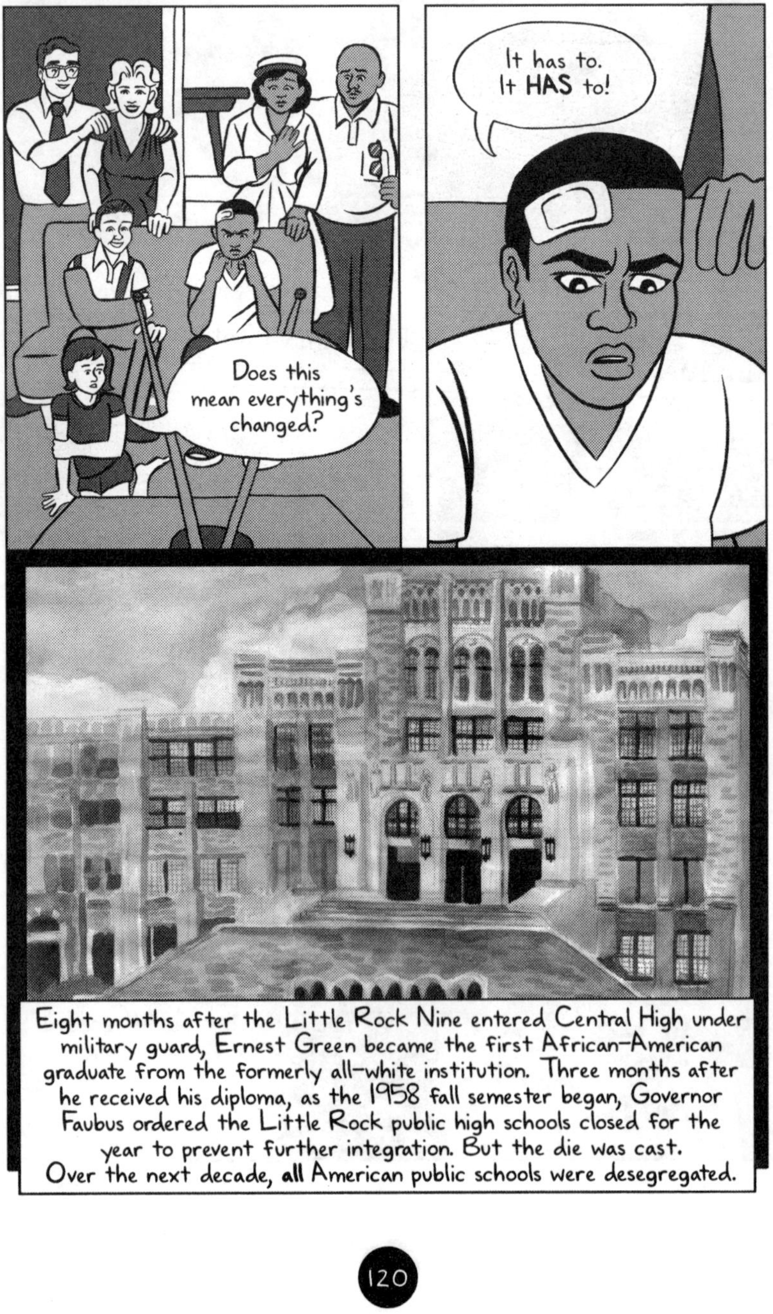
Does this mean everything's changed?
It has to. It HAS to!
Eight months after the Little Rock Nine entered Central High under military guard, Ernest Green became the first African-American graduate from the formerly all-white institution. Three months after he received his diploma, as the 1958 fall semester began, Governor Faubus ordered the Little Rock public high schools closed for the year to prevent further integration. But the die was cast. Over the next decade, **all** American public schools were desegregated.

MARSHALL POE

is an American historian and the author of many nonfiction works. He is currently a writer and analyst at the *Atlantic*. Marshall lives in Iowa City, Iowa.

ELLEN LINDNER'S

comics and illustrations have appeared in a range of independent magazines and anthologies. She splits her time between New York state and London, England.

ALADDIN GOES GRAPHIC...
don't miss any of Aladdin's exciting graphic novels!

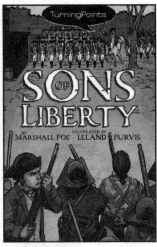